Teaching World Affairs
in American Schools

A CASE BOOK

Teaching World Affairs in American Schools

A CASE BOOK

EDITOR

Samuel Everett
Associate Professor of Education
The City College of New York

CO-EDITOR

Christian O. Arndt
Professor of International Educational Relations
School of Education, New York University

FOREWORD BY WILLIAM HEARD KILPATRICK

Harper & Brothers : New York

IN MEMORIAM

CHARLES LESLIE CUSHMAN, dreamer and builder, philosopher, pioneer, prophet, and friend—you came to a staid old city and stirred it to knowledge of itself and its potential destiny. You came to a proud old profession and taught its members to turn again to all men with the kindness of understanding.

Yours was the greatness that believes every man to be great if he will but be so.

The strength of your listening was a creative force that now dwells with us.

Your courage burned a path in which we follow. Your brilliant, fertile, patient mind has set us tasks we shall be all our lives completing.

For your genius, for the lesson of your way of life and work, for your friendship, we thank you this day.

—HELEN C. BAILEY

THE ADVISORY CASE BOOK
COMMITTEE

CONTENTS

FOREWORD

by William Heard Kilpatrick

WHAT is here said will be limited to two main lines of thought, first, the present world situation and our country's necessary part therein; and, second, the consequent demand that our citizens be more adequately educated for the part they must now play in these world affairs.

Never before in our history has the world situation held for our country such dire threats, or demanded of us such responsible action. On the one hand, the free democratic world is anxious to live at peace —on terms of fairness and justice with the rest of the world. Opposed stands the Communist group determined by power and guile to rule the whole world. Beside these opposing forces stand perhaps one-third of mankind troubled and bewildered as to how to free themselves from ignorance, poverty, hunger, and exploiting feudalism, uncertain whether to believe the alluring Communist promises or to follow the slower but more realistic advice of the free Western world. It is in this situation that our country, contrary to all our past history, has had thrust upon it the highest degree of leadership in the free world, a task and degree of responsibility quite new to our people.

Throughout our history, up to the close of World War II, the prevailing mood of the American people was against international commitments. An apparent exception was our Monroe doctrine, but this was really a device to keep selfish European aims out of our continent. In intent we had consistently followed Washington's advice against "entangling alliances," and had accordingly held ourselves aloof from any part in European or Asiatic ambitions and disputes.

However, by 1900 our people had begun increasingly to consider the possibility of world commitment against wars. Accordingly we took active part in the 1899 and 1907 Hague Peace Conferences and in the establishment of the Permanent Court of Arbitration at The

Hague. When World War I broke out in 1914, there was organized in this country, largely under the influence of ex-President William H. Taft, the "League to Enforce Peace," which hoped for an effective world organization against war. In May 1916, President Woodrow Wilson espoused the cause of a "League of Nations"; and after the war, under Wilson's influence, a "Covenant" for such a League was written as part of the Treaty of Versailles. For reasons not now convincing, the Senate of the United States refused to ratify the "Covenant" and the League was organized without our membership.

It is too late now to ask what "might have been" had our country entered wholeheartedly into the League, whether the invasion of Manchuria and Ethiopia and Finland might have been prevented and World War II averted. It is the future, not the past, that concerns us— specifically, whether World War III can be averted.

There was a time, not long ago, when social intercourse was so limited that Americans could apparently ignore, in large part at any rate, both Europe and Asia. But now the oceans no longer keep the continents apart. The airplane and radio communications have together brought all the parts of the world into such close relationship that the world is now one society in a degree never before true. What happens in some dark corner may start a conflict which might not stop until hydrogen bombs had destroyed most of the world. The risk and the threat are together appalling.

The military problem, urgent though it is, is not, however, the task confronted in this book. Rather we are here concerned with educating our people, not only the younger ones from the kindergarten through undergraduate college but also the adult population, to a proper understanding and appreciation of world affairs, that civilization may be adequately supported and improved. Specifically, we wish the free world so to understand and think and act that the presently "undeveloped" countries may be helped, as they see things, to solve their problems of poverty and hunger and so escape the blandishments of Communism.

The problem next in importance is that we of this country and the whole free world may live such a favorable example of freedom that the people behind the Iron Curtain will also accept a true democracy as their way of life instead of the dictatorship they now suffer.

This then is the social situation which confronts us of the United States and the rest of the free world. The most serious aspect of all for us of this country is the greater responsibility we now must carry in the matter of leadership. Do we have sufficient wisdom of thought and self-control to do our full and proper part in helping the free world to decide what it shall best do? Has our diplomatic service had sufficient experience to enable it to do its proper part? And at home, have we, for example, learned how to conduct our political campaigns in a way to impress other countries favorably? Are enough of our people sufficiently sensitive to what is involved under our new degree of responsibility to demand that our representatives in Washington act with discernment and discretion?

A partial answer to these questions is seen in the fact that at best only about 51 per cent of our people take the trouble to vote. Thus it is clear that we are failing in essential social attitudes and concern. Man cannot live on a basis of selfish individualism, either personal or national. As was said of old, "no man liveth to himself" and "we are members one of another." Man lives adequately only as a real member of society. This means, as every right thinking person must see, that the human individual profits *by* and *from* his social relationships. And this means that each one owes it to the rest to do his social part in the social whole. In this way morality becomes a social necessity, and he who fails to do his social part is immoral. He is living selfishly at the expense of others.

These are some of the factors in our situation which make special new demands on education. While the primary concern here is with elementary and secondary education, the same demands force us to consider also both the undergraduate college and a wider adult education. From all these considerations conscious education must accept in a new sense and degree the obligation to educate all to clearer and more reliable thinking in social and political affairs, to greater sensitivity to the social scene both at home and abroad, to firmer commitment to the discharge of our full duty to the common welfare. The building of the needed social intelligence and socially moral character —these must become the principal duty of teaching from the kindergarten up through college to our citizens at large.

In discharging this duty educators must avoid indoctrination. It is open-minded study that we must seek; for we live in a precarious and changing world. We must develop characters able and disposed to face each new situation on its merits, for the future cannot be foretold.

It is this needed understanding and open-minded intelligence which this book would foster. The many accounts of actual experiences will be suggestive to sensitive teachers. To them I heartily commend the book. Also I commend both contributors and editors for the excellent collection here made available.

PREFACE: DESIGN OF THE STUDY

W<small>HAT</small> responsibilities do American schools have for education for world affairs? And what are the schools in the United States now doing? The John Dewey Society, in a recent publication, *Education for a World Society*, took a forthright position with regard to the first of these questions. This publication, *Teaching World Affairs in American Schools: A Case Book*, is intended to throw some light on the second.

The current study was authorized by the Executive Board of the John Dewey Society in 1953. The membership was subsequently canvassed for the names of people in schools and colleges who were thought to be engaged in promising practices in international education. Comparable requests were made of the members of an informally organized national group known as the "Conference of Professors of Curriculum, Supervision and Instruction."

The response was most gratifying. It became apparent that many teachers in various sections of the country are seriously engaged in some school or college work of the type sought. A Case Book Committee was established, the members of which also became engaged in locating, and sometimes editing, descriptions of promising practice. The Committee feels a real sense of appreciation to those who submitted material and to all who contributed in any way to the success of the study.

As will be seen, the preponderance of examples in this book come from certain public school systems and not every section of the country is represented. The location of members of the Case Book Committee is responsible for this. The quality and number of descriptions received would seem to indicate that many more could have been located and described.

Contributors were asked to write brief, rather than comprehensive, descriptions, varying from 500 to 1200 words in length, with titles which in each case emphasized a theme or major idea.

In his letter requesting descriptive articles, the chairman also included a Check List, "Suggested Purposes, Content, and Activities Appropriate for Inclusion in the Proposed Publication." This statement was also made available to members of the Case Book Committee. The list included a statement of the suggested areas in which examples might fall.

A copy of this Check List may be found in the Appendix. It was compiled as the result of a careful analysis of the John Dewey Society's 1951 Yearbook, *Education for a World Society,* which contains many leads for promising school practice. This earlier publication, and the current Case Book, may with profit be used together by teachers and curriculum workers.

The plan initially was to separate classroom teaching examples from those which described courses of study. But this has not been done in the final organization. The explanation is to be found in the nature of the descriptions of classroom teaching and courses of study actually received.

The examples clearly showed that in all sections of the country from which material was received elementary and junior high school teachers are predominantly using an activity type of program in education for world affairs. These descriptions reflect considerable knowledge of children and concern for the learning process in classrooms. Content and materials are included, but are usually not given a central place. Conversely, secondary school teachers tend to stress content and sources, while giving less space to learning activities. To have followed the initial plan would have resulted in a presentation of practically all examples of "Classroom Teaching" from elementary and junior high schools, with practically all senior high examples organized in a "Course of Study" section. Hence, the material is integrated in chapters titled, "Classroom Teaching and Learning in Public Schools."

The reader may find of special interest the fact that a good number of school systems have established district, city, or county-wide committees and programs in promoting education for world affairs. Schools are also cooperating with civic agencies. Such examples are presented under the heading, "Systemwide School and Community Services."

A statement of ideational orientation precedes each chapter. Inasmuch as education for world affairs is continuous and developmental, these introductions are cumulative in nature and should be read with this in mind. Little evaluation of examples is presented in these initial orientations. The evaluation of individual cases is left to the reader, using the ideational orientation which seems appropriate to him. General evaluative remarks appear in Part V, *"Evaluation and a Look Ahead."*

In order to maintain an uninterrupted flow of ideas throughout the book, authors and their schools are listed at the end of the volume. In a number of cases the original order of the descriptions has been changed or cuts may have been made. The editors take full responsibility for these alterations. They have tried, in all cases, to preserve the meaning of the original material.

It is the hope of the Advisory Committee that the design of the study, *Teaching World Affairs in American Schools: A Case Book,* may suggest to groups of educators in other countries that somewhat similar surveys be made, perhaps by National UNESCO Committees. If this were done, educators all over the world would profit and national programs would benefit greatly. In addition, citizens everywhere who believe in the necessity of international understanding would perhaps then see more clearly the necessity of supporting local attempts of schools and colleges to become increasingly important instruments in the building of a more cooperative and peaceful world.

SAMUEL EVERETT
CHRISTIAN O. ARNDT

Part I

CLASSROOM TEACHING AND LEARNING IN PUBLIC SCHOOLS

CHAPTER 1

Elementary School

WHAT kind of person do we wish to develop in teaching about world affairs in elementary schools? This question penetrates to the heart of classroom teaching and learning for international understanding.

In American elementary schools we desire to develop children who feel a sense of security in their schools, their families, and their home communities. A feeling of security, of being loved and wanted, is perhaps the best insulation against intolerance. The concept of the self should not be one of antagonism toward others, which is easily transferred from immediate contacts with persons to distrust and fear of peoples far away.

The feeling of personal security easily leads children to want to know more about the world of nature and the world of people. It disposes them to exploration and to the use of the scientific method of inquiry, rather than to scapegoating and to rationalization of emotionalized prejudice. Music, literature, and arts and crafts further stimulate the imagination, as does the full utilization of people and other resources in school and community.

With the development of a sense of personal security, the democratic values of respect for others regardless of differences, of cooperation and the participation of all in policy-making, are accepted as a natural heritage. Children seek to find out about other lands and peoples. Their curiosity is insatiable. Strange ways of life are exciting to discover. They are not ways of living to be feared and condemned. More likenesses are discovered than differences. Differences, when found, may give insight into differences at home. And so the search for evidence, the exciting adventure of learning, goes on.

These are some of the attitudes and types of behavior which teachers are attempting to develop in children in American elementary schools. In the process, knowledge of peoples abroad grows in extent and depth. The critical evaluation of social questions is begun as such

3

differences are found both in the United States and abroad. These questions are explored in a democratic context. The development of a tolerant attitude toward differences, tolerance even in the face of abuse, is sought. Children come to love and understand their own country, not less but more, through such experiences. They begin to develop that awareness of time and of history which has helped to make all people what they are today.

The examples of practice found in this chapter are only a few of many that could have been described. They illustrate the achievement of some of the purposes sought in a democratic orientation toward world affairs.

"The Heart Can Push the Sea and Land"

First-graders, like the Elephant's Child, are full of "satiable curiosity." They thrive in an atmosphere where the answer to their "Why?" or "How?" and "I wonder . . ." is "Let's find out."

In the Du Pont Primary School, Old Hickory, Tennessee, many simple books are used to build interest in the world, to establish attitudes concerning people, to help in finding answers to questions.

No particular technique is required but the teacher should know books so well that she can put her finger on the right book at the teachable moment. She needs to be sensitive to the situations or ideas in books. As she reads she conveys to children her own feelings as well as those of the author.

Most books will be read to first-graders for two reasons. Young children can not yet read many desirable books with understanding. And a "reading to" situation establishes rapport and warm-hearted feeling in a shared experience. Enough such experiences will do much to establish the attitudes with which international understanding is concerned.

Something further is required of this teacher who would use books with six-year-olds. She must know their interests and needs, for where these are involved six-year-olds are cooperative and positive in their action.

First-graders are interested in themselves. If you find one of them before a mirror you will see long, searching looks, much stretching and tiptoeing. For first-graders want to grow up. Good books to read to them are *A Growing Story* by Ruth Krauss, *When Will the World*

Be Mine? by Miriam Schlein, *Wait Till the Moon Is Full* by Margaret Wise Brown, *One Morning in Maine* by Robert McClosky, *A Hole Is To Dig* by Ruth Krauss.

If first-graders who are self-centered can be expected to be more positive in their approach to life, and they can, it is likewise important that they like their families—that they feel the warm, caring-about relationship of fathers and mothers, brothers and sisters. And so we read to them *The Bundle Book* by Ruth Krauss, *Runaway Bunny* by Margaret Wise Brown, *In My Mother's House* by Ann Nolan Clark, *We Are a Family* by Inez Hogan, *Ferdinand* by Munro Leaf, *The Country Bunny and the Little Gold Shoes* by Du Bose Heyward.

Space ships today, trips to the moon tomorrow! First-graders will want books about these, too. Virginia Burton and others have books about machines which contribute to our community life. An understanding of machines is necessary, but it is even more important that children learn to feel at home in the natural world, for here they may find permanence and stability amid social change. Books like *Green Eyes* by A. Birnbaum, *Johnny Maple-Leaf* by Alvin Tresselt, *Go with the Sun* by Miriam Schlein, and *All Around You* by Jeanne Bendick, have a concept of recurring seasons, and the night-and-day cycle, which give an assurance to the six-year-old that the world will be here tomorrow. Specific interests in the world may demand such books as those written by Herbert Zim and Robert McClung. *Let's Go Outdoors* by Harriet Huntingdon is always of use in making first-graders feel at home in the natural world.

Coupled with this interest in the natural world is an interest in history and geography. It would be hard to find a better conception of an island than the one pictured in *The Little Island* by Golden MacDonald. There are perhaps few better histories of time, as it has evolved in our country, than is found in *The Little House* by Virginia Burton. This feeling of continuity of time is necessary to secure feelings in children so important to international understanding. Secure children are receptive. Their tendency is to be kind.

First-graders can learn about problems which other children have solved and perhaps come to feel less baffled about their own. Books which can be used to advantage are: *Two Is a Team* by Lorraine and Jerrold Beim, *The Carrot Seed* by Ruth Krauss, *The Quiet Mother and the Noisy Little Boy* by Charlotte Zolotow, *Finders Keepers* by Will and Nicholas, and *A Story About Ping* by Marjorie Flack.

The world touches the six-year-old at many points today. It may be a Korean news account on television. It may be that he is going to or coming from Japan. Or perhaps his sister brings home a guest from college who "really and truly lives in India." Wherever the point of contact, books may be found that extend experiences, that make the unknown become the known. It is important that these books present the people in a sensitive manner, as the following do: *Who's Upside Down?* by Crockett Johnson, *The Village Tree* by Taro Yashima, *Down Down the Mountain* by Ellis Credle, *Looking—For—Something* by Ann Nolan Clark, *Rain in the Winds* by Claire and George Louden, *The Five Chinese Brothers* by Claire Bishop, and *Madeline* by Bemelmans.

Another area of great importance to true understanding is the construction of meanings within and without context. Situations and comparisons can change meanings, and a beginning of this understanding can be given small children from such books as *Fast Is Not a Ladybug* and *Shapes* by Miriam Schlein, and *How Big Is Big?* by Herman and Nina Scheider.

Nothing reveals the values we hold quite as much as does our laughter. So we must give children books with laugh-provoking incidents—books like *Curious George* by H. H. Rey. Like the children in the poem by Dorothy Aldis, our sixes may laugh until their cheeks are tight and their stomachs are sore. Like the children in the poem they may not be able to remember what they're laughing about. But those of us who choose books for children can try to see to it that they do not learn to laugh at other people. We can try to help them become persons who know that all of us need not look alike, walk alike, or talk alike or think alike to be human.

You will remember what Ruth Krauss said in *The Big World and the Little House:* "The little house had become a home. Home is the way people feel about a place. Some people feel that way about a room, which is just part of a house. Some people feel that way about a corner—which is just part of a room that is part of a house. Some people feel that way about the whole world." We may hope each of the sixes we teach is becoming a person who feels at home in the world.

Books will help in this process. Some will be factual. Some will be about animals and people and their feelings, for we believe

The heart can push the sea and land
Farther away on either hand
        —EDNA ST. VINCENT MILLAY, *Renaissance*

Our first-graders are not unlike the snowshoe rabbit who said to
his mother, "I understand all that you have taught me to understand."

Beginning American Life in an American School: The Story of Tikva

In early November, Tikva came from Israel to Oak Lane Country
Day School in Philadelphia to begin American life in an American
school. The story of what has happened to her since she has been at
Oak Lane is an inspiring one. It is a testament to understanding
teachers, warm and loving American foster parents, friendly, sensitive classmates, and Tikva's own great courage and spirit. But even
more important, perhaps, is what has happened to Tikva's school-
mates. Accepting a new person with whom one cannot communicate,
who seems "different," can be an unwelcome experience. If, however, the project is undertaken with a recognition of the gains that
can accrue to all the participants, then a great deal of good can be
derived.

Seated in a circle, at a time during the school day reserved for
talking over important plans, the girls and boys of the fourth grade
listened to the teacher talk sympathetically but factually about a
little girl, eleven years old, whose parents had died during the war,
who had just come to America, didn't know any English, and was
thinking of coming to school. The eyes of the children grew more
and more round. Eagerness and excitement jiggled them in their
chairs. When the teacher stopped talking, the questions flew: "Will
she come here?" "In our class?" "We could help her a lot, couldn't
we?" Here was the first good that Tikva brought to these children,
the good of being able to offer to do something big for someone
one doesn't even know or, to put it in more important-sounding
words, the ability to volunteer service to humanity.

"Now, what shall we do; how can we best help Tikva?" asked the
teacher. The children thought deeply. "We can help her find where
everything belongs." "We can teach her lots of words just by pointing to things and saying their names." "We'll try to show her that

we like her." "We'll give her a chance to do things." "We mustn't all rush at her or make too much fuss." And here was the second good: nine-year-olds planning together ways to help someone they have never met or, in more technical language, an opportunity for constructive planning for a hitherto unexperienced relationship.

A few days later Tikva and her new mother came to school. The children rushed in, trying to help. They were constantly at the new child's side. Tikva was something like the bottle under a funnel. All day long children poured in everything they could, to fill her up with "a good feeling."

But the one-way funnel didn't last long, hardly twenty-four hours. Tikva had a lot to offer, too. She was able to express her spirit of fun by the way she handled herself. She "mugged," as it were, and the children laughed with her, discovering, without putting it into conscious thought, that one doesn't have to know your language or your ways in order to be interesting and enjoyable.

It wasn't always easy for Tikva, but, as she herself wrote later, "The more I learned, the more I was interested." She learned quickly. She remembered the words the children taught her. She began to write stories, to find her way about, to do things for herself.

In January Tikva moved up to the sixth grade. A fourth-grader, writing a story about her, said: "We thought maybe we had taught her too well because she had gone so fast, but we were glad for her."

To the sixth-graders, too, Tikva was something special, but with a difference. She was their age, and by now she could speak their language and join in their games. In addition she was able to help some of them with Sunday School Hebrew homework, and could answer many questions about how other people live. Her new classmates began to rely on her for information, and grew to respect the contributions of knowledge and friendship that people from other lands have to offer.

Do we honestly assert that Tikva taught her classmates to: give service to humanity; plan constructively for people they don't know; appreciate the intellectual and emotional ties that can bind all peoples together; be sensitive to the needs of others; respect the contributions of other cultures to our world? Of course not! To acquire these feelings is the goal of a lifetime, not the happening of a portion of a school year. But Tikva, we believe, by giving a successful experience in each of these feelings to her classmates, and in a degree to the whole school, pushed open the gates leading down these pathways to better world understandings. A small step along each way was taken by each child. And the second step is never as hard as the first.

Developing a Democratic Climate

World understanding in an elementary school requires first of all a climate throughout the school which will free teachers and children to make the greatest use of their capacities to respect themselves so that they may respect others; to free themselves of artificial distinctions, economic and social, that keep people apart; and to enable them to work with others toward a common goal.

In the Robert J. Vance School, New Britain, Connecticut, a laboratory school of the Teachers College of Connecticut, teachers are making a sincere effort to create the climate and to provide the experiences necessary to develop the desired ideals. The program is unspectacular, stressing day-by-day living together in friendship rather than costly or energy-consuming programs.

Children enter school with simple concepts of geography and politics and their horizons do not extend much beyond their immediate neighborhood. It is the job of the school to widen the horizon of each child as much as possible. The habits and attitudes for understanding others are the same, no matter how narrow or wide are the horizons. Honest respect for the achievements of others, always realizing that people are not alike and have varying abilities, is encouraged. The kindergarten child whose ability to express himself verbally is not well developed may win the respect of his entire class by being the first to be able to skip.

Bulletin boards displaying IMPROVED WORK are used and every child, no matter how little ability he has, may find his paper on this board, with the whole class sensing what an achievement it is for him that his paper now has only two mistakes. When a sixth-grade class wrote letters of invitation to an original play, the letter of the boy with the poorest writing ability was unanimously chosen because "he's been working so hard and his writing has improved so much." One fifth-grader sent for the principal to come and join in their joy because, "Freddy hit a home run." Everyone in the class had been trying to help Freddy (a brilliant boy, but physically immature) to gain the skills necessary to play ball well and now felt a justifiable pride in his achievements.

All rules and regulations of the school are based on consideration of others. As often as possible children have a part in formulating these rules and, whenever this is not possible, the reasons for the rules are carefully discussed with the children. Children walk through the halls rather than run, which they would so much rather do, because they might bump into someone and hurt him if they ran. Children talk in soft voices in the halls because they might disturb classes which are working hard. Children try to leave the lavatories clean because it makes it pleasanter for others to find them that way and "besides the janitor has to work so hard and he's so helpful to us that we ought to help him."

In the teaching of social studies as many source materials as possible are used. The teachers believe it is important to learn that books, newspapers, and magazines are written by people who write from their own point of view. Authors stress their own interests and tend to minimize those subjects in which their interest is not so great. Only by using many sources can the whole truth be found.

Teachers are alert to the many sources of help available in the community and elsewhere. Libraries and museums are used extensively. People in the community who have colored slides, or movies, and articles to show from other parts of our own country or other countries are invited to school. Besides being of tremendous value in helping us to understand life in other places, these visitors help children to appreciate the courage shown by those who left their own country to come and settle in a strange land. They come to realize a little more the contributions different groups of people have made to America. The school has been fortunate enough to be able to entertain many visitors from foreign countries.

Each year the whole school unites in celebrating the birthday of the United Nations. The parents have donated a United Nations flag and a sixth-grade class made a set of 12-by-18-inch flags, one for each member nation. Every room has some interesting display for the occasion. The sixth-grade classes have, for example, made a study of the organization and work of the United Nations. During one United Nations week a television set was rented and each class had a chance to see the United Nations in action. An important part of the birthday celebration is the birthday gift of money from the school toward some part of the work of the organization. One year the school entertained for a day eight children who were natives of other countries and whose fathers were employed by the United Nations.

The political structure and work of the United Nations is difficult for some elementary school children to grasp. But the fundamental ideal of nations joining together to talk over problems peacefully, and to work together for a common goal, are simple enough ideas to be grasped by all. A first grade, for instance, was having a serious discussion about the misbehavior of one child. The children finally came to the conclusion that he needed help and that it was up to each of them as members of his school family to help. A little girl's face lit up and she exclaimed, "We're just like the UN."

In a sixth grade a boy asked, "What good is the Security Council anyway when it hasn't power enough to settle all questions?" He was reminded of an incident which had happened several days previously when a group of boys were brought to the office by the Junior Patrol because they had been fighting on the playground. At first the boys glared at each other in anger. But when each one was allowed to tell his story, all began to cool down and finally grinned sheepishly. One boy spoke for all when he said, "Sounds sort of silly now." With this background in mind, the questioner gained a measure of understanding for the value of the frank airing of problems, even when applied to international affairs.

The concept of a world united for peace may seem too idealistic for many adults. But to children who have lived in a school community where people work together peacefully without sacrificing individuality it seems both sensible and possible.

Spot the News

To meet the need for teaching about World Affairs and World Geography, a fifth grade in the William Randolph School in Asheville, North Carolina, has found the following effective.

On a large bulletin board there appears an up-to-date world map with the title, SPOT THE NEWS, in large letters above it. The teacher placed the map on the bulletin board during one weekend. On Monday morning several pupils noticed it and commented on its bright colors. They pointed out places with which they were familiar. The map was left up all week. References were made to it at different times, and a great deal of interest was shown because it was a world map. During the week pupils located places that came up in their class work, and some pointed out places they had visited.

The following Monday morning the teacher came in with several newspaper clippings, "spotted" each one on the map, and then put the clippings on the bulletin board. Immediately there was a chorus of "May we bring in news reports, too?" The project was off to a good start.

Each morning about fifteen minutes is devoted to world news. Anyone who has an interesting news report may give it. The student gives an oral report of the news event to the class. The class has the privilege of asking questions for further details.

After the first report was given, these comments were heard: "He read it." "He didn't face the class." "That word wasn't pronounced correctly." The comments led to a discussion about judging the reports. The class working together developed the following standards:

1. News items must be told and not read.
2. The person reporting must be familiar with all details.
3. Face the class and speak in a clear, distinct voice.
4. Hold pictures, clippings, etc., to the front so that all the class may see.
5. Use correct English.
6. Pronounce all words correctly.
7. News items must be of general interest.
8. Do not use crime and sensational stories.

The person giving the report has to learn as much as he can about the topic to be able to answer questions and give details. When the report is finished, each child goes to the bulletin board and locates the place mentioned in the news item. Using twine with a pin in one end, the pin is placed on the spot on the world map where the news happened. The other end of the string leads to the newspaper clipping which is thumb-tacked on the board around the map. Until the student can "spot the news" where the event took place, he is not permitted to post his clipping on the bulletin board. All clippings are removed at the end of each week.

These news reports are subsequently related to regular social studies work. For example, a report on the St. Lawrence Seaway led to a study of the need and use of this seaway by both the United

States and Canada, the relationship between these two countries, and the Congressional bill authorizing the seaway. This study was further related to the three branches of the government in the United States, with particular emphasis on the two houses of Congress, on how and where bills are introduced and passed, and on the power of the veto.

A "Spot the News" report on the bill to make Alaska and Hawaii states led to a study of Alaska and Hawaii, their population, area, resources, industries, and present ability to govern themselves as states. Films on both Alaska and Hawaii were used to supplement the text.

The news report period is correlated with English in setting up standards for giving oral reports. The reports are aimed at helping the pupil develop the ability to stand before a group and speak clearly and distinctly, using good English, correct pronunciation, and good enunciation.

Through its "Spot the News" program, this fifth grade is learning more about World Geography and World Affairs.

Teaching World Affairs in a University Elementary School

Placed at the center of the school plant at the entrance to Community Hall stands the symbol which represents the major goal toward which the staff of the University Elementary School, University of California at Los Angeles, moves as it works to educate its children. Struck in copper by sculptor Bernard Rosenthal are three animals: a regal giraffe looking toward the south, a deer with stars on its horns facing east, and a llama with its eyes turned westward. The feet of each animal are planted firmly in a thick copper base.

As the younger children from three to five years pass the statue there are smiles and comments, such as: "Oh, look at the monkeys." "I know what that animal is. It is a big giraffe! My papa showed me one at the circus!" "That is a deer. I saw one in the mountains. But its horns were different!" Pointing to the llama, "What is this?" At this age they like and enjoy the animals for their own sake.

As the children mature they continue to find interest in the animals. Their remarks indicate the widening and deepening of concepts regarding them: "I saw a whole herd of giraffes running swiftly, all moving together. They live in Africa. Their long necks help them eat the leaves high on the trees." "This llama looks more like a camel! My sister in the sixth grade was the Silver Llama in a play about Peru a long time ago."

By the time children have reached the age of nine or ten most of their remarks show a growing interest in the statue as a whole: "There are hundreds of animals in the world. Why were these selected?" "Remember when Miss Kunugi was here, she told us about the Shinto shrine in her garden to the Fox God. Maybe these animals represent certain religions." "Notice, these animals are not looking at each other. I wonder why? Maybe they don't like each other!"

The pupils of the University Elementary School observe that the animals symbolize the three great land bodies of the world: the giraffe, the Southern World of people and things; the deer, the Eastern World; and the llama, the Western World. Each animal differs in part because the environment in which he grew differed from the other two. The peoples of each section of the world become what they are through living in their particular environments. Food, clothing, shelter, weapons, tools, recreation, records, communication, education, and religion vary and this may lead to difficulties. The thick copper base represents the body of common principles created by the peoples of the world to promote world unity.

The statue symbolizes a world community in which the separate sections move in certain directions because of different physical and cultural developments. But, at the same time, the world community works together to resolve differences which interfere with the promotion of peace and harmony in the world as a whole.

The social studies program of the University Elementary School is built upon the needs and desires children feel and satisfy as they interact with an ever-widening environment. From three to eight years their experiences are centered in home, immediate neighborhood, and the expanded community. At this stage, children are acquiring meanings and growing concepts of their relationships to members of the family and to people outside the family group.

As the children have experiences they develop attitudes of liking people who help them, of appreciating the work of others, of being interested in and respecting people who differ from them in appearance, ideas, and economic status. At the same time, they develop increasingly habits and skills essential to communication and the securing of information which satisfies curiosity. By eight years of age children have met personally people of various cultural and racial backgrounds. Also, in studies centered in transportation, they have become acquainted with places and people outside their own community.

In studies such as "How We Secure Our Bread" pupils not only learn how bread is made and distributed in their own community, but also in the nation and in some areas of the world, such as Mexico, Israel, and China. They satisfy their curiosity as to how bread was made long ago! Thus the concepts and understandings of life in other places and times are in the process of being built. They learn why cereals differ in various regions. Meanings and initial concepts are formed which in time develop into the major concept, "What man does to satisfy his basic needs in any one place or time depends upon his physical environment and cultural development." They learn that people the world over are alike in many respects. They love their children, they eat, build houses, care for crops. By the time they reach eight, with teachers who understand concept building through the process of generalization, they are "on the way" to the acquisition of a sound background of understandings, attitudes and skills essential to facing problems in the larger world.

During the eight-, nine-, and ten-year period the children continue to build the patterns of behavior which make them increasingly one with a world which has been extended to include many parts of the earth. They may become interested in life studies of Hopis, Navahos, Mexicans, Chinese, Japanese, Bagandas of Uganda, Samoans, early Hebrews, early Californians, early colonists of Plymouth, the pioneers who pushed forward the Western Frontier. Which of these studies they undertake depends upon the specific interests of each group. In the three years at the University Elementary School, only six of these studies can be completed fully with the comparative relationships which are involved.

Such excursions into the lives of other peoples involve helping the children to make some of the cultural patterns of the people part of themselves. Through "becoming" the people, through building a typical shelter, growing, processing and eating different food, experimenting with fibers for cloth, making clothing, creating tools and weapons, children acquire meanings which enable them to fashion the particular responses that generate attitudes and build skills. These experiences drive them to feel deeply and act efficiently in behalf of people should the occasion demand it.

A study of the United Nations without prior discussion of class-room and school problems would have little meaning and hence be of little use. Thus the approach to the subject is simple, direct, and meaningful, and only later will the room become filled with books, posters, flags, and maps. Before the close of the semester the children take a look at the long growing-up period this world has had. They trace the history of slavery, of citizenship, of charters and constitutions, of religious and racial discrimination, and they see in the United Nations the latest effort being made to help the world community grow up without greed, selfishness, or discrimination, and to work toward the creation of a happier and more peaceful world.

That cooperative action, as demonstrated in the United Nations, can become a living and working concept is demonstrated by one sixth-grade class which drew up a Charter of Children's Rights at the University Elementary School. This class had been studying the United Nations. They discovered that its purpose is to help the people and countries all over the world work together. They thought that a good place to start helping people work together was in their own school, so they wrote their own charter.

Charter of Children's Rights
University Elementary School Standards

Preamble:
We the students of the A6 class have written these suggestions to make our school a better place to learn and to work together.

There should not be any sign of discrimination, prejudice or segregation in this school.

Let all children, no matter who they are, have a fair chance in our school.

Try to be friendly with all of your classmates. Find all the good points in your friends. Forget their bad points. Play games with them and have other group activities with them at recess and noon hour as well as lesson time.

Do your best to be friendly with new people and try to get along with them. Show them around the school and teach them games that they don't know.

All students should be able to have student offices such as Council and class monitor duties.

Try not to tease people who are making as good a try as they can in the classroom or on the playground.

Let everybody have a fair chance on the playground.

There should not be any one person who can "lock" a game or be the "boss" of any game.

There should not be any one person who can be put out of a game because of his race, creed, color or sex.

If someone is not a very good player he or she should be given a chance to learn. Soon they will become better.

Be cooperative with your Team Captain.

We hope that these suggestions will help all of us and all of those who will come to our school later to get along together better.

Education of this kind is real and vital. The understandings and attitudes which result enable children to think more responsibly and make wiser decisions in matters which affect the peoples of the world.

Pacific Peoples Made Meaningful

Living as they do on the eastern shore of the Pacific Ocean and being so close to its blue waters, the sixth-graders of the Ynez School, Alhambra, California, naturally wonder what lies on the other side.

A study of the islands and the peoples of the Pacific is listed as part of the prescribed curriculum. But how to bring this to the children? What do they need to know of this part of the world? How much is necessary to give them an understanding?

Fortunately, a teacher in this school knew the islanders as people, not characters from a book. He wanted the children to feel the same way. He had come to appreciate their way of life, their history, their art and music, and he wanted the class to develop this appreciation. He wanted his students to see and understand these Pacific inhabitants as they really exist.

The factual basis of the study did not present major difficulties. The vastness of the ocean, the climate, with all its ramifications, the types of islands, the three native classifications were of prime importance. The class considered how the environment dictated their way of living. They noted the similarities and the differences of the various cultures. The Viking-like history of these people and their more recent impact on world affairs in World War II, demanded their attention. The customs, the music, and the arts and crafts of these people warranted special study.

But to bring the student to a closer relationship to the study was the foremost task. A field trip served this purpose. The class toured Los Angeles harbor by boat for two hours. The children were eye witnesses to foreign ships unloading raw materials from across the sea. They noted rubber, pineapple, sugar, coconuts, and other goods being unloaded. They checked for manufactured articles that were being exported.

Early in the study each student composed and mailed a letter to a student in the Feleti Memorial School in Pago Pago, Samoa. The answers were later to prove a high point in the semester. For the day-to-day portion of the unit each pupil was assigned an island, or island group, on which to report. The *National Geographic* magazine was the backbone of the research material.

Recent visitors to the islands were twice invited to the classroom. The room environment was enriched by artifacts of Pacific culture, since many fathers, uncles, and brothers had served in the Pacific during the war. The audio-visual department provided excellent films.

How bring this study to a significant and successful close? The pupils had spent a considerable length of time on Hawaii. The children had even adopted a Hawaiian slang expression for their motto, "Hiki No," for "can do!" They had discussed, at length, this melting pot at "The Crossroads of the Pacific." Together they had examined her racial strains, her unique fusion of the East and West. All felt that it would be fine if they could bring a little bit of Hawaii right into the classroom. The luau was the perfect answer. Here was a feast typically native, yet more and more being enjoyed by the mala-hinis from the mainland.

A two-hour tape recording of *Hawaii Calls* radio program supplied the musical background. Parents supplied fresh pineapple, coconuts, papayas, bananas, and pineapple juice. The cafeteria supplied a dinner of boiled rice, roast pork, and yams. Class members brought large banana leaves from which they ate. The room was tastefully decorated with many flowers and the children, barefooted, were arrayed in Hawaiian shirts and skirts and bedecked with flowers in their hair and leis they had fashioned themselves. The teacher, in a bright aloha shirt, provided an additional native touch by opening the coconuts in approved island fashion.

For two hours these mainland boys and girls were vicariously living a part of an alien life. They knew what lay beyond the waves. They knew and appreciated what fun and laughter could belong to any boy or girl in his or her own environment. Nor would they soon forget.

How Japanese and Americans Depend upon Each Other

At the start of the spring term, a class in the McCall School of Philadelphia entered into a discussion of current events. Repeatedly the concept of the interdependence of nations was mentioned. The teacher had informed the children that the work of the term in social studies might well be centered around Asia and the Pacific area. The children welcomed this topic because of the Korean War and the news from the Far East. Teacher and children began cooperatively to develop a list of the countries of this area that they might study.

The problem became personal in nature when it was discovered that a good portion of the class had relatives serving in the Armed Forces who were, or had been, stationed in Japan. Pupils and teacher listed thirty-two items which they felt they should know about Japan, in order to understand the people and their activities and to learn how Americans and Japanese are mutually interdependent.

The information obtained through discussion was then organized under four headings:

1. People: living, education, religion
2. Trade and Industry
3. History and Government
4. Geography: physical environment and resources

The members of the class decided they could best meet this problem by organizing committees to explore each of these areas. Each pupil was given the opportunity to choose his committee, but if one committee was filled, the pupil had to accept a second or third choice. Committees elected their own chairman.

It was agreed that each child would carry on research. Then the committee would meet, listen to the information reported, and decide which items should be used in a report to the entire group. Upon completing this phase, the groups felt that they would like to meet with the teacher in order to plan the presentation of the report. Some of the committees presented their reports in puppet plays, booklets, a frieze, homemade movies, and dramatizations.

Also included in the project was a display of Japanese products, materials, costumes, and some festival decorations and symbols. The display was quite large, as the entire school became interested. The faculty and children from other classes loaned valuable materials.

The social studies collaborator heard about this unit and upon seeing a notice in the newspaper of a talk by Harumi Takeuchi, First Secretary of the Japanese Embassy, Washington, D.C., suggested the value of utilizing a resource person in further developing the unit. The World Affairs Council of Philadelphia was approached about obtaining the Honorable Mr. Takeuchi. The World Affairs Council then contacted Washington, D.C., in order to obtain the services of Mr. Takeuchi.

On his arrival with his family, at the McCall School, he was greeted by seven children dressed in traditional Japanese clothing. He listened to the reports and was invited to participate. Mr. Takeuchi then spoke of his homeland, developing and strengthening many understandings concerning the interdependence of the United States and Japan.

The participation of Mr. Takeuchi with his wife and child throughout the morning provided the children with an educational experience in social living they may never forget.

Following this culminating activity, each committee then reassembled in order to make changes in its report in accordance with the information gained through Mr. Takeuchi's visit. The revised reports were then presented to the class, in order that each child could understand better the total picture involved in the unit, "How the Japanese and Americans Depend on Each Other." This report was then drawn up in outline form as a permanent record to be consulted and used when planning the next units.

The entire unit was evaluated in terms of what had been discovered, how ideas had changed in the light of new information, and how and why Japan was important, not only to our country but also to us as individuals.

Chinese Are People

In the Forbes School of Pittsburgh there are fifty children of Chinese origin. They are lively and seem happy among themselves but remain aloof from other pupils and from the ordinary community life of the school. Teachers watch for opportunities to assimilate this group of Chinese children into the school community and at the same time awaken in the rest of the school society some awareness of the richness of Chinese culture.

Mr. Lee, one of the Forbes School parents, had visited a teacher of the sixth grade during Education Week and showed great interest in what his children were learning at school. Soon after, Tommy Lee came dancing into the art room singing a Chinese song. Tommy and his sisters were asked to sing before the class. These incidents, Mr. Lee's visit to school and Tommy Lee's songs, seemed to be the natural opportunity to begin a study of the Chinese people.

The usual pupil committees were formed to find out about the Chinese people, their accomplishments, their art and the painstaking work required to produce it, their agricultural life involving the raising of rice and tea, their festivals and wedding customs. The teacher herself found it necessary to do a great deal of research in order to guide the work of the children intelligently.

The resources of the community were used extensively. A visit was made to the Chinese Merchants' Associated, located in the Chinese section of the city, where Mr. Lee answered questions and children gained a knowledge and appreciation of Chinese businesses, customs, and religious beliefs. A trip to the Chinese Room, University of Pittsburgh, was a stimulating and informative experience. An excursion to the Carnegie Institute was made to see such things as jades, ivories, and mandarin coats. The children had lunch at a Chinese restaurant operated by a parent. He invited the class to enjoy rice cakes and tea served in traditional Chinese style. These visits stimulated great interest in the contributions China has made to the world.

Many art activities made this study meaningful to both children and teacher. Table models were constructed showing typical street scenes in China. Cardboard and clay were used as the base of the construction. An original puppet show was put on, using a story written by one class from knowledge gained in its studies of China and its people. The children made paper sculpture, showing the usual methods of transportation and ordinary occupations of present-day China. A wall hanging of silk was painted by a group of children somewhat after the Chinese fashion, telling their version of a Chinese story.

The study closed with a party given by the Chinese mothers in their native costumes. These mothers also provided and served the food. Although the activities in this unit centered around art experiences, the children gained much knowledge usually associated with social studies, such as library techniques, research reading, and knowledge of other academic-subject fields.

The unit on China helped the children gain a more complete understanding of Chinese life and to discover that Chinese boys and girls love their homes and families and enjoy games and fun just as they themselves do. Working together, offering an occasional helping hand to a Chinese classmate, and sharing materials were part of the classroom activity. People in the school community gained respect for people of another race when they saw how Chinese and white Americans worked together to accomplish goals which all had helped to determine.

A Study of Today's India

A group of children in the George Gray School, Wilmington, Delaware, became much interested in India as they discussed the news together each morning. They asked, "Why are they saying that what happens to India will affect the whole world?"

After talking together about what was happening in India, the class decided that much more information about the people of India was needed to understand better what was happening and why it had meaning for us. The pupils made a list of the following questions they wanted to have answered:

1. In what kind of homes do the people of India live?
2. What do they eat?
3. Is it true that many children of India never have enough to eat?
4. What are their religious beliefs?
5. Is it true that they think cows are holy?
6. What educational advantages do Indians have?
7. What is their form of government?
8. What kind of work do they do for a living?

The next step was to decide where to find information that would help in answering these questions. Some members of the group had already gathered information from the television and radio. To this were added the following sources:

1. Maps and globes
2. Encyclopedias
3. Books and pictures from our classroom and the school library
4. Daily newspapers
5. The news and magazine sections of the Sunday papers
6. Weekly magazines
7. People who have lived in India

The children decided that someone who had recently lived in India could give a true picture of how the people lived. Through the school principal an exchange student was located who had spent the previous winter living with a farm family near Delhi, India.

With the aid of colored slides, which were taken during his stay in India, this student gave the class a vivid picture of the home life and the constant struggle for existence of the farming population of India, which comprises about 85 per cent of the population. The children asked many questions of their visitor about what they saw in the pictures and about his relationships with the people. They learned that because of primitive farming tools, and the dry and rainy seasons, the people of India failed to raise enough food to feed themselves and that, in consequence, many were hungry most of the time. As the visitor explained the American Point Four and Technical Assistance programs with which the United States is aiding India, these terms became more meaningful. When the illustrated talk was finished, many of the questions which had puzzled the children were answered. The children were beginning to understand why there is so much unrest in India.

An article in their *Weekly Reader* on India's objection to United States military aid to Pakistan was read, and posted on the bulletin board was an article from a morning paper on the same subject. After reading both, the class divided into Indians and Pakistanis. They debated whether the United States was right or wrong in the action taken, according to the viewpoint of the respective countries. During the debate, the world map was used to make clear the location of India and Pakistan. Their nearness to Communist China and Russia was noted. These places thus began to have real meaning to the children.

A newspaper article, about hundreds of Hindus being trampled to death rushing to bathe in the holy waters of the Ganges during a religious bathing festival, led the children to the encyclopedia to learn more about the religions of India. Discussion of the reports on the various religions, superstitions, and the high rate of illiteracy of the Indian people enhanced their understanding of India's needs.

A scrapbook of newspaper and magazine articles on India was made to use for later reference, or just to be re-read when needed. A large map of India was also constructed on which pupils showed the leading industries and the leading exports and imports, so that they could get a clearer picture of the kinds of work the people of India do, the food they eat, and the countries with which they trade.

Graphs were made showing the daily consumption of nourishing foods in India and in the United States, as well as of the yearly death rates in the United States and India. The relationship between a nourishing diet and the health of a people was thus clearly suggested. A chart was developed showing the ways in which the United States had helped India in her food production and health program. The class thought that what it had learned about India was important enough to share with other sixth-grade groups and they arranged a sharing program.

The children acquired many insights from these activities. They began to think of India as a country of 360,000,000 people rather than as a spot on the map. They became acquainted with the customs of these people, learning how they dressed, what they ate and what they wore, how they felt about other peoples, and how quickly Indian children had to grow up and accept responsibilities.

They began to understand that when people are hungry, unlearned, sick, and afraid, they are likely to have a kindly feeling toward those who help them overcome these difficulties.

They learned something of the moral obligation of the more fortunate toward those less fortunate.

They gained an appreciation of how rapidly the world is changing, as they found it difficult to find up-to-date material on India except from newscasts on television and radio and from daily newspapers, current magazines, and people who have recently visited India.

They acquired an increased interest in reading the daily papers and current magazines and in watching television newscasts to learn about what is happening in the United States as well as in other parts of the world.

They realized India's strength as a leader among the nations of

Southeastern Asia, and that whether she remains a free, democratic nation, or falls under the domination of Communism, will greatly influence all of Southeast Asia and eventually the entire world.

How Young Americans Attempted to
Solve the Trieste Problem

When the F. Read School in Philadelphia opened for the fall term, newspapers, radio, and television were carrying news of disturbance in Trieste. Parents in the Read School neighborhood are predominantly Italian. Many were engaged in indignant discussions which showed antagonism against Yugoslavia. "Trieste was a part of the Old Roman Empire when no one had even heard about Yugoslavia!" The "battle of words" was on, and the children in the sixth-grade class were caught up in it. This matter concerned them closely, their parents having kept the traditions of the Old Country alive in their hearts and in their homes.

"What are our parents arguing about?" they asked the teacher. The map was studied. The children saw the location of Trieste in relation to Italy, to Yugoslavia, and to Europe. This led to more questions. "Why is Italy ready to go to war over one seaport, when there are other Italian seaports nearby?" "Why does Yugoslavia want the Port of Trieste?" "In what ways does its location make it important?" "Why is Russia interested?" "Does this problem affect Europe?" "How?" "Why are we, as Americans, concerned over this problem?" "What part should our country take in the Trieste dispute?" "Does this problem concern the other people of the world?" "What part should we take in world problems?" "What can children do?"

Thus it was that the children decided to try to "solve" the Trieste Problem. But how? Where should they go for information? Newspaper items, magazine articles, and books were found and a bibliography was begun. Letters were sent to publishing companies, to the Italian Steamship Line, to the embassies concerned, to the United Nations, and to the United States Printing Office.

The information obtained was insufficient to solve the problem. This necessitated finding other sources of help. Under the caption, "Resource People," were listed the people who might help: a teacher who had vacationed in Italy last summer and who had returned with a wealth of pictures and information; a parent of one of the children in the class, who took frequent trips to Italy; a child who had just returned from a visit to the southern part of Italy. This was fine, but information from these sources would probably be one-sided.

"Isn't there someone who can tell us how all the people involved feel, the residents of Trieste, the Italians, and the Yugoslavs?" "Couldn't Mr. Hanusey help?" Mr. Hanusey, a social studies collaborator, could and did. Through him the World Affairs Council was contacted. Mrs. Flounders discussed the situation from the viewpoint of the residents of Trieste. Miss Ely, who had spent some months in Yugoslavia, gave the Yugoslav's viewpoint.

Many more questions arose, involving: the history, the government, the people, their homes, their manners and customs, their beliefs, their education, the ways in which they earned a living. Answers to these questions and many more were necessary for a better understanding. It was necessary to reorganize the class plan.

To understand the culture of the people, the class went to the Commercial Museum, to the Museum of Art, and to an Italian bakery. A soldier uncle of one of the children, stationed in Trieste with the Army of Occupation, sent a letter home telling about Trieste, the people, and what our government had done to improve the port. He seemed to be writing about Philadelphia. People seemed to be very much the same the world over. Their problems were our problems.

In order to keep their study impartial and make it effective, the children saw that it was necessary to feel and think as Italians, Yugoslavs, and Triestines, as well as Americans. And so they took an imaginary trip, first to Italy, then to Yugoslavia, and lastly to Trieste. They were interested in the people of the towns and mountain villages, as well as the cities. Children's diaries were literary gems by this time, for vocabulary had kept pace with other learning. Drawings, graphs, maps, dressed dolls, and miniature homes were made. To illustrate what the children felt it was necessary to know to understand the Trieste problem, for example, songs were sung, poetry was written, and dances were learned.

Facts were constantly being evaluated, added, eliminated, and reorganized. The class plan now had five areas:

1. Questions Concerning Geography and History
2. Questions Concerning the People
3. Questions Concerning Earning a Living

4. Questions Concerning the United States
5. Questions Concerning the World

Committees studied each area. Soon the information was as complete as the children could make it. In order to have a clear and orderly picture of the problem, the committees wrote and presented a "You Are There" skit.

The day came when the class felt it could make some recommendations. Again the committees went to work, and from their combined efforts recommendations were written. "Now that we have a solution to our problem, what shall we do with it?" the teacher asked. And so they decided to send it to John Foster Dulles, Secretary of State. This, they thought, was to be the final culmination of their work, but there was another yet to come. That took place the day Mr. Dulles took time out from a busy day personally to encourage a sixth-grade's interest in world affairs.

Hi Neighbor

In the unit, "Hi Neighbor," the sixth-grade pupils of the Platt Elementary School, Grand Island, Nebraska, come to realize that in the present century the peoples of the world are next-door neighbors. They study how communication, transportation, and power have brought this about. They learn how these basic factors have helped the United States become one of the world's leaders.

An imaginative air tour of five countries of the world furnished the structure for the unit. The social economic life of each country was studied. The aim was to discover how communication, transportation, and power are affecting the lives of people. In addition, facts were sought concerning races and religions in each country, so as to gain a broader background of the need for world understanding.

Attitudes and understandings emerged as the children engaged in carrying out the activities of the unit. In Brazil they saw a new frontier being developed through the use of modern means of transportation and communication. In France, India, and China they realized that further development of power could help increase the potential of each country. When they "traveled to Israel" they were amazed by the twentieth-century pioneers who had gone from the oxcart to jet planes in a matter of a few years.

During the study of these countries emphasis was placed on the following attitudes and understandings which it was hoped would become more a part of their way of life:

1. To recognize and respect the worth of an individual regardless of race, color or creed
2. To respect the religious beliefs of other people
3. To appreciate the contribution of other cultures
4. To accept a feeling of responsibility for improving standards of living in the world
5. To accept the conviction that world problems must be solved through mutual efforts and understandings
6. To gain an understanding of the people of the world, their problems, their needs, their desires, and their cultures
7. To gain an understanding of how modern developments have caused these problems and will in the same sense combat them
8. To develop an understanding of why people in different countries live as they do and what other countries of the world can do to help these people
9. To understand better the forces of communication, power, and transportation and how they have affected the world
10. To enrich the child's understanding of the United Nations and how this organization is working to better our world and help to overcome its problems
11. To develop an appreciation of what the other countries of the world have contributed to human society as a whole

Stress was placed on having pupils seek answers to the various problems they formulated. The study of each country was begun with a familiarization trip which focused attention on the way the people lived. Following this orientation, the pupils formulated their questions to bring out the impact of the basic forces on people's lives. The effort to solve their problems carried the pupils to many resources. Many of the materials used in this unit were obtained from the Nebraska Air-Age Education Division, University of Nebraska, major airline companies, foreign embassies, consulates, and private industries engaged in business in foreign countries. Several social studies textbooks were also used for reference.

Activities included drawings, production maps, construction, graphs, reports, inviting resource persons to visit the class, preparation of various foods, making field trips, and collecting models and specimens.

One group surveyed, "What our forefathers contributed toward the development of the United States." As the discussion went on it soon became apparent to the members of the group that some nationalities did contribute more than others. This was soon faced squarely by David, who said, "What difference does it make whether your folks contributed more than mine, or if they came from a different country? It was the participation, cooperation, and sharing of all groups that helped make America what it is today."

One particular discussion centered on, "What happenings have caused the Jewish people in Israel to seek a different way of life?" The discussion was mainly concerned with the persecution of the Jewish people. One of the Protestant girls compared the Jews with our own forefathers and Pilgrims, and the problems they had before they could establish a secure home.

In the unit "Hi Neighbor," pupils not only learned that Americans today can travel anywhere on the globe in fifty hours. They sensed as well that in the future this time may well be cut to a day or less. Some of them, at least, began to think of themselves as world travelers and as ambassadors of good will and understanding.

Sixth-Graders Study Foreign Lands

This is a resume of the study of "Old World Lands" by the sixth-graders at Belvoir School in Shawnee County, Kansas. The principal encourages imaginative and creative teaching methods which give the teachers confidence in undertaking and doing something which is new to them.

At the beginning of the school term the children were led into a discussion of the purposes of studying foreign lands. In these discussions of goals and purposes the children stated not only the usual goals of learning to read maps and to reason geographically, but also the goal of a "better understanding of the people of the world and how they are like us."

The class chose first to make a brief study of Kansas in order to be better prepared to make comparisons of industries, occupations of the people, climatic conditions, geography of each country, and its schools.

After studying Kansas, the first discussions of foreign lands were centered about the United Nations. The materials used were the state-adopted textbook, *Old World Lands,* encyclopedias, current newspapers, and magazines. The children clipped pictures and news stories from newspapers and magazines for class discussion and for the bulletin board. Kings, queens, presidents, and prime ministers were included in the picture collection.

The school has rather meagre source material and the teacher was at a loss as to what more he could use to stimulate interest. One day when the class was reading its newspapers he showed them a copy of a Chinese newspaper. The response was almost electrifying. "What do newspapers in India, England, Italy, Saudi Arabia look like?" they asked.

While the interest was high a letter was sent to Senator Andrew Scheoppel inquiring how to secure copies of foreign newspapers. The Senator sent a copy of the Official Diplomatic List. From the diplomatic list each child chose an Embassy to which to write and was assigned one other country. For a few days the group studied sentence structure and letter writing. Each child then wrote a letter to the ambassadors of the country or countries for which he was responsible. In each letter copies of a foreign newspaper, bulletins, and pamphlets were requested. Each child mailed his own letter.

While they waited for answers to these requests, the class learned how to read and apply information given in the legends of maps. The class thus began to be acquainted with the countries of Europe, Asia, and Africa.

When the newspapers arrived, some of which included translations of a paragraph or two, each was compared with American newspapers. It was discovered that other peoples in the world are also interested in foreign news. In many of the papers the picture of Vice-President Richard Nixon appeared. The children discovered advertisements of familiar American brands and saw pictures of foreign commodities. They found advertisements of motion pictures and other entertainment. They looked at the "comic" sections and wondered about the plot of an apparent serial story. They drew the conclusion that these people, like ourselves, are interested in foreign news, commodities, and entertainment.

With the newspapers came vast amounts of informational and educational bulletins, pamphlets, and folders. These greatly increased available source material. Each of the children adopted "his own countries" and asked for the privilege of making special reports.

The whole group again studied sentence structure and how best to make oral reports. There was great interest in selecting material thought to be important and interesting. One child, discovering that in France teachers are quite strict and that children learn "facts," asked, "But what if they don't believe or can't understand the 'facts'?" This led to discussion of the "what" and the "why" of what we believe. Another boy discovered that Kansas wheat was developed from the wheat of Turkey and Southern Russia.

One outgrowth of the collection of foreign newspapers was a study of Spanish. Three fifteen-minute periods a week are now devoted to this. The children are enjoying learning the names of common objects, colors, numbers, and common phrases and sentences. The teacher's purpose in teaching Spanish, in addition to showing the children that there is such a thing as a language barrier, is to show them the importance of correct pronunciation of words. A fact which many of the children have discovered and which they find interesting is that in many schools of the countries of the "old" world English is a required subject.

The children wrote the appropriate "thank you" letters and many requested the names of children with whom they could correspond. As replies were received, the class studied the "friendly" letter as a means of carrying the good will of Americans to the children of the world. It is to be hoped that this group of good-will ambassadors will be more effective than some of this older generation have been.

This group of sixth-grade children maintained a high rate of interest in the study of the usual skills, such as map reading, geographic reasoning, sentence structure, letter writing, and oral reports. They seem also to have developed an unusual understanding and tolerance for their associates. Again it is hoped that such understanding and tolerance will carry over into adult life and will reach out to the peoples of the world.

How Air Transportation Affects
Social Living

In a sixth-grade social studies class of the Clara Barton School, Long Beach, California, questions arose about the increased speed of modern aircraft on world travel. A boy asked, "If, in the winter, I took a commercial plane from Long Beach, where it's warm, to New York, where it might be cold and snowy, what kind of clothes would I wear?" Before anyone could answer, a girl of obvious Scandinavian lineage went on, "And what happens if someone is going from New York to Sweden where it is even colder? I wonder how the people in Sweden are dressed?"

After the class had shared comments and ideas it was agreed that a "flight" from Long Beach to Stockholm should be made. As a result of the discussion and class receptiveness to the idea, a Planning Committee was set up. Committees were also organized on an interest basis.

The Planning Committee suggested the route which was approved by the group. They chose the countries in which they were particularly interested, namely, America, Portugal, Spain, France, England, Belgium, Holland, Germany, Denmark, Norway, and Sweden.

By the time "D-Day" (Departure Day) arrived, everyone knew the location of the countries to be visited and about how long it would take to get to them by air. The departure was from New York. The spirit of friendliness at the beginning continued to pervade the atmosphere in every country the children visited. Each "official representative" gave a friendly welcome and an interesting report on his country stressing the typical areas, food, and customs. Opportunity was given to the visitors to ask questions.

There was emphasis on the likenesses between countries and on the things they had in common. One representative answered, when someone remarked about the difference in language, "We talk about the same things you do only we say them in words that are easy for us to understand." It was interesting to hear comments such as, "Gee, I didn't know people in Holland rode in streetcars, wore leather shoes, and suits and dresses like ours." This was the observation of a sixth-grade boy after experiences in reading, conversing with other people, and seeing audio-visual aids.

In the evaluation that followed the children's return from their imaginary trip perhaps the major insight gained was that more was gained by working together and sharing information than would have been possible had each individual made a trip alone, with no opportunity to share his insights with others. Learning accomplished through shared experience is a positive factor in the development of clear conceptions and understandings. One girl concisely phrased this when she remarked, "If all the countries we have visited would share their ideas as we have done, *everyone* in the world would benefit and be happier and no one would get mad and want what someone else has."

This was a happy experience for the children. It was also one in which they felt they had acquired a better understanding of the people of other nations. One does not know how long the new attitudes will last. In the multiplication of many such experiences, however, children should continue to broaden their horizons and appreciations.

Sixth-Grade Children Study Europe

Before the beginning of a study of Europe the sixth-grade boys and girls of the William Randolph School, Asheville, North Carolina, discussed with their teacher what they already knew about the countries of Europe. There were many and varied opinions. Some said the people looked different, dressed differently, had darker skins, ate unusual foods, and spoke different languages. Others thought they were not so different.

A few boys and girls said they knew children who had come from Europe and had seen people from European countries. One boy said that his parents had come from Europe, and one girl said that her grandparents had emigrated from Europe. During the discussion the children came to the realization that they were descendants of Europeans.

The children could hardly wait to find out from their parents the countries from which their ancestors had come. The next day the discussion was even livelier. Each child selected a country on which he would like to do special research. Usually he selected one from which his ancestors came. Others, who had been unable to learn about their ancestry, selected countries because they were curious about them, or because they knew someone there, or were otherwise interested in a particular area. Among the countries chosen were Norway, Sweden, Greece, Germany, Switzerland, Italy, France, Spain, Ireland, and England. From three to six pupils worked together on each country.

The pupils next discussed the best sources of information. They decided to use first their geography text, *Nations Overseas,* and their history text, *Builders of the Old World*. Some suggested that the encyclopedias would provide basic material. To get interesting details they thought it would be necessary to go to the school library and the city library for stories and pictures.

All agreed that the most recent information could be found in newspapers and current magazines, and through listening to radio or television. Each morning reports were made to the class on information or news read in newspapers and heard on television or radio. It was soon found that the collection of news items, pictures, maps, and other information made it necessary to make a scrapbook.

It was discovered that *Young Citizen,* their weekly newspaper, not only contained world news, pictures, and maps, but pronunciation helps for difficult words. The children came to look forward to it to see who could find the most information and best clippings for his scrapbook.

Sometimes the class discovered that neighboring countries were having problems or disagreements. The pupils who represented these countries had panel discussions or debates to try to clarify the reasons for these problems. One of the discussions was concerning the old issue of who should have the Saar, France or Germany. Since that problem seems to be one of the issues that keep Germany and France from being friends, pupils found it an interesting and important problem for study. Another problem of interest was that of sending freedom pamphlets in balloons from West Germany to East Germany. "Why were the balloons needed?" "What might be gained through their use?"

One period a week was chosen to teach a game played by children in one of the European countries. Pupils learned to play *Bag Race* from Holland, *Blarney Stone* from Ireland, *Lucky Leaf* from Italy, *Fire on the Mountain* from Scotland, *Dodger Tag* from England, *Exchange* from France, and *Barley Break* from Germany. They also discovered that many of the games they had been playing originated in Europe. *Spanish Fly* turned out to be what they had always called *Follow the Leader.* The book used here was *Games Around the World* by Sarah Hunt.

The class learned two folk dances for which they made their own costumes from crepe paper. These were *Clappdans,* a Swedish folk dance, and *Chimes of Dunkirk,* a folk dance from Switzerland. Later these two dances were presented on a variety program given by the school and sponsored by the Parent Teachers Association.

Dramatizing stories proved to be one of the most interesting activities. The three stories enjoyed most were: *The Pied Piper, The Wise Men of Gotham,* and *The Three Golden Oranges.* The best

European story collection was found in the book, *The Crowded House,* by Fan Kissen. Not only did the pupils learn more literature, they advanced in oral reading, expression, and diction as well. The children especially enjoyed putting the stories on the tape recorder as they read them, and playing them back for their class, as well as for other classes, to hear.

From their music textbook the children learned and often sang *The Spanish Cavalier; Ah, Lovely Meadows,* a Czech folk song; and *Cockles and Mussels,* an Irish folk song. The one they enjoyed most was *Mountain Stream,* a Swiss song. The class created dances to the rhythm of *Mountain Stream* and seemed to enjoy the words and music more because they were reminded of their own mountainous region of western North Carolina.

Maps were drawn of Europe and its countries. Pictures were painted, dolls dressed, and clay models made—all to help the class understand the dress, habits, and customs of the people of Europe. Some original poems were written. Others were read and collected for scrapbooks. Movies such as: *Children of Holland, Norwegian Children, French Children,* and *English Children* were viewed and discussed. Many filmstrips were used as well.

Some of the people who talked to the class about European countries were: a neighbor who had lived in Scotland; a father from Germany and one from Sweden; and a friend from England. During this study two exchange teachers, one from The Netherlands and one from Germany, visited the school and met with the class. The children were delighted to have these rich sources of information and bombarded the visitors with questions. Probably one of the greatest helps was one of the teachers in the school whose father and mother were from Greece. Although she had not been to Greece, she had studied the language and was very helpful in pronouncing difficult names. She also brought authentic costumes of ancient Greece as well as dolls and other souvenirs from Greece.

Invitations to parents to hear the review of this study were made on a map in the form of the country studied by each group. For refreshments, foods representative of the different countries were served. These included: for Greece, ripe olives; Spain, green olives; Sweden, cheese; France, grape juice; England, teacakes. The program was concluded with songs and dances of the countries studied.

CHAPTER 2

Junior High School

THE basic values to be sought in education for world affairs in junior high schools are fundamentally those sought in elementary schools. It is important to develop self-respecting, self-reliant, individuals who are not prone to work off personal feelings of aggression in antagonism toward minority groups and strange peoples. Respect for others regardless of the many differences of race, religion, nationality, sex, intelligence, and social economic status is of paramount importance in a democratic society and in education for democratic living at all levels.

The spirit of inquiry, the desire to explore the world and its peoples, characteristic of younger children, is also apparent in early adolescence. In junior high schools use of the careful method of inquiry is increasingly possible. More facts are sought. Distinctions between fact and opinion are made. Sources are evaluated in a conscious attempt to find the truth. Different interpretations of facts are weighed. The importance of tentative judgment becomes more consciously apparent.

There are at least three aspects of teaching and learning in junior high schools which make any type of international education difficult. First, boys and girls are in the early adolescent stage of development. Second, the expectations of parents and citizens for these youth are somewhat different than those they hold for younger children. Third, the climate of public opinion in a time of continuing world crisis often makes education for world affairs hard to achieve.

Early adolescence, as all parents and teachers know, is apt to be a difficult period. Boys and girls are seeking to break away from adult direction. At times these young people act and think as adults and at others as children. They are sometimes visibly dependent on parents and teachers. At other times, they may become defiant even of suggestions made by adults which are interpreted as authoritative pronouncements. Under such circumstances respect for others, and the careful use of the fact-finding techniques of impartial inquiry, are difficult. When there is added to this the predisposition in early adolescence to emotionalized fixations on particular individuals and ideas, advancing democratic values in the classroom can be extremely difficult.

The second problem of significance in teaching and learning for world affairs in junior high schools arises from the normal expectations of parents. Sons and daughters are becoming adults. As adults they should be developing "sound ideas" on questions of foreign policy and in relation to international problems of all kinds. "Sound ideas," naturally interpreted by the parents as their ideas, are not always based upon a knowledge of facts, or even upon a respect for factual evidence. Under such circumstances teachers may find it difficult to do an honest job of inquiry with their students. They may find the achieving of other democratic values equally difficult.

A third factor affecting the achievement of truly democratic purposes is the state of public opinion in a time of uncertainty regarding national and international affairs. That we are living in such a time is apparent to all. There appear to be no final answers to our international difficulties. But too often people seem to need and try to seek final answers.

Teachers in junior high schools are more subject now than formerly to the pressures of public opinion which affect the higher levels of education. An honest search for understanding and for evidence in the schools in some places has been subject to attack by people who, in varying degrees, are concerned and frightened by the uncertainties in the international scene. Local bigots take advantage of the current situation to attack teaching, the schools, and even the use of intelligence. Some of these attacks have been successful. Others have not. Under such circumstances teachers everywhere tend to become "careful." This means that they may consciously or unconsciously cease to do an honest job of education. And where intellectual honesty is curtailed the educative process may become but a limited form of propaganda or a dreary march through a text.

The descriptions of the ways in which some junior high school pupils and teachers have sought to achieve democratic values are presented in this chapter. It has proven to be almost impossible to obtain descriptions of situations in which teachers and schools have been under attack or where attacks are feared. Participants in such situations are naturally hesitant to evaluate the conditions which coerce them.

The descriptions that follow are, therefore, largely success stories. The reader will, however, be able to evaluate each in terms of educational values which he thinks to be important. In the descriptions, one needs to look at the results achieved with a healthy skepticism.

Attitudes Based on Values Held in Common

The abstract, remote, foreign world must necessarily remain mysterious and strange when one's first impressions are of different racial groups, bizarre dress, unintelligible language, odd customs, and sinister gods. Others are always foreign, different, and somewhat ridiculous when we ourselves are the standard. Such an attitude, more than any other, stands in the way of world understanding. And such an attitude, as expressed in current nationalistic extremes, is the inevitable consequence of placing primary concern on the superficial artifacts of a culture.

The matrix from which human brotherhood can stem is in the realm of values held in common. While information has worth as a tool, any program which aims only that far has failed. Information, and all forms of secondary experience, can further develop attitudes already begun. But without the compelling understanding of how we act, why we behave as we do, and how the actions of those about us develop, we cannot hope to reach for the empathy basic to real world understanding. And no externally imposed, teacher planned and dominated program can create or evoke such feelings from many children.

In line with these beliefs the emphasis in the early weeks of the work of the first-year core group in the Tappan Junior High School lay in the creation of an atmosphere in which policy could be cooperatively formulated without dominance or trepidation. The same problems of organization, communication, and administration were present as in any community which seeks to be self-governing. Certain problems had to be solved if planned procedures were to be developed for meeting the group's needs. The class inquired into the ways other groups have organized. Existent forms of government, national and international, supplied the answer.

Pupils and teacher asked themselves what would be needed if they were to operate democratically, and whether it was a possibility in their circumstances. Slowly a pattern of classroom operation emerged. In certain areas it was possible for the teacher to relinquish his veto over group decisions. On some questions parents were consulted. Effective channels of communication between home and school had to be established. In many small ways the classroom problems of procedure were unique, but in many larger ways all could see the resemblance to the problems faced by the First Continental Congress, as well as by the League of Nations and the United Nations.

Each time the class group examined its own operation the members became more aware of the value of an ability and willingness to look at things from the other fellow's points of view. Principles of procedure were only a rough guide. The interpretation necessary to apply principles successfully to particular cases was only achieved when the parties in conflict were able and willing to examine all points of view from the standpoint of their worth in achieving the goals of the whole group.

It became apparent that selfish antagonisms invariably reduced all efforts to futility, as did prejudicial dogmatism. Soon the group was interpreting international conference successes and deadlocks in the light of its own experiences. These boys and girls began to see clearly that much of international frustration grew from a persistent unwillingness to discuss basic points of view. They came to know, also, that people who do not understand the values they hold in common flounder. They sometimes wondered, as the representatives of international bodies must also wonder, if they could hope to succeed in their cooperative efforts.

Once this critical understanding and appreciation of values and their function and importance for individuals, groups, and societies were grasped, the class had the unifying thread upon which the beads of factual information about the world could be strung.

Members of the class began painting a 22- by 12-foot mural map of the world on the back wall of their classroom. To obtain information on the various countries, each student wrote to the embassies of two major world powers. In addition to locating countries on the map, the group was able to see in the mural the talents of each class member expressed in a form pleasing to all. As individuals and as groups, the class found that the map offered opportunities to work out problems of group association which they had earlier identified.

When the mural was finished, the class file of information from the countries was complete. This was supplemented with UNESCO materials on seventy world powers. Each student summarized his data on the two countries he initially investigated and provided each of his classmates with mimeographed outlines. Charts were made showing vital information. These were hung around the room.

The group liked the one painted wall so much that they went ahead and painted the rest of the room and refinished the blackboards, all in accordance with the latest information which could be obtained on lighting and color harmony. Then, so the whole room would be dynamically drawn into the map, they connected the pictures and charts to their appropriate countries with colored yarn.

The embassies contacted helped the project further by showing how class members could get in touch with pen pals in their countries. When individuals began sending and receiving letters on their own, the desire to understand others grew considerably. As the letter file grew and the storehouse of information expanded, this junior high school group realized that they understood others as much through what they told about themselves as through what others wrote to them. The more they told their pen-pals about their own lives, the more they were able to understand what each was trying to say.

Letters grew more personal and more private. Soon, students were talking about what their friends abroad thought of what they were doing in class. Many of the questions which came through the mail were questions raised earlier in class. Questions and problems replaced queries in letters about climate and geography. Pictures of parents and friends, homes, and favorite scenes replaced national monuments and public buildings. The pen-pals began to see what it was that each treasured and believed. Pupils began to understand other's values and were amazed at how much they had in common. They came to believe, finally, that it would be possible to live peacefully and productively with their friends overseas regardless of such disagreements as they or their governments might have from time to time.

It Is Interesting to Be Different

Direct correspondence between American pupils and the boys and girls of other countries can be most rewarding.* Pen-pals convey a real understanding of how other peoples live and think. To quote a Finnish correspondent, "We are building a bridge of friendship."

Research has its place, but it is frequently a cold substitute for the mysterious envelope bearing strange stamps. At first, only a few members of the seventh-grade class of the Cecil Avenue School, Delano, California, wrote letters. But as letters began to arrive and were shared with the whole group, more and more boys and girls joined the ranks. Soon pictures and scrapbooks were exchanged, and intolerance, if any, was lessened or disappeared in the natural process of understanding and comradeship.

We have too long minimized the differences between national and ethnic groups, in the mistaken idea that it is always necessary to hunt for common factors. At the Cecil Avenue School it is believed that people should acknowledge their differences and point them up as the possible reason for the particular contributions made to civilization by a given national or ethnic group. Students very often concluded that it is more interesting to be different, especially after discussing American achievements and differences.

Exchange teachers and students, as well as foreign-born residents in the vicinity, were asked to visit school to show articles from their homelands, and best of all, to answer the many questions in the minds of the boys and girls. If these questions sometimes sounded naive, it should be realized that not only do some pupils have strange notions about other places and peoples but, equally, some teachers need to revise their concepts. Perhaps teachers should shamefacedly admit that, in the past, too much emphasis has been placed on: windmills in Holland which have been replaced by modern pumps; colorful costumes in European countries, now seldom seen except on festive occasions; igloos in Alaska, where they are actually rare.

If young people learn to respect a representative of a national or ethnic group, that feeling tends to be transferred to the whole group. And tolerance grows from respect. Sound judgment must be exer-

* This method of contact is fostered by The International Friendship League, 40 Mount Vernon Street, Boston 8, Massachusetts. Those interested may write for information.

cised, therefore, in the selection of foreign-born representatives to visit classes.

In the upper grades of the Cecil Avenue School pupils learn to appreciate the contributions made to modern civilization by the peoples of other cultures without losing pride in their own. The techniques used to reach this goal include the study and performance of folk dances, folk music, and classical music. Art in its many forms is used to contribute to the pleasure of new experiences for students. Local families with treasured handcraft articles made abroad are proud to display them before a class. In this way students arrive at the conclusion that America is a little of every other place in the world. This gives them a feeling of kinship with other peoples. A "family tree" is another device used in this school to show boys and girls how diverse were the homelands of their forebears. They enjoy this personal research problem.

October is especially utilized to teach about the United Nations. The agencies which are having some measure of success are stressed, such as those dealing with international health, communication, and technical aid to underdeveloped areas. In the case of political questions it is freely admitted that achievements have not been as great. Here, as elsewhere in the school, pupils are led to face facts in the belief that intellectual honesty takes courage and that the world needs more of this quality.

The community surrounding the school is made up of minority groups. Many of the texts and materials available have been found to be inappropriate for local pupils. Children commonly come from homes where little or no English is spoken. The curriculum used in the past, therefore, frustrated both pupils and teachers. A revision of the coverage of study to make this meaningful to pupils is now under way and, in this venture, education for international understanding will assume its rightful place. Better relations with adults, particularly with the foreign-born, should aid in understanding that it is "interesting to be different," especially in a culture that has developed respect for difference into a unifying thread.

First Steps in World Understanding

In the spring of the year a young teacher of a seventh grade in the County of San Bernardino, California, began to make plans for the fall. Since he was in a school in a mountainous region similar to Scandinavia, he believed that the boys and girls would be interested in a study of these North European countries. Here seemed to be an opportunity for relating local mountain culture, and ways of making a living, to foreign lands.

Throughout the summer the teacher gathered material and information in order to develop a unit for the fall. When school started he was ready to present an experience unit. The main purpose was to compare the industries, geography, and government of the United States with those of the Scandinavian countries. He thought, "How can this help but be a successful experience with all the work which has gone into it?"

But after two weeks of school the children were completely frustrated! The teacher spent hours trying to figure out what was wrong. In analyzing the situation he finally realized that he had failed to take into account the most important part of any school, the children.

He had a group of mountain boys and girls, each one of whom was a rugged individualist. There seemed to be no feeling of cooperation in them. The children were extremely cruel in their remarks to one another. They needed to learn and understand the meaning of kindness and cooperation among themselves, with people in the neighborhood, and with other people in the world.

With this realization a new approach was made to the unit. Much time was spent in group discussions about the nationalities of the different children in the room. They talked about how each individual had a different appearance, but how basically they were much alike. They read about the boys and girls of Scandinavia, learned some of their songs and dances, and talked about how important cooperation was to the people of Norway, Denmark, and Sweden, in order that these small countries might survive. The class enjoyed stories by Hans Christian Andersen and learned that children all over the world read and enjoy them, also. Class members talked about the folk tales told to small children in Scandinavia and compared them with their own folk tales. Stories of the Vikings were read and discussed. For several weeks the pupils re-lived the many adventures of Lief and Lucky. One girl in the class wrote to a girl in Denmark and established a fine friendship.

After many weeks of activities and group discussions, important changes occurred. Much of the pettiness had disappeared. Members of the class began to ask if they might work in committees. Team games became popular, rather than something forced upon them. They were ready to study and compare the fishing, lumber and mining of the Scandinavian countries. They talked about the main cities and harbors. They learned about the Lapplanders and longed to see the beauty of the Midnight Sun. Some of the children gave reports told to them by their Scandinavian parents who had been to the land of their ancestors. Perhaps the greatest sense of achievement came to the teacher when as a culminating experience the class went to a Swedish restaurant for a smorgasbord dinner where, with complete ease and mutual respect and courtesy, they sat and ate together.

How many facts about Scandinavia will remain with these pupils as they grow older no one can predict. But this seems certain: through the study of a foreign people and their ways of living these children learned much about the meaning of cooperation and kindness. This was their first step in world understanding.

Common Ends Are Sought in Different Ways

In the Tappan Junior High School in Ann Arbor, Michigan, seventh-grade social studies and English are combined in a unified studies course. In the past the social studies aspect of the integrated course has had the title, "Man and His Environment." It is in the unified studies work that education for world affairs is to be found.

Each teacher and class plan separately the units to be covered during the school year. These plans have varied greatly, ranging from an historical to a modern geographical approach. In spite of the variety of approachs, there has been an amazing similarity in information gained. All classes acquire basic geographical understandings, such as the effect of climate and types of land on the economic ways of life, methods of transportation and communication, shelter, foods, clothing, and outstanding physical characteristics. Governments, religions, music, art, literature, industry, and history are commonly compared with those in the United States. All classes stress interdependence of geographic areas and the subsequent need for co-operation among nations in our modern society.

Topics have been grouped differently in the various classes. For example, one group may study Our Neighbors, the British Commonwealth, Lands Behind the Iron Curtain, Africa, and Islands of the World. Another class may study these topics by continents; while a third may take an entirely different approach and do its research under the headings of Food, Shelter, Clothing, Transportation, Communication, Power, Governments, and How People Express Themselves in their religions, art, music, and other cultural forms. Still another list of topics may include Early Civilizations, Mediterranean Contributions, Medieval Times, The Age of Expansion and The Industrial World.

Pupils engage in a variety of activities. They exchange letters, make models of buildings and vehicles of transportation, cook foods of other lands, and give style shows dressed in different costumes. Flour maps, animated maps, charts, and graphs are made. Coin collections are of great interest. Heroes of other lands make an impression as does the study of world champions in athletic events.

Efforts made in the past to build regional and world organizations make a fine background for understanding the League of Nations and the United Nations. Information and understanding of the problems of living man are stressed in current events work. Children participate in clothing drives for people abroad, aid in missionary programs, as well as help with the Crusade for Europe and other worthy causes.

Resources beyond the scope of any single teacher are many times made available by using the qualifications of other personnel in the same building. Art and music teachers help immeasurably in supplying opportunities for students to work with the art forms of different countries and to learn the songs and hear the music of these places. One of the mathematics teachers helped the unified studies geography program by building his units on charts and graphs using materials students had located in their social studies classes. These students were much more impressed with the value of their information than they had been before and the information had more meaning for them.

The amount of "world understanding" developed in any class depends largely upon the degree to which the teacher understands the world and on the ability of that person to provide vital learning experiences for the pupils.

Mexican Puppet Show

A tin mask as a wall decoration, a fragment of a stone god used as a paper weight, a woven belt worn in a group of clothes-conscious teen-agers—such casually displayed materials are familiar means of motivation in elementary and junior high schools. Combined with one teacher's quite apparent post-holiday enthusiasm for Mexico, they served to stimulate a series of projects on various grade levels in the Linden School, Pittsburgh, Pennsylvania, of which the most significant was a marionette show produced by the eighth-grade class.

Like most tourists, this teacher had been duly prepared for her journey to Mexico by a spate of pamphlets which depicted the quaint and the picturesque. Like most art-minded travelers she was awake to the beauties of the archeological remnants, the living traditions in the crafts, and the vitality of contemporary production in the fine arts. She had read of the inspiring campaign against illiteracy. But nothing had prepared her for the friendliness of the Mexicans, for their industriousness, for their sensitivity, for their aspiration and growth. Her own belated recognition that here were people of whom even the well-intentioned visitor frequently knows only the superficial aspects was what prompted the puppet show project and gave it real value to the children involved.

The marionette show offers a natural opportunity for the sympathetic acquisition of knowledge of another culture. It is a world in miniature and in action. In its creation, and in subsequent dramatization, not merely appearances of objects but reasons for and uses of objects become important. Similarities to and differences from familiar ideas and objects are accepted as merely incidental by children who identify themselves with characters who, for the moment, they genuinely are. But before this happy stage is reached the many steps of construction and production offer exciting challenges and gratifying outcomes.

The search for a script encouraged this eighth-grade group to read some twenty books. This wealth of sympathetic material about Mexico, written especially for children, was briefed by committees and analyzed primarily for suitability to marionette production. This purposeful reading, of course, expanded background information and shaped attitudes. Eventually the choice fell to *The Least One,* by Ruth

Sawyer—a book rich in Mexican folklore and universal in the appeal of its story of a boy and his pet. Dialogue from the book was supplemented, in the English class, with additional dialogue to fill gaps created by the deletion of narration and description.

To recount the establishment of scale for the production, the improvization of a stage, the making of marionette parts in a relatively formal classroom with fixed desks but movable children, the group activity which brought forth wardrobe and wigs, the challenging use of salvage materials, the group appreciation of the contribution of even the least capable child, the assumption of responsibility and leadership by those best able to lead, would be to tell more than a twice-told tale to many a teacher.

More pertinent was the discussion, not of technical or aesthetic problems, but of the "how" and "why" of Mexico itself, the growing use of Spanish phrases of courtesy gleaned from reading and references to a Spanish-English phrase book, and the pride with which the class sang in Spanish for a lovely Mexican friend who was passing through the city and who impressed them by her smart, modern dress and her honest answers to their questions.

The finished performance for a mother-and-daughter afternoon, and a father-and-son night with the Mexican Counsul as a guest, was gratifying, but less so than the children's question, "What can we send to a Mexican school?" The opportunity presented for the international exchange of children's drawings through the Junior Red Cross offered a simple and practical solution, for at that time choice of destination was possible. While there was a scattering of requests for various countries—"so that we can learn about them the same way"—the overwhelming choice of the entire school was Mexico, "so they will know we are interested in them," "so they will learn about us, too," and "so that they will know we are their friends."

The facts, geography, and statistics learned by this eighth-grade group may be forgotten, but some of the warmth of the experience, and the sense of identification with friendly people, will remain. This may happen to but one child; yet it will be important that one more person in the adult world of tomorrow will know that somewhere else in the world are old friends and, however far away, good neighbors.

"Lights! Camera! Action!"

A teacher of ninth-year social studies of Junior High School 52 in New York City faced the difficult problem of using appropriate content and method in working with his Spanish-speaking pupils. After discussions with the principal, other teachers, and the pupils, it was decided to study the different national and racial groups in the immediate neighborhood in order to learn about the United Nations. The principal suggested that a motion picture might even be made. The response of the class was enthusiastic.

Pupils and teacher planned the project in seven phases:

1. Getting the facts
2. Working out conclusions
3. Putting these conclusions in sequence
4. Writing a scenario
5. Shooting the picture
6. Writing the script
7. Preparing the program for presentation

Money for films had to be obtained from the School Senate, an elected body with the sole right to spend student funds.

To get the facts, the pupils prepared, mimeographed, and distributed a questionnaire for parents. The respondents were asked to state the land of their origin, their religious belief, and their comments on the people who were their neighbors. Committees of students then went about the community for random interviews asking people, "How do you think this community could be improved?" This question was designed to elicit prejudiced opinion that might not appear in the responses to the questionnaire.

The tabulated results produced some interesting indications as to the nature of the community and the opinions of the various groups about minorities. The findings led the boys to serious thought about intergroup relations. Some students gave cogent reasons for differentiating between the feelings of adults and those of children. Before the project was finished the relation between living together in a neighborhood and in a world of nations became clear.

Conclusions were drawn up in the form of propositions. These were put in order, and relevant scenes, illustrating each proposition, were worked out. For example, the film opens as follows:

Proposition	*Scene*
The United States is a nation of immigrants. They come from all lands and are of all races and creeds. Our city and our community represent many people.	Titles and credits. Class working on project showing boys of different ethnic origin. The American Flag. Statue of Liberty. New York skyline. Panorama of our community. Street scenes. People at work. Churches and synagogues.

The United Nations was included, along with the great document upon which it is based.

Shooting the picture was an exciting experience. No one knew too much about the technique. Everybody asked advice and gave it. There were underexposed and overexposed sections. Saturdays and Sundays were used to get shots of churches and synagogues in action.

After the film had been cut and edited, the class wrote the script. Every section had to be timed. The script had to be revised, lengthened here and shortened there, to fit the timing. There was strong pressure to put the script on a sound track but this was not done as it was desirable that the students, in the many presentations of the film, have the experience of speaking before audiences.

The students, the faculty, and the community took great pride in the film presentation. Representatives from the Board of Education and community groups came to see it. Interest in the undertaking led the students to master much specific knowledge and acquire many skills. Teachers of other subject areas integrated their work with this project. In addition to the social studies, mathematics, language arts, and science played functional roles. Perhaps even more important was the experience in democratic cooperation, in organizing, in planning, as well as in criticism and self-evaluation. In the making of a motion picture, these boys not only learned much about the United Nations and what it stands for, but also made part of themselves the concepts of brotherhood which derive their meaning through daily living.

From the United Nations
to the United States

The pupils of an 8A core class in the Bartlett Junior High School in Philadelphia were afraid of, and yet fascinated by, *war*. Their insecurity was shown by such remarks as "Are those planes ours?" when hearing engines drone in the distance. But the ambition of many boys was to join the air force or other defense services.

The pupils were also intrigued by the United Nations. Here was an organization, conceived during a war, fighting for *peace!* They willingly studied the complicated machinery of the organization and its functions. They read, recited, discussed, and argued about the Universal Declaration of Human Rights. Greater understanding of today's tensions developed. Names that had been mouthed, read, and forgotten became people, familiar and remembered, representing ideas and philosophies.

Going back through the history of the United Nations, the class became involved in trying to understand the issues and alliances of World War II, and, later, of the Korean conflict. From this stemmed a growing desire to study United States history, to find out the causes of the wars the United States had fought. They wanted to study the methods of treaty-making, the results of these agreements and the ensuing problems.

The class drew up a skeleton outline for a restudy, war by war, of military and social phases of American history.

A. When did the war take place?
1. Picture of life at that time
2. Declaration of War
3. Open warfare
4. Peace treaty and armistice
B. Who were involved?
1. Countries and their alliances
2. Reasons for these alliances
C. Why did it start?
1. Pre-war differences of opinions
2. Pre-war tensions
3. Incidents leading up to declaration of war

D. Where did it take place?
   1. First battle or attack
   2. Important events
   3. Turning points of the war
E. Results
   1. Peace treaty
   2. Political, economic, and geographic results

Committees were formed, using sociometrics, first through interest, then with social choices. Each committee specialized in separate areas, the Revolutionary Period, The Civil War, World War I, World War II, and the Korean conflict.

References and resources used included the class and school libraries, newspapers, news magazines, the World Affairs Council of Philadelphia, radio and television programs. Each group was responsible for keeping a written account of committee meetings, in addition to giving an oral report. Each committee was given a bulletin board and the responsibility for organizing and presenting illustrative material in its areas. Each committee was also responsible for preparing a written report, including a bibliography.

The pupils read a good deal outside of history as such. They read biographies of Washington, Revere, Lincoln, the Roosevelts. They read novels about the particular age they were studying. They brought in the picture history of World War II, and newspapers saved from September 1, 1939, D-Day, and the V-Days.

Oral reports to the class took the form of a play, written, directed, and given by one group; a panel discussion; a TV quiz show, concentrating on information; and a "Dragnet" presentation of World War I. They marked the change in methods of warfare: transportation, communications, and weapons. They noted the change in the foreign policy of the United States, in conjunction with its physical, political, economic, and technical growth. They saw the change in the size of the world, from small separate communities to dependent, overlapping countries, where everyone, regardless of geographical isolation, must be sensitive to every political, economic, or cultural tremor anywhere. They saw the beginning of the atomic age, and discussed its implications for peace and war.

When returning to the present, pupils were able to discuss and think more intelligently about possible United States recognition of Red China, the Berlin Conference, the social and political crisis in

South Africa, and the pros and cons of possible United States intervention in French Indo-China.

After moving on to other projects, interest has continued in world happenings. A class reporter pin-points new events and a strong desire has developed to visit the United Nations headquarters in New York.

A United Nations Building Project

A United Nations Building Project, carried on by the seventh grade of the Arroyo Grande Union Elementary School, Arroyo Grande, California, provided a unique opportunity for students to gain an understanding of international cooperation on a democratic basis. It also gave the teacher an excellent opportunity to correlate work of various subjects into one teaching unit.

The mathematics involved provided an opportunity for the pupils to have learning experiences in mechanical drawing, planning, and construction. English was brought into play when letters requesting information were written to various members of the United Nations. All such information was placed in notebooks and provided the basis for oral reports. Geography was also brought into play when the student searched out information as to the location, industries, imports, and exports of United Nations member countries. History was involved when the pupils studied the history of governments, political parties, wars, social problems, customs, habits, and the attempts of the United Nations to bring about world peace.

Each student in the class of thirty chose two members of the United Nations to study. Each wrote letters to gather information answering the following questions: "What are the country's resources?" "Why did they join the United Nations?" "What are their imports and exports?" "Who are their delegates?" Questions were asked, also, concerning habits, customs, and home life. Committees were chosen by the class to dramatize and give a detailed explanation of the organization and structure of the United Nations.

When it was decided to construct to scale the United Nations Buildings the pupils elected a chief engineer who, in turn, appointed an engineer for each of the three buildings. These engineers then selected communities to help them with their tasks. Every pupil was given an opportunity to take part in the construction of the United

Nations buildings. Buildings were constructed on a scale of one-eighth of an inch equaling one foot. The Secretariat building actually now stands 5 feet 8 inches tall. The buildings have chairs, tables, desks, and all types of furniture built to scale.

These seventh-grade pupils also printed their own newspaper, *The United Nations Press*. One pupil wrote an article telling of the progress and cost of constructing the buildings. Another wrote an article concerning customs and habits. Articles were written on foreign cars and social problems of member nations. A fashion column appeared, with drawings depicting the various costumes worn by the peoples who comprised the member nations. And articles were written on up-to-date problems confronting the United Nations.

In undertaking this study the pupils became increasingly aware of the great need for, and the importance of, the work done by this international organization. There developed a desire to know more about the United Nations, to understand its aims and ideals. The maximum creative resources of pupils and teacher were called forth in this United Nations Building Project.

A Ninth-Grade Class Studies the United Nations

A teacher of the Lincoln Junior High School of Santa Monica, California, previously set the classroom environment for a study of the United Nations by preparing an attractive attention-getting bulletin board display on UNESCO in action throughout the world. She also read letters from the state board of education, the local board of education, and the school principal, inviting the students to prepare a school assembly with the theme of brotherhood in keeping with National Brotherhood Week.

This build-up was sufficient to lead the children to accept enthusiastically the invitation to put on an assembly program. They decided to write a play for National Brotherhood Week to show its relation to the United Nations and UNESCO and its meaning for the community and world. They also planned to make individual notebooks and to carry on supplementary activity for extra credit, such as making a set of United Nations flags, or authentically costumed manikins of people from United Nations countries. These were later contributed to the school library.

The individual notebooks included thumbnail sketches of member nations of the United Nations, providing in each case such information as historical and cultural backgrounds, as well as data on government and industry. Illustrations were added in the form of pictures, maps, flags, and news clippings.

One week was spent in research and discussion of information about the *what, why, who, when,* and *how* of the United Nations. Hearing her daughter talk about the interesting work being undertaken in the class, prompted a mother to offer the group the use of any or all of the costumes she had collected during her stay in the Far East and the Orient. She accepted an invitation to talk to the class about these countries and display and model the costumes. This experience added interest and the students decided to end the play with a parade of costumes.

In planning the play each student wrote a few lines expressing his idea of an appropriate theme. After hearing each read, several of those thought to be the best were listed on the blackboard. After much discussion the class selected a theme, which was then developed by the author with the aid of a consulting committee. Since several other themes seemed to tie in closely with the main idea, it was subsequently decided to make the play a group of dream sequences. The cast of characters was chosen by tryouts, and rehearsals began. In two more weeks the play was ready for the student body assembly.

The title of the play was *The World: A Brotherhood.* It centered upon a teen-age junior high school girl who, having just begun the study of the United Nations and UNESCO, has four dreams. Its theme suggested that kindness and understanding begin in the home, emphasizing that brotherly love unites, whereas hate and envy destroy. A dream, "Pride and Racial Prejudice," brought out the fact that children are not race conscious, accepting people as they are; that it is the adults who seem to initiate prejudices against minority groups. In "A Family Cares" sequence, an American family sent a CARE parcel of food to a German family in need, thus emphasizing the value in helping those who are less fortunate. In the "Parade of Costumes" each person appeared in costume, the narrator announcing the country and type of costume and telling something of interest about each.

At the end, the little girl who had these dreams awakened with a broader understanding of the purpose of the United Nations and UNESCO.

Why We Believe as We Do

Many seventh-grade classes in the Bartlett Junior High School have shown a spontaneous desire to study the various religions. One group went so far as to draw up a petition, even before the class had an opportunity to go through the usual procedure of choosing a unit. Its interest was recognized and the class subsequently made an outline of what it felt should be covered. This included the study of primitive forms of worship, the history of the Judeo-Christian system, Oriental religions, religion in art, and the history of the struggle for religious liberty.

The class was then divided into groups based on interest and sociometric studies. Each committee was responsible for drawing up an outline to guide its work. The committees obtained information from the class and school libraries, filmstrips, films, the Fellowship Commission, and religious leaders in the community. They made several trips to the main city library to supplement their work. *Life* magazine was running a series of religious articles at the time and these proved extremely helpful. One group copied clerical dress from photographs and drawings, and later made puppets of the clergy wearing these outfits. These figures were used in presenting information to the class as a whole through a play which the group wrote and produced.

The entire class took a guided tour through the Art Museum, concentrating on religious paintings, sculpture, and *objets d'art*. The committee was able to obtain a rather extensive collection of inexpensive prints at the Museum, to add to photographs cut from magazines. The music department cooperated by assisting in a study of religious music: chorals, oratorios, songs, and symphonies.

The students tried at all times to write the facts in their own words, to read and interpret, to discern between fact and opinion.

When class members felt they had gotten all they could from the printed page, they listed such questions as these from their outlines which were still unanswered: "How do churches raise money?" "How do the clergy dress?" "How do the worshippers dress?" "What articles are used in the rituals?" "What is the significance of these?"

"What is the significance of the decorations or objects placed around the house of worship?" "Is there any historical significance to the design of the house of worship?"

Arrangements were next made for the entire group to visit churches. The children received written permission from their parents to go on all trips. They did not attend services. They went on tours through the buildings. They received the utmost cooperation from the religions institutions visited. They toured the Cathedral of Peter and Paul, Congregation Rodeph Sholom, and Christ Church. In each case, the architecture, historical significance, ornaments and dress, were explained, indeed, all questions were answered.

At the completion of the study, there was greater understanding on the part of the children. They celebrated Russian Easter, sang Christmas carols, and stayed home from school on Yom Kippur. There was greater understanding, also, of the music and painting created through the love of God, regardless of the ritual used.

The World's Living Religions

A seventh-grade core class in the Metcalf Laboratory School at Illinois State Normal University, Normal, Illinois, became interested in the topic "Seeking Religious Freedoms in New Lands," while studying the history of the thirteen colonies in America. The children were especially impressed by the intolerance shown toward faiths different from that of the majority. Questions such as these were asked, "Why weren't the colonists more tolerant than their former European religious leaders?" And "Who is a Christian?" The regular teacher, aided by a student teacher, helped the children find answers to their questions and problems and share their experiences with the members of their class.

Since the study was student-initiated, the boys and girls entered upon the research with enthusiastic eagerness. Each child made a study of his own religion. Through role playing the pupils learned to make effective telephone and personal interviews. They wrote letters inviting resource people in the community to speak to the class. These included ministers, missionaries, a rabbi, a priest, and college students from abroad who were of differing faiths.

The children engaged in committee work in preparing reports and in preparation for panel discussions. They interviewed the visitors, studied books on their respective religions, and made a class and campus survey of religion.

An interchurch visitation program was undertaken. Each child invited a number of his classmates to be his guests at Sunday School and at worship services. The rabbi and priest invited the entire class to visit their places of worship.

These seventh-grade pupils formulated the following guide for the study of their own religions:

1. Name of their church and its officials
2. The doctrines or creed of the church
3. The sacraments and forms of worship
4. The religious events on the church calendar
5. The number of active world and local members
6. The church program for bringing about greater religious harmony with other religious groups
7. The church program for promoting world peace
8. The ways in which the church helps me to become a happier individual and a better citizen

Following the study of their own religions pupils chose to learn something about the following: Taoism, Confucianism, Buddhism, Judaism, Hinduism, Shintoism, Zoroastrianism, Islam, and the Greek and Russian Orthodox creeds. The outline developed in this case included: the origin of the religion, its organization, doctrine, and the forms of its worship.

As the unit progressed through the year religious movies, songs, poems, literature, and art masterpieces were enjoyed. During the Lenten season, the children learned Bible verses and prayers of their own selection. The teacher read a biography of Pope Pius, emphasizing his role as a world leader for peace.

This study was favorably received by the parents and the community in general. There seemed to be no conflict with the objectives of public education. The unit was an additional way by which to broaden the public school curriculum to meet the interests and needs of children. No final written or oral examination was given.

A Ninth-Grade Unit on the U.S.S.R.

The pupils of a ninth-grade social studies class of the Johns Hill Junior High School of Decatur, Illinois, first became interested in

Russia when, as seventh-graders, they had followed Congressman Peter F. Mack's around-the-world flight in their classroom work and shared his disappointment when the "Iron Curtain" wasn't raised for his proposed visit to Moscow. They decided two years later to find out all they could about Soviet Russia.

When they started to study this unit, teacher and pupils decided they wanted to know the geography and history of modern Russia. They wanted to know the structure of government, and to learn about the peoples and the armed forces of this great land mass of Europe and Asia. They agreed that they wished to compare each phase of their study with the United States. The class planned and devoted six weeks to the unit.

A general chairman was selected for each two-week phase of study. After considerable discussion the class felt that the geographical research should be done by committees. These were established for the topics of natural resources, climate, communication and transportation, peoples and their distribution, and recently acquired territories. Each committee selected one member to act as its librarian. The committee librarians conferred with the school librarian, who helped them find pertinent materials. Materials were brought to the classroom for use.

Reports were given by each committee to the class. Pictorial graphs of the systems of transportation and communication were made. Pictures were collected and arranged attractively on the bulletin board. Maps and charts were drawn to show the diversity and location of the U.S.S.R.'s natural resources. A display table was set up with samples of minerals, even including uranium. The climatic belts were charted on the globe. Outline maps were used to show the division of the sixteen republics and the acquisitions of the U.S.S.R. Notes were taken on their research and reports and notebooks kept.

In order to assure brevity and clarity, the teacher presented to the class the historical factual information essential for an understanding and balanced judgment of past and present events. Each student was given mimeographed sheets which gave a thumbnail chronological overview of Russian history from 862 A.D. to the present. These stressed significant dates. Emphasis was placed upon the coming of Bolshevism and the construction of the Socialist State.

Communism and democracy were defined and their philosophies explored. A comparison was made of the functions and operations of our political parties with those of the single Communist Party. It was necessary to become familiar with new words and personalities such as Comintern, collectivization, purges, Lenin, Stalin, and Trotsky.

Huge charts were made by class members to compare the present-day governmental structure of Russia with that of the United States. Russia's central government was compared with our federal government, the provincial with our states, and the local with our county and city governments.

Curiosity concerning the biographies of top U.S.S.R. leaders was so strong that the class requested that a good reader be selected daily to read a brief biography of a top personality. For their audience reading, the class selected the following:

1. In Public Affairs: Stalin, Molotov, Malenkov, and Beria
2. In Military Affairs: Zhukov and Konev
3. In Economy: Mikoyan
4. In the Press and Communication: Ilya Ehrenburg
5. In Sciences: Trofim Lysenko

It was easy to find apparently authentic material on Russia before World War II but the facts on the years since the war were difficult to track down. Volumes of information, much of it contradictory and unsubstantiated, have been published in periodicals since the war, and the class had to analyze a great deal of material to collect facts they could accept as true for a panel discussion in which life under a dictatorship was compared with that of life in a democracy. Other subjects treated in panel discussions included the family, the position of women, education, labor, housing, recreation, the press, free speech, the right to assemble, justice, and religion.

As a research problem, each pupil wrote a paper of 500 to 1000 words. The class agreed that each person should use at least three references. Pupils were taught how to make a bibliography and each was required to submit one with his paper. Papers dealt with everything from biography of leaders to statements on basic economic problems in Russia.

Because the class felt that the people of Decatur should share in their findings on the U.S.S.R., the class decided to use their scheduled thirty minutes on television for this purpose. The resulting telecast over WTVP, Channel 17, consisted of three program divisions.

Part 1 was a panel composed of eleven students and their chairman. They discussed the geography of the U.S.S.R. Part 2 was composed of two students who discussed Democracy and Communism. Charts were used to compare the governmental structure under each political system. Part 3 was a forum composed of ten students and a chairman. This group compared the freedoms enjoyed in a democracy with those in a dictatorship and showed the effects on life under each system.

The television program attracted such favorable comment that the Decatur chapter of the American Association of University Women invited the class to present this program on two radio broadcasts over local radio stations, WDZ and WSOY.

During the study one student wrote a one-act play entitled *Escape*. The play had four scenes with ten characters. *Escape* depicted life behind the Iron Curtain and the valiant, successful efforts to get out of the country. It was presented as a live broadcast over WDZ.

In the class' evaluations of this unit, students reported that the most surprising fact they learned from their study was that Russia, although supposedly Communistic, had only a small percentage of party members. They also were amazed at the great diversity of land and peoples in Russia.

Many parents and citizens in the Decatur community have stated that the unit on the U.S.S.R. was worthwhile educationally. They often add that the experiences in research, the telecast, and the radio broadcasts were, and probably will continue to be, a high point in the lives of many of the pupils.

This Johns Hill Junior High School class won a Principal School Award in the 1954 Freedom Awards of the Freedom Foundation, at Valley Forge, for its outstanding performance in this unit.

International Trade Can Lead to World Understanding

An English class of the Cavert Junior High School, Nashville, Tennessee, came to the unit on international trade direct from their literary experience with the theme of Coleridge's *The Ancient Mariner:*

> He prayeth best, who loveth best
> All things both great and small;

For the dear God who loveth us,
He made and loveth all.

This was the theme which served as a springboard for the global thinking required by the international trade unit.

The unit itself was initiated through an attitude test on various phases of international trade. This same test was administered at the end of the unit to determine changes in attitudes brought about as the result of study and research.

The first three weeks of eight weeks of study were spent sensitizing the class to problems of international trade. This was done through displays of imports, visual aids, audiovisual aids, a current events bulletin board entitled "World Trade in the News," wide general reading, and class discussions. Films on the importance of international trade included *World Trade for Better Living, Our Shrinking World, Made in U.S.A.,* and *Stuff for Stuff.* The filmstrip *Keystone of Prosperity: America's Foreign Trade* served a like purpose.

The rise in the cost of coffee stimulated interest in Brazil, her economy, and her role in international trade. In preparation for a guest speaker from Brazil the class arranged a Brazilian display, featuring a products map, samples of her chief exports, books, magazines, and pamphlets presenting life there and the results of Point Four aid.

As the students became aware of problems related to international trade, further resource people were brought to the classroom to clarify issues. Guest speakers included the following: a representative from The League of Women Voters, who presented the League's view on international trade policies; Nashville's U.S. Customs Officer, who explained customs procedure and the recent simplification of customs; a U.S. Army Captain recently returned from Germany, who spoke on the reconstruction program in Germany and conditions in Western Europe today; an exchange student, who gave a German's view of Germany's reconstruction; an Hawaiian exchange teacher, who showed slides depicting life in Hawaii and explained her role in world trade.

The class chairman introduced speakers and made the concluding remarks. Buzz sessions or question-and-answer periods followed the speeches. Thank you notes were sent to all speakers.

Interest in seeing for themselves a phase of their city's role in international trade took the entire class on a tour of one of Nashville's largest warehouses. Here they viewed great quantities of imported foodstuffs. The director of the coffee division, who spoke to the group on cultivation, processing, and exporting of coffee, pointed out the complete dependence of the United States on imported coffee and Brazil's economic dependence on her coffee export.

Class members tried to think of themselves as a group of responsible citizens interested in one of the vital issues of the day, rather than as members of an English class. Five committees were organized on the basis of interest in a specific phase of international trade. The committees set up for intensive study were:

1. Significance of International Trade
2. Difficulties in International Trade
3. United States Contributions to a Freer Trade Policy
4. International Contributions to a Freer Trade Policy
5. Tennessee's Role in International Trade

Each committee used the problem-solving approach. Members read widely, made personal and group field trips to importers and exporters, conducted interviews, took opinion polls, and wrote letters to Congressmen, Senators, and members of the Randall Commission. They gained basic economic understandings and concepts which were shared from time to time with the entire class. Their findings were presented through oral reports, group discussions, panels, junior town meetings, debates, skits, creative writing, graphs, charts, posters, models, and a sand table.

Illustrated class diaries were kept by the secretary and by each committee. Logs were kept by recorders. Each student prepared his own illustrated notebook. This contained creative writing, copies of letters sent and received, notes on speeches, recordings, films, reading and current events.

Student enthusiasm ran high throughout the unit but reached its highest peak in the culminating activity, which was attended by representatives of interested groups in the community, including college students and teachers. By this time the classroom had taken on an international trade atmosphere. Each committee had prepared a bulletin board summarizing through visual aids the important concepts related to its area of study. The culminating activity consisted of committee reports presented through different media.

Skill in the proper use of research tools and techniques was developed as the students read widely, distinguished fact from opinion, and read current material on international trade with understanding. The habit of listening responsively and critically for persuasive techniques and bias was formed. Enrichment of vocabulary resulted from the many new terms encountered in the study.

The students were better prepared by their study to face the economic world through these understandings: (1) higher standards of living are made possible by international trade; (2) the more industrialized a nation becomes the more dependent it is on other nations for raw materials and markets; (3) high trade barriers cause international tensions; and (4) the more prosperous other nations become the more they can buy from us.

Developing alongside such international economic understandings were an appreciation of the skills of peoples in all parts of the world; an awakened sensitivity to the problems, needs, and aspirations of other peoples; a desire to weigh legislation concerning international trade in the light of its probable effects on peoples throughout the world; a willingness to cooperate with other peoples in an attempt to solve international economic problems; and the recognition that, "We are all fellow-passengers on the same planet and are all equally responsible for the happiness and well-being of the world in which we happen to live."

World Trade: One Approach to International Understanding

The girls in a core class of intellectually gifted pupils at the Elizabeth Barret Browning Junior High School, New York City, were beginning a study of world trade. They regularly discussed the issues of the day. Some of these they took up briefly, while others were chosen for study in depth. As they collected and analyzed news stories pertinent to world trade, they began to sense the broad scope of the problem. Questions listed for further study were:

1. The problem of East-West Trade and its effect on our relations not only with the Soviet bloc but also with our allies
2. Problems related to specific industries in the United States which were seeking protection through tariff and quota arrangements (e.g., the Briar Pipes case)

3. Problems related to the slogan popular with our friends, "Trade Not Aid"

In trying to discuss these and other problems, the pupils raised other questions:

1. If we should lower our tariffs would it reduce our national revenue and thereby necessitate rises in taxes?
2. If we were to allow other countries to send their goods into our country wouldn't that ruin some of our industries and cause unemployment and depression?
3. Why should we import cheese when we can make our own?
4. Wouldn't it be better if we were self-sufficient? Could we be self-sufficient if we wanted to?
5. If we did more trading with our allies, would we be able to drop our foreign aid program?
6. How do we pay for imports? How does international trade actually work?

It became increasingly evident that there were wide areas in which not only the knowledge of the pupils was inadequate but also that of the teacher. Here, then, was a good point at which to invite an expert to come into the classroom.

Mr. Lawrence Senesh, an economist who has specialized in the study of international economics, agreed to come to visit the class and to talk about some of the fundamentals of international trade. This turned out to be a unique educational experience. The visitor was not only an expert in his field, he was also a master at working with children. He explored, with the students, the reasons why man engages in trade. He avoided abstract definitions, using instead questions such as these:

1. Why does your father not make his own shoes?
2. Why do the people of North Dakota buy oranges from California or Florida?
3. Why does the United States not produce its own uranium?

Thus the concept of an international division of labor, growing out of differences in climate, physical features, resources, and technology, was made clear.

The speaker had literally brought with him a bag full of tricks. In a large paper sack, he had stored "money" of a variety of colors to represent the currencies of different nations, and many toys to be used as items for trade. To these realia he added a rich sense of humor and a knowing way with youth. Soon students were acting out situations of bilateral trade, of multilateral trade, of currency exchanges and balance. They were thinking through the problems posed by these situations and they were drawing significant generalizations.

At this stage in the proceedings the students had become ardent crusaders for the "free trade" position. It was so simple, as they saw it! Wasn't it obvious to everyone that it would be best if each nation produced those goods for which it is best suited and traded for whatever else it needed? Wasn't it obvious that such an arrangement would mean greater abundance for all, higher living standards throughout the world and an economic foundation for international peace?

The guest quickly sensed the oversimplification in the class' thinking and carried the discussion to a consideration of some of the complicating factors in the picture.

1. The unequal distribution of natural resources
2. Variations in national currencies and problems of currency manipulation
3. Differences in labor costs
4. Political difficulties (e.g., the East-West division)
5. Problems of state trading and international monopolistic practices
6. The restrictive practices of nations (e.g., tariff walls and quota systems)

Of course, none of these concepts was dealt with in detail at this meeting, nor did students reach complete understanding. The pupils knew enough by now, however, to be certain what it was that they wanted to study. After further discussion at subsequent class sessions, the class worded its core problem in this way:

In the light of contemporary political and economic difficulties, how can we promote world trade in the interest of a rising world standard of living as a foundation for world peace?

The class decided, in the interest of efficiency in using the human resources within the group, to divide the problem into subtopics, each of which would be investigated by a committee of students. These five major committees were established:

1. What is Meant by International Trade?
2. How International Trade is Conducted

3. Present Difficulties in World Trade
4. Ways to Promote Freer Trade
5. Promoting World Trade by Developing Underdeveloped Countries

And so all set to work. The extensive classroom library of books, pamphlets, magazine articles, research papers, and speeches came into full use, as did the school and public libraries. The school and district film libraries were culled for appropriate films and filmstrips. Those found were used and others were borrowed from the central film library at the Board of Education.

Although the class did extensive reading, one of the most rewarding aspects of the project was the extent to which the groups were able to use effectively the resources of the community. New York is a port city. It is also the world's capital city. Thus, it is a place rich in resources. None of the class knew how welcome they were to use these resources, however, until they tried. It is important to note that through careful pre-planning and follow-up, training in disciplined research was never relaxed during the field experience.

The class visited the Customs Court and sat in on a hearing. They also spent over an hour, at the luncheon recess, talking to the Chief Justice of the Court. Here students saw that complicated customs regulations can choke off trade almost as effectively as a tariff levy. On another day, a committee interviewed a cheese importer from the Netherlands and learned that a quota can be equally impeding to trade.

A committee was invited to sit in on the annual conference of the National Social Welfare Assembly. This organization is a federation of private philanthropic organizations which operate in foreign fields (e.g., CARE, Jewish Joint Distribution Committee, Federation of Protestant Welfare Agencies, National Catholic Welfare Conference, American Friends Service Committee, American Red Cross). Here students learned that governments are not the only agencies through which aid to other people is made available. They learned that men of good will feel responsible for their fellow man.

There were many other field trips but of special significance was the one experienced by the committee concerned with the problem of underdeveloped countries. A day was spent at the United Nations following a briefing by a staff member at the United States Mission on United States policy at the United Nations, with special reference to the relationship between the United States technical assistance program and the technical assistance program of the United Nations. The group learned how these programs complement each other. They learned of the "shirt sleeve" work being done by Americans in co-operation with others. They saw that we are not the only people with technical know-how, that we learn as well as teach.

At luncheon this group listened to a member of the Israeli delegation speak on technical assistance problems in the Middle East. Here the pupils obtained a graphic picture of how war and the threat of war act to retard man's progress. After luncheon they sat in on a session of the Economic and Social Council. They saw dramatized before them the problem of communication among people. They also saw men reaching over the barriers of language and culture in an effort to find satisfying solutions to common problems.

Finally, the group had a conference with the education director of the United Nations. She was a lovely lady from the Philippines. She spoke in eloquent terms of the work of the United Nations in her own country and in other countries where living standards are low. Children saw before them living proof, in the person of one who would be a credit to any country, that it is folly to equate low living standards with inferiority.

Students who had started out that morning merely as eager fact hunters, were, by the end of the day, concerned young citizens. Places on the map had ceased to be mere jigsaw puzzle pieces, colored in bright hues and labelled with names once recited by rote in school. They had become real places peopled by real human beings who faced real and vitally pressing problems. One cannot soon forget the look of shock, pain and compassion on a thirteen-year-old's face as she said, in speaking of the per capita income per year of a family in one of the underdeveloped areas, "How can they live? My mother spends just about that much each week just for food for our family."

Such concern was apparent in the culminating activity when the class members presented to each other and to many adult visitors the findings of their study. Posters and other visual materials were about the room. Pupils were now no longer content merely to spout facts. They interpreted facts in terms of their meaning in the lives of people. The maturity and authority with which they handled difficult problems was heart-warming.

Teachers often wonder if what they think is good seems equally good to the children involved. Seldom is it possible to arrive at a valid answer. In the case of this project, however, there seemed to be at least a partial answer. Some six months after the project was over, after the girls had been graduated from junior high school and had scattered among many different high schools, and after a summer vacation, several students were invited to evaluate their project before an audience of educators, and business and labor leaders. They had no preliminary meeting and their discussion was completely unrehearsed. Here is a part of the stenographic record of their discussion:

Before we studied this topic we had a tendency to form little, I guess you call them cliques, groups of people going off to one side and talking to each other. I think this topic brought us all together because we learned to work as a class.

We didn't just use textbooks and abstract things. We worked with real things.

Since we worked in that way, it became more real to us and we realized that it was not something that you read about in textbooks which maybe does exist or doesn't exist, and maybe the textbook was dated 1939 and maybe it wasn't, and maybe those things aren't here now. But these things really are, and they are in front of us and they have to exist because we see them.

One of the most important things in the way we studied world trade was that we did everything ourselves. When we had a problem in trade, we took articles and actually worked it out ourselves.

Not only did we get information from the booklets, but we got it from the source from which it came. If we were studying about quota restrictions on cheese, we went to the cheese manufacturers and we spoke with them and they gave us their side of it. We went to both sides and we heard each person's views.

I know with all the girls it is practically the only thing they remember that we studied last year, and one of the reasons was because we were so interested. It was all so new and happening right then.

And you might say also we got so carried away in the topic we never —really this is the truth—we never thought about marks until we got them.

A senator came out with a statement that we should go it alone and . . . I remember we were very proud of ourselves because here we were in the 9th grade and couldn't even vote, but we could challenge something that was said by so famous a man.

When I thought how every single nation, including those not at war, suffered, it just didn't make sense. If arguments could be settled peacefully—I don't know of any special way of ending wars—but if arguments could be settled peacefully, it would be more ideal and everybody would profit; everyone would prosper.

Out of the mouths of babes. . . .

CHAPTER 3

Senior High School

LEARNING is a continuous process. Education for world affairs does not stop at any particular age. It continues throughout life, conditioned by age changes, but is not fundamentally different at any level. The democratic values, processes, and procedures of importance in earlier education are also of importance in senior high schools. Social pressures in a time of crisis, to which attention was called in the introduction of Chapter 2, inescapably affect teaching and learning in senior high schools.

Certain unique conditions affect education for world affairs in American senior high schools as well as in the earlier grades. Such conditions result from both the age and intellectual ability of learners and from historical circumstances.

Senior high school boys and girls are reaching adulthood. Where home and school conditions have been favorable, the great majority are capable of intellectual effort beyond that possible at an earlier age. Under expert guidance such students can do research of a superior quality. They can go beyond naive acceptance of facts, and the rationalization of emotionalized prejudice. But such conditions are far from universal.

Hundreds of thousands of senior high school students come from homes and schools which make learning difficult. Broken homes, homes which produce instability of mind and character, homes where there appear to be few, if any, intellectual interests—such conditions where they exist are not conducive to good education of any kind. Moreover, where the earlier school experience has been poor, senior high school students are further handicapped. An inferior quality of education leaves little on which to build.

At least two other important factors affect the quality of education for world affairs in American senior high schools—namely, the quality of teaching and of curricula. Where teachers and administrators are alert, experimental, and devoted to the achievement of democratic values, and where curricula are continuously subject to evaluation and improvement, the achievement of a superior degree of understanding of the peoples of the world and our relation to them are possible. But where narrow textbook teaching is prevalent, and where expert knowledge of both students and the modern world seem to be largely absent, education for world affairs suffers.

It is perhaps pertinent at this point to call attention to the recurrent failure of many senior high schools to refine and develop the clearly conceived concept of personality development which is so well illustrated in the descriptions of practice found in Part I, Chapter 1, of this book. This conception of education might well be continued in more high schools with the difference that study and activities would be more complex and the processes of intellectualization more mature. Why, the reader of this book may well ask, do not more senior high school teachers follow up and build upon the groundwork so well laid in many elementary schools?

In this chapter are found a number of examples of teaching and learning in senior high schools from various sections of the United States. They were located through the use of the same research methods by which the examples from elementary and junior high schools presented in earlier chapters were discovered.

At the Crossroads of the Pacific

McKinley High School in Hawaii has developed various channels for promoting world understanding on the part of students. Special attention is given to world relationships in the curriculum of the sophomore and senior years. The tenth-grade social studies work is primarily the study of world history, with emphasis on present-day world problems. On the twelfth-grade level one semester is devoted to international relationships, with emphasis on promoting peace.

To bring the peoples of the world and their problems closer to students, there is a well-planned program of audio-visual materials used in connection with these courses.

Student forums on problems of relations with other countries are conducted. These are sometimes given before one or two classrooms and sometimes before larger groups of students of the same class level. Representative students of the school participate in the high school conferences promoted by the Institute of Pacific and Asian Affairs. They attend monthly regional meetings which are held on Saturday mornings. Near the close of the school year an annual conference is held in which all public and private high schools in Honolulu take part.

Another channel through which students on the three class levels learn about the peoples of the world and their problems is by reading and discussing the news in publications designed for the use of high school students. Those who are the better readers use the *American Observer,* while the slower readers use the publications written in simpler language.

Many students take part in essay and oratorical contests conducted by World Brotherhood and by local community organizations. An eleventh-grade boy recently won first place in the Territory in the essay contest on, "What the United Nations Means to Me." He then made the Youth Pilgrimage to the United Nations. Second place in this same contest also went to a McKinley student. Entering these contests is voluntary.

To give pupils an appreciation of cultures, especially Pacific and Asian cultures, trips are made to the Art Academy for lectures. More extended tours are made, also.

Through the school government students give attention to other peoples and their needs. This organization maintains a World Relations Committee which directs monthly drives for money to support adopted children. McKinley has had eight of these. Currently fifteen dollars per month is being sent to a child in France for his support. Part of the funds collected through these drives is used for CARE packages for war-ravaged countries. Frequently, tool and plow packages are sent.

The pupils of McKinley also sponsor an annual "Lima Kokua Drive," which is a clothing drive for war-torn countries. Over 100,000 pieces of clothing have been collected each year. In the last drive the clothes were sent to Korea. Other collections have been made of books and school supplies for the Philippines and Korea.

Through the Assembly Committee the school government sponsors Kiwanis World Travel Films, World Brotherhood assemblies, and assemblies which show the cultural contributions of various races in Hawaii.

A newspaper, *The Daily Pinion,* is published by the students. This activity, too, does much to promote world understanding. Each year *The Daily Pinion* enters the contest sponsored by World Brotherhood. This newspaper gives publicity to all student world relations activities and publishes interviews with visitors who come from all parts of the world. In 1952 and again in 1954 the *Pinion* won the Freedom Foundation Award.

A booklet of students' creative work, *Ka Hana Kaulana,* is published annually. One section of it is devoted to World Brotherhood. Copies of this publication were sent last year to many nations which have World Brotherhood organizations.

The students of McKinley High School have always displayed much interest in international understanding and in helping people all over the world. This interest may be traced in part to the cosmopolitan character of the student body and in part to the fact that it is located at the Crossroads of the Pacific where representatives of many nations meet.

Building World-Mindedness

At the Philadelphia High School for Girls, which is a college preparatory school of almost 1200, pupils find it natural to be world-conscious. Many elements contribute to an atmosphere of interest in, and concern for, people from other lands. There are usually in the school a dozen or more foreign-born girls from Europe, Asia, and the other Americas. Members of the faculty have for years been inveterate travelers, who return each summer with slides and interesting experiences to relate. The principal has a background of living in Chile, Brazil, and Europe, and of working in International Relations Seminars of the American Friend's Service Committee. The school also enjoys a continuous stream of visitors from many foreign countries.

Classroom work is deliberately related to the understanding of other cultures. Spanish, French, and German classes are conducted from the very beginning and throughout four years. Spanish students correspond with boys and girls in Mexico and celebrate Pan-American Day. French students exchange letters, pictures, school work, and scrap books with an affiliated school in Besancon. Two teachers recently visited Besancon and a French girl will spend a term at

Girls' High. The School Affiliation Committee, one of the organizations sponsored by the French Department, raised money for this purpose by showing French films after school. Each term there is a language assembly, in which the Bible is read in a different foreign language. In turn, songs and plays are given in French, Spanish, and German. The German plays are written by a native-born department member.

Girls' High School fellowship carries beyond the classroom or auditorium, into the homes of teachers and students. An especially memorable occasion was the visit of twenty-five Danish teachers to Philadelphia. They were entertained at the Ocean City home of a member of the Girls' High School faculty, with all the neighbors joining to furnish ice cubes, roasted turkeys, blueberries, and Jersey tomatoes for a typical American meal. This elicited a warm toast to America from the Danes and led to plans for visits to Denmark by the hosts.

A State Department-sponsored teacher from Great Britain spent a year at the school and one of the girls was an exchange student at Moreton Hall, in Shropshire, for a term.

The Social Studies Department furthers understanding of other nations, in class and extraclass activities. A student from Girls' High School served as President at a model Congress at Temple University recently.

A school Service Club has officially adopted a Korean orphan, Im Moo Sung, to whom cards and gifts are sent on his birthday and at Christmas. Letters received from him are printed in the school newspaper.

The World Affairs Club has members from all grades, and of many different backgrounds. It tries to stimulate all possible interest in world affairs. In its three years of existence, it has had as speakers representatives of fifty-seven countries who have been students of the University of Pennsylvania. Through talking with them, Girls' High School students have in many ways been lead to see their own country in a more comprehensive way.

Use of Student Activities and Rich Resources

Cooperatively planned experiences have enriched the lives of the boys and girls of Germantown High School in Philadelphia and have also provided an inspiration to its teachers. This school has enlisted the services of many people who, through travel, the position they occupy, or because of special interests, are qualified to make clear the fact that understanding the many peoples of the world is an essential step toward the achievement of international harmony.

The head of the foreign relations department of a large corporation recently spent the greater part of a day speaking, during various periods, to as many of the language students as could crowd into the largest available room. An officer in the Naval Reserve recounted his experiences in South America. A young Germantown High School student from Ecuador, described life in Latin America and played some of its music. Several foreign students from the University of Pennsylvania have also enriched the language program by speaking to classes about their native countries.

The foreign language club provides opportunities for reaching many students. Five members of the faculty who have traveled extensively have addressed the club. Interesting descriptions of life abroad have been presented by the school's French exchange student and by one of its own students who studied in Germany.

The maintenance of relations with Germantown's two affiliated schools, in Prades, France, and Kaufbeuren, Germany, stimulates many interesting activities. A form containing instructions for writing letters to these schools has been developed. This is distributed each term by members of the student committee to all tenth-grade home rooms. Stamps and International Mailing Coupons for a pre-paid reply are available at the school store.

Each department in the school has faculty representation on the affiliation committee and an effort is made to have a department make one major contribution to each affiliated school each year. Contributions may range from notebooks or scrapbooks developed by a class to a collection of money for some worthy gift. Publicity for the program is provided through a special bulletin board on which Christmas, New Year, and French "April Fish" cards are exhibited.

A library showcase displays articles from abroad and has aided in the circulation of some of the popular French magazines. Two sets of slides from the German affiliated school have been shown in school assemblies. When a local radio station featured the music of Pablo Casals, who lives in Prades, the home of one of the affiliated schools, Germantown students spoke on the program.

As a natural sequel to the program of foreign school affiliations, an exchange student program has been developed at Germantown. The American Field Service and the United States State Department selected the first exchange student, a boy from Germantown's affiliated school, the Oberrealschule mit Gymnasium, in Kaufbeuren, Germany. The parents of one of the seniors volunteered to take the boy into their home, and the Germantown Mothers Association made an appropriation toward his expenses. The Students Association agreed to pay all expenses of school activities and dues.

The seventeen-year-old foreign student, Herbert Arnold, was welcomed by his American foster family early in August, 1952. Within a short time after the opening of school in September he had become quite at home. He played on the varsity soccer team which won the city championship. Students became well acquainted with him through his assembly talks in which, with the aid of slides from his home school, he described German schools to his American classmates. He was elected to the cabinet of the Students Association and learned the part American students take in school government.

In the summer of 1953, the Germantown High School received a scholarship from the American Field Service for one of its own students who, under the summer program of the Field Service, spent six weeks with a family in Ludwigsburg. In 1954 this opportunity was extended to another student who lived with a family in Kaufbeuren, Bavaria. During the school year 1953–1954, another European student, this time a girl from Nice, France, lived in Germantown and attended the school.

Germantown High has always regarded its assembly as an opportunity for its citizens to work on common problems and to share mutual interests and experiences. Many assemblies have been planned to contribute to the individual student's growth in world-mindedness. Several of the programs which have carried out this idea are:

1. A United Nations Day assembly, with a colorful flag display, and a message on world cooperation by a dynamic speaker
2. Several assemblies featuring the school affiliations program, and the exchange students
3. A town meeting program, prepared for later re-broadcast on the radio, on the implications of the war in Indo-China

Germantown High was fortunate recently in having an exchange teacher in the English Department from Epsom, England. With

seemingly little effort, she fitted into the life of the school, participating in practically every phase of school activities. This teacher
endeared herself, not only to the staff and students but also to the
community. She spoke with wit and candor before civic, professional,
and cultural organizations and to each she brought a realistic picture
of English culture and education.

Germantown High School's dance group has contributed significantly to the school's development of an international consciousness.
One of the first countries interpreted through the dance was Spain.
One member of the group was so intrigued with Spanish dance forms
that she won parental consent for a summer tour of that country to
study them at first hand. A United Nations ballet was choreographed
by this group. Hours were spent in discussing manners and customs,
in making appropriate costumes, and in arranging snatches of descriptive music for each country.

Working with the World Affairs Council of Philadelphia, Germantown students have attended city-wide conferences, participated
in round table discussions, and heard outstanding speakers. On one
occasion the program took the form of a Model United Nations in
which Germantown students took part as delegates, committee members, and observers.

Social studies classes regularly observe a television program, *The
World at Your Door*, sponsored by the Philadelphia Public Schools.
Through these and other programs in the social studies curriculum
students receive stimulation in thinking, reasoning, and discussion.
The long-range value, while not immediately apparent, is the development of life-long interest and an active participation in world
affairs.

Working at International Understanding

The work of Richmond High School, Richmond, Indiana, in the
field of world affairs is of two kinds, curricular and extracurricular.
In the curricular field there are two courses in area studies, as well
as a course in World Geography. The area studies are called American Neighbors and Pacific Relations.

The American Neighbors course consists of the study of the geography, the native peoples, and the Spanish colonial period of Latin
America. The wars for independence, relations with the United

States, products, trade, and education are studied. The study of our northern neighbor, Canada, takes about a third of the class time. The study of Canada includes historical background, geography, mineral resources and their uses, relations with the United States, as well as travel and recreational advantages. International understanding is one of the main goals of the course. It is classified as a citizenship course by the Indiana State Department of Public Instruction.

In Pacific Relations, units on geography, peoples, culture, and economics introduce the course. There is a great deal of study of the Pacific area on relief and political maps. Next the specific areas are studied in detail. These include U.S.S.R., China, Japan, India, and Australia. Again, relations with the United States are always kept in mind. The understanding of the peoples of these lands is emphasized. This is also considered to be a citizenship course and, along with American Neighbors, is approved by the State Department of Public Instruction and may be taught in any high school in Indiana.

As the result of the development of these courses a teacher of the Richmond High School was asked to serve on the State Curriculum Committee. Subsequently, the work done in this school led to the organization of committees and subcommittees in the eastern part of Indiana to write a course of study in World History. Bulletin 191 was produced which incorporates short units in the areas of Latin America, Canada, and the Far East. These were developed so that they can be taught either with the World History course or as short units in other social studies offerings.

In the Richmond High School, in conjunction with text study, returned tourists and travelers help in international understanding. There are three colleges in the community whose foreign students frequently come to share information about their countries. Usually the procedure is for the foreign student to give a short talk and then allow pupils to ask questions. Frequently, the foreign students bring articles from their home countries. Again the emphasis is on understanding how the people live.

A social studies teacher of the school has recently been able to give students more personal help in the understanding of world affairs as she has traveled in thirteen European countries and Canada. She studied at the Institute for English Speaking Teachers at the University of Oslo, Norway, at the University of Innsbruck Summer Session at Mayrhofen, Austria, and took the Holiday Course at the University of Copenhagen, Denmark. Additional insight into world affairs was gained by this teacher in visiting the Vienna Command, where her husband is stationed with the United States Air Force.

Much helpful information comes from the Department of the Army bulletin called *Ambassadors All*. In this bulletin such subjects as "We Judge Foreign Countries by Foreign Visitors" and "Children Help Relations Abroad" show the need for understanding on the part of Americans who go to live abroad. Since there have been 1,500,000 servicemen stationed in 63 countries, it is important that schools help pupils understand how Americans should live when abroad.

The school has a club called the Social Studies Forum for pupils interested in world affairs. Assemblies are held on United Nations Day, Pan American Day, and other similar occasions. Club members sometimes entertain foreign students from local colleges in their homes and take them to various places of interest in the community. Twice a year the Social Studies Forum sponsors a party and picnic for members and foreign students from Earlham College in Richmond, and Miami University and Western College in Oxford, Ohio. There is informal dancing and recreation at these affairs, after which correspondence and future social events develop.

Students Construct a Questionnaire on World Affairs

A teacher in the Lindsay Senior High School, Lindsay, California, describes his experience in working with high school pupils in the construction of a public opinion questionnaire. The project he reported concerns the problem of whether or not the United States should send troops to fight the Communist menace in Indo-China.

This project was initiated in class discussions, which were based on reading of newspapers, current event papers, and magazines. Varying opinions were expressed by students on the advisability of United States active participation in the Indo-China situation:

It would just be another Korea and we cannot afford to become involved in another war to drain away our strength.

We must eventually fight the Communists. Why not now while we can fight with the French to help us.

We should exhaust every possibility short of war first, but let's be realistic. We are not likely to win at a conference what we are already losing on the battlefield.

To aid the French in Indo-China would put us in the bad position of supporting colonialism.

Such divergent shades of opinion served as the basis for making a worth-while public opinion questionnaire.

It has been found in the Lindsay Senior High School that more learning will result, and interest will be extended beyond the mere tabulation of results, if a questionnaire includes a brief statement of the problem, followed by a list of possible solutions, with student-written statements supporting each solution.

In writing accurate and persuasive supporting statements, pupils must engage in considerable study. For example, in the case of the Indo-China problem they needed to know something about the background of European interests in Southeast Asia, the importance of this area to the free world, and the likely response the Communist nations would make to a proposed free world policy.

When sufficient study has been carried on, students submit statements supporting each possible solution. The best statements, or combinations of statements, are then selected by the class and the questionnaire duplicated in adequate numbers.

A trial run of the questionnaire is then carried on in the student body. This allows for changes to be made for the sake of clarity. It has also been found to be of interest to compare the results of this sampling with those of the public at large.

Care is necessary, even in the trial run. A large classroom, such as a study hall, is a good situation, since there is an atmosphere of seriousness which may not be present in more informal gatherings. It also removes the respondents as much as possible from the influence of friends. By contacting a full schedule of such classes, a large percentage of the student body can be included.

When the questionnaire has been revised, it is then given to the general public. Several procedures have been used here. Service clubs may be contacted at their regular meetings. This allows for an oral presentation of the arguments supporting each solution. Care should be taken, however, that the arguments be read, lest individual students influence the results through their oratorical ability. If this procedure is used, some provision must be made for sampling other economic groups of the community, since a sampling based on service club membership alone would undoubtedly result in an unrealistic picture of community opinion.

The sampling may be done in a door-to-door or street-corner canvas.

Once the results are obtained they can be forwarded to the appropriate representatives of the people interested in the problem and to the public press and radio. It is desirable to carry out this step since it increases the importance of the project in the eyes of the students and therefore encourages them to take pride in their work.

The educational values of this experience have been found to be many. Students are stimulated to delve deeper into a problem than they would if the activity ceased at the classroom-discussion stage. A richer understanding of the complex make-up of current problems is achieved and appreciation of different points of view result. Furthermore, by actually doing something with the results of the poll, students develop a sense of personal responsibility to the community for the quality and accuracy of their work. By no means secondary are the valuable experiences in writing, meeting the public, and developing personal opinions based upon tangible evidence. In addition, the project may actually help to educate the community, since a reading of the statements supporting the various proposed solutions is in itself a learning experience.

Building a Classroom Environment for World Affairs

Since World History, a required tenth-grade course, is only one semester in length in Chico Senior High School, Chico, California, students keep up with world events through all subjects in the curriculum. One of the most important tasks of the social studies teacher, therefore, is building an environment that will "carry over" into other classes. This may be done through student-produced murals.

In Chico High School a teacher and his social studies students fell heir to a sewing room. How to create an atmosphere that would aid in the study of world affairs became their problem. Since the room had abundant blank wall space, it was decided that a wall mural, depicting the course of man's desire for order and self-government, was the solution.

A committee of ten was selected and one class period each week was devoted to the choice of suitable events from the history of the world to carry out the theme. After four weeks of research and consultation, the committee decided upon the following:

SCENE 1.   "Cro-Magnon Man" (the first artist)
SCENE 2.   "The Code of Hammurabi and the Twelve Tables of the Romans" (examples of the first law codes)
SCENE 3.   "Signing of the Magna Carta" (inroads on monarchial authority)
SCENE 4.   "The Declaration of Independence" (the right of the people to control their government)
SCENE 5.   "The United Nations Declaration of Human Rights" (man's hope for future peace)

After selecting the scenes, the committee subdivided into groups of two, and each twosome chose the scene it wished to paint. Rough drafts were first sketched on manila paper. These were then transferred to the wall with carbon. Before final alterations and painting, the subcommittees consulted the art teacher and devoted much time to library research to find the most appropriate colors for their scenes.

When the mural was completed, class discussion brought many comments on the values of this work, such as:

Man's history has direction. Man is always striving for a better way of life.
By seeing some of man's accomplishments and studying about these advancements we are better able to appreciate our own heritage.
Liberty and human rights bring responsibilities with them.
These scenes tend to make history live in the classroom.
It was an opportunity for creative art.
Future classes will benefit from the "air of history" in this room.

The project stimulated interest in other classes and another group volunteered to decorate a wall with famous scenes from American historical literature.

Art Class Activity

Art students in the Chicago public schools have developed twenty-one Pan American murals, featuring each of the twenty-one Pan American nations. These murals were unveiled at a Pan American festival held at the International House in celebration of Pan American Day. Students from these nations, as well as the art students who produced the murals, were invited. The festival featured a program, dance, and reception.

Students had to acquire a great deal of knowledge about Latin

American nations before they could express the culture of these countries in murals. Actual mingling with Latin Americans at the celebration, in an atmosphere of warmth and good fellowship, led to a recognition of the idealism of all people who search for "the good life." A questioning attitude developed in this project, of wanting to explore many questions and many ideas related to inter-American relations.

The murals were later exhibited in schools and museums in various parts of the United States. They were photographed and slide reproductions made. These slides have been used in illustrated lectures to show both the role of art in human relations and techniques of mural painting.

A Course on World Cultures

What do we expect to learn in a class on World Cultures? Why is it important? The tenth-, eleventh-, and twelfth-grade members of a World Cultures class at the University School of The Ohio State University sought answers to such questions as these.

The essential groundwork of respect for others in our increasingly interdependent world led students to compare but not to sit in judgment in the study of various peoples. Attention in each case was focused on the following:

1. Geographical description, government
2. Customs, religion, social problems
3. The arts, literature, language
4. Economic situation, world relationships

The following aids were found to be very desirable in carrying on the course:

1. Speakers, foreign whenever possible, or Americans who had lived in foreign lands
2. Films, obtainable from many sources
3. Slides
4. Records
5. Fiction books depicting the lives of foreign peoples
6. Art exhibits

With the large numbers of exchange students, visitors, D.P.'s, and war brides in this country, the class was not hampered by lack of speakers. They also made extensive use of films.

Members of the class initially agreed that their main stress was to be on the modern world, with history used only insofar as it contributed to their understanding of the present. The study of Greece and Italy, for example, led them into history and aroused an interest in philosophy and concepts which have had significance in the Western world.

In its study of related groups of countries, the class divided itself at times into sections, each of which later shared its findings with the whole group. At other times, individual students agreed to do research on specific countries. In one unit, each student made a special preparation of a specified topic and led the discussion on the day when that topic was a general assignment. In another unit, there was a free choice study; each student wrote a report on his own special interests.

All kept up to date through the constant use of a world map. The map proved helpful in choosing each unit as it gave visual guidance for thinking. Other effective devices were crossword puzzles of names and terms in current news and mimeographed sheets of names and terms to be identified. An attempt was made, also, to learn a little of the language and religion of each country, in an effort to interpret more effectively the people's patterns of thought.

The students felt, as they moved on through the course, that they were becoming progressively better prepared to advance their newly found understandings of, and feelings of friendship with, other peoples.

International Understanding Through Literature

The course, International Understanding, is required for one semester in the twelfth grade at Stockton College, Stockton, California. The purpose of the course is to encourage understanding of other people and their way of life as a basis for living together in a changing world.

Studies are made of the recent history and current problems of nations, though concentration is on the tension areas of Europe, Asia, and Africa. Whenever possible, attention is centered on the actual lives of the people and their problems, rather than just on political and economic structure.

One of the most potent instruments for understanding people is literature, for the reader finds himself identified with the emotions and problems of other people. There are enough good travel stories, novels, and biographies available to permit the formation of a list that provides students with opportunity to select books that fit their reading level and interests. Stockton College students are required to read a minimum of two books and make a report on each. The report consists of a brief summary of the book along with an explanation of what was learned.

At the end of each semester the students vote on the value of the books which they read. Their list of recommendations is submitted to members of the class the following semester. Some of the favorites on the list are Hersey's *Hiroshima,* Steinbeck's *Russian Journal,* Koestler's *Darkness at Noon,* Paton's *Cry the Beloved Country,* and William O. Douglas' travel stories.

The students point out that no one is prepared to decide on the use of atomic weapons until he has an intimate understanding of the effect of an atomic explosion on human life. *Hiroshima* gives the reader a poignant, even traumatic, illustration. A dimension of understanding is obtained that would not be possible through a factual, scientific explanation.

The *Russian Journal* gives the students a picture of the Russian as a person, not simply as a Communist. The book helps correct the conventional stereotypes that Americans often have of Russians. *Darkness at Noon,* like an ominous echo of *1984,* vividly delineates the ruthlessness of a totalitarian system. Students mature enough to read *Cry the Beloved Country* respond with a deeper human involvement in the South African conflict than they would to factual news reports. Perceptive travel stories like Douglas' *Beyond the High Himalayas* permit a sympathetic understanding of people that is hardly obtainable from the conventional textbook.

Teaching international understanding through literature is successful for a number of reasons. The students enjoy the reading, if they find a book that fits their reading level. If the reading list is broad enough, students usually find a book they like and the teacher therefore meets the individual differences of a normally heterogeneous class. Since the reading is coupled with a report demanding discrimination of the important values of the story, each person has both a language experience and an exercise in judgment.

Term papers are usually required as one of the main outside assignments and considerable latitude is given in the choice of a topic. This assignment is of most value when each person is required to put all the writing into his own words, instead of yielding to the common scissors-and-paste temptation. The assignment provides a further way of meeting individual differences. Some students write original imaginative stories based on their studies of other people and their culture. Practically everyone writes on some country, a prominent leader, or an international problem. Before papers are handed in, each student presents the substance of his paper orally and discusses it with the class. Knowledge is thus shared and students gain a better sense of the justification of their efforts than they would by having the teacher only see their papers.

Topics covered in class include American foreign policy, political ideologies, national problems, causes of war, current events, and the United Nations. Students assist in curriculum planning and usually request that special emphasis be given to Russia and the problem of Communism. Some material is presented by the teacher and the salient problems are always discussed. Students often take areas of a topic and then study material and have panel discussions. Some of the controversial problems are presented through formal debates.

Students usually enjoy the International Understanding course because they are aware of the importance of such understanding as a prerequisite for peace in a world that is becoming smaller and more interdependent. They become aware of the vast power that nations possess and the vital need for an intelligent foreign policy in a world where mistakes can bring mutual annihilation to nations. They learn to recognize the obligation they have to people less fortunate than themselves and gain a more realistic understanding of themselves and their relations to other people.

World Literature Is Used in Teaching International Understanding

Counterpoised in history with the names of kings, queens, and military leaders are the names of the world's great writers. Writers, too, formed and expressed the news and the views of their time. Immortality belongs to them, not to the rulers, whether the latter were considered as deities, despots, or dictators. Agamemnon lives because of Homer and Aeschylus, not because of his skills in war or wedlock. Shakespeare eclipses a complete line of egocentric and eccentric Tudors. Machiavelli's name has become a dictionary-listed adjective, while the Borgias and the Mussolinis receive progressively less space in history texts.

There is a coordinated program of English and social studies in high schools of Kern County Union High School and Junior College District, California. Accenting a theme, "Developing American Citizenship in the World in Which We Live," historical facts and world literature selections are taught as concurrent and complementary materials. It is assumed that any understanding of the present-day world must be based on a study of man's past. The course, therefore, is a historical survey from the Egyptian culture through the hot and cold wars of today.

Often literature seems more effective in teaching an understanding of the past and the present than does a study of historical facts. Students can understand more easily the limiting and tragic effects of Spain's isolation—an isolation geographical, industrial, and cultural—when it is told partially through the tragi-comic peccadilloes of Don Quixote, rather than told entirely through the study of charts, graphs, and statistics.

The principal aids used in this two-hour coordinated program, in addition to standard history texts and periodicals, are selections from world literature appropriate to the units. Some of the readings recently used and the units of study they have emphasized are detailed below.

One of the primary objectives in the study of the Greeks is to show them as the builders of a great culture, as the dreamers who, in a time of wars and conquest, caught briefly a vision of democracy, dreamed briefly a concept of the individual worth of all men. The literature used to supplement this objective included sections of two plays by Aeschylus, *Prometheus Bound* and the *Orestia* trilogy. The former was considered as the attempt to define the relationship between a too-stern god and helpless man, or between unbridled power and individual freedom. Sections of the *Oresteia* were studied to illustrate the establishment of law and justice to replace tyranny and fear. The embryo of the democratic idea appears when Athena, goddess of wisdom, decreed:

> Let no one be uncurbed by law
> Or curbed by tyranny.

Shakespeare's tragedy, *Julius Caesar,* was read in a study of the Romans which accented their achievements in empire, insofar as these resulted in government and law. The students, after reading the play, held panel discussions and wrote papers, pro or con, on Brutus as the loyal Roman who "loved Caesar not less but Rome more." Or papers criticized Antony as loyal to his friends, even when his loyalties might better have been transferred to the people, and noted that this criticism had sometimes been made of Harry S. Truman when he was President of the United States.

Parts of *Don Quixote* were read in the unit of study on Spain. After discussing the humor and the pathos of Cervante's quaint hero —a hero because he followed his convictions, a tragedy because his life was an anachronism—the students wrote reports of a present-day Don Quixote trying to promote idealism and chivalry in Franco's Spain or in the United States. One person pictured an interplanetary Don Quixote skipping about in a space ship.

Selections from Machiavelli's *The Prince* were used in the study of an unhappy Italy. It was pointed out that Machiavelli was no original villain but merely a recorder, a non-hypocrite in a time and land of hypocrites. In addition to tracing the sorrows which the following of his harsh and bitter philosophy brought Italy under the Fascist regime, the students discussed contemporary Congressmen who seem to subscribe to his theory that the end justifies the means.

The writings of Rudyard Kipling and of Alan Paton were used in studying European colonial empires and the tragedies and problems these decaying empires present. Kipling's then prophetic *Recessional* was read as the epitaph to an age. The students unanimously agreed that Ghandi and others had relieved Kipling's "white man" of his burden.

The writings of the contemporary Paton were read as poignant and powerful expressions of the crisis approaching in racial-torn South Africa. More peremptory than any headline or political battles, or race riots, is his summarizing statement of the white man's dilemma:

Cry the beloved country, for the unborn child that is the inheritor of our fear. Let him not love the earth too deeply. Let him not laugh too gladly. . . . For fear will rob him of all if he gives too much.

The tragedy of millions forever in bondage, passed like cattle from master to master, was emphasized in the unit of study on the Russians. To illustrate this dramatically, a play adapted from a short story by Efim Zozulya, "A Tale About Ak and Humanity," was used. Pupils discussed how the play, which tells on an allegorical level of the awful butchery during the Revolution in the mad, blind attempt to "create a better life," is no more unbelievable or basically tragic than much of the propaganda to which the Russian people are even now subjected. Students wrote papers on what our policy toward the Russians might be after discussing the theme, stated by the play's unhappy hero, Ak, when he rebels at the "necessary" killing of "human rubbish."

Necessarily, on the tenth-grade level, all of these literary topics are discussed in a much more simplified and detailed manner than presented here. As stated, only parts of the writings were used. These parts, however, help in the twofold and interrelated job of teaching both an appreciation of world literature selections and an understanding of nations through a study of the writers' statements of people's problems, their fears, and their hopes.

A Unit on Strategic Areas and the United Nations

Most teaching about the United Nations is deductive. It tends to present the structural organization of the United Nations in diagrammatical form and then proceeds to state the purpose of each of the several agencies. The work of the agencies may next be studied. Often the charter is read and the statements of the various suborganizations examined. Sometimes an historical approach precedes the formal study of the United Nations organization. At other times the charter is looked at in relation to other notable documents. Often this kind of formal study is called a unit when in reality its unity is thematic rather than developmental. The ironic thing is that this formal, logical treatment is often repeated once more when the United Nations is included in other courses to be taken by the same students.

At the Bridgeville High School, Bridgeville, Delaware, the inductive approach has been used in a core program, for seniors, called Social Living. These boys and girls come from lower-middle-class homes. Few ever go to college. Reading levels may be as low as third grade.

These pupils read newspaper headlines, and hear of world events on the radio, television, and in the movies. The teacher begins his study of the United Nations by asking pupils to list some of the "trouble spots" of the world. Even before 1950 such areas as Berlin, Egypt, Indonesia, Israel, Iran, Pakistan, and Korea were listed. The class discovered that such spots, which they learned to call "strategic areas," were comparatively unknown to them.

The study then began with individual and committee reports on resources, trade, and culture of these areas. The nature of the "crisis" within each was investigated by the class. This inquiry took several weeks, with an extra week to pool findings and dig up some generalizations as to what conditions generally provoke "crises."

In this study period, it was appropriate to ask why some crises were brought before the United Nations. "What constituted a United Nations case?" "How does the United Nations operate to meet the challenge of a strategic area?" "How successful have efforts been to cope with sore spots?"

Out of such questions as these there came the realization that power blocks had already formed among nations, with some nations like India, more or less on the fence. It was learned that the very large nations have a "following" of smaller nations which, if not satellites, tend literally to be drawn into more powerful dynamic orbits. "Why does the United States sometimes go outside the framework of the United Nations to achieve some of its aims?" "Why, on other occasions, has it called upon the United Nations to handle a case?"

Problems of colonialism were studied to see how they are constantly involved in the work of the United Nations, including the work of UNESCO. The problem of how to raise the productivity of unindustrialized countries, without westernizing them or exploiting them came up. This was especially stressed for those countries that have just won their sovereignty. The controversy over the adequacy of the world food supply in relation to the growing population was investigated.

All these larger issues made the class search into what the United Nations is doing. The work of the various agencies and their activities emerged from the study rather than from a listing and description of one after the other, with no thread to hold them together. Finally, the class studied how various groups in the United States regarded the United Nations, and how public opinion of these groups has fluctuated at different times.

Inductively, then, the changing attitude of the United States toward internationalism grew. History came out of the study as a kind of summation, or review, bringing the subject of global thinking back to present crises.

Current Events and a Unit on the United Nations

In a United States History class in the Chico Senior High School, Chico, California, pupils became so interested in current world happenings that they wanted further opportunity to discuss them. Their request was granted and fifteen minutes of each class session were reserved for this purpose. The following rules were jointly agreed upon:

1. The discussion should be led by a student volunteer.
2. The leader must choose his own topic, and announce it a week in advance, thus enabling a schedule of "coming attractions" to be prepared.
3. All members of the class were expected to acquaint themselves with a variety of references on the topic.
4. Outside authorities should be invited to participate whenever possible so that the true facts would be presented.

When this procedure had been in operation for several weeks, the actions of certain members of the United Nations came up for discussion, together with the need for tolerance of another country's way of life. Many students felt that they harbored mistaken concepts of other countries. Consequently, those who were corresponding with residents in these nations wrote for information. They also asked the opinion of their pen-pals on other topics the class was discussing.

In the exchange of ideas that followed, the class members found there was much they could do to participate actively in world affairs. They raised money to help a Dutch family which had lost everything in a flood. They gathered books and fashion magazines for a Filipino couple who taught school and also owned a small dress shop. They subscribed to a well-known nature publication for an Indonesian boy whose hobby was bee-keeping. They also secured pamphlets about their own community from the local Chamber of Commerce and sent these abroad.

This class came to agree that what happens in the world can affect everyone and that "history" means much more than just what is written down in a textbook. Many lasting friendships were made with correspondents overseas. The class summarized these discussions, and their work in United States history, with the following student-prepared unit on the United Nations.

THE UNITED NATIONS: INSTRUMENT FOR WORLD PEACE
Committee 1. *The Organization of the United Nations*

A. Material to be covered:
 1. Tracing back in American history the efforts toward building a world organization
 2. The beginning of the United Nations and its "Charter"
  a. Comparison of the Charter with the Constitution of the United States
  b. The importance of the veto power
 3. What the machinery of the United Nations is and what it does
  a. Main organs
   (1) General Assembly
   (2) Security Council
   (3) International Court of Justice
   (4) Economic and Social Council
   (5) Trusteeship Council
   (6) Secretariat
  b. Specialized agencies
 4. Headquarters of the United Nations—how it operates
 5. The UN flag
 6. UN radio broadcasts and publications
B. Visual aids and activities:
 1. Ladder showing steps toward a world peace organization
 2. Cartoons: "Russia Uses the Veto," "Young But Growing," etc.
 3. Colored drawing of the flag
 4. Bulletin board showing the UN headquarters and some of the sessions

Committee 2. *Leaders of the United Nations and
the Countries They Represent*

A. Material to be covered:
 1. Brief sketches of the important leaders of the UN

2. Number of countries having membership in the UN today—brief descriptions of the policies followed by these nations
3. What new countries should be admitted to further world peace:
   a. East and West Germany
   b. Japan
   c. Red China
   d. Others
B. Visual aids and activities:
   1. A map of the world showing present day members of the UN and location of UN headquarters buildings (Pictures of the leading delegates might be pasted around border of map.)

Committee 3. *Successes and Failures of the United Nations*

A. Material to be covered:
   1. Strength of the UN and what it has accomplished
   2. Its weaknesses and its failures
   3. A comparison of the UN with the League of Nations
   4. A comparison of the UN with NATO
   5. Is the United Nations the surest road to world peace?
B. Visual aids and activities:
   1. A large chart of the UN's record, showing its successes on one side in black and its probable failures on the other side in red
   2. Illustrations of the UN's actions in Korea
   3. Use of the magazines and newspapers brought in by the class to compile a scrapbook of the UN's activities since the opening of its second session
   4. A panel discussion: Resolved, the UN should be transformed into a world state

Committee 4. *Youth and the United Nations*

A. Material to be covered:
   1. Attitudes of youth toward the UN
   2. What can be accomplished by "pen pals"
   3. What the youth of other nations are doing about the UN
   4. Anything youth can do to help keep the peace
B. Visual aids and activities:
   1. Contacting some of the foreign students attending Chico State College to ask them to speak to our class (or, if this isn't possible, to ask them to tell you something about the youth of their nation)
   2. Interviewing professors at Chico State about their views on the UN and its activities
   3. Choosing a representative group of adults and youths, and finding

out how much they know about the UN. See whether they hold any hope for its future, and decide which group is best-informed on the subject of the UN

Carrying the United Nations to the People

A teacher in the Morocco High School in Morocco, Indiana, began teaching about the United Nations at the community level. Her initial effort was participation in a workshop of six sessions which was sponsored by a church organization. Among the people in the group were officers of civic and social clubs. These included such varied organizations as the American Legion Auxiliary, Parent Teacher Associations, Farm Bureau, Lion's Club, Methodist Men's Club, Hi-Y, Literary Club, and Methodist Woman's Society. Invitations to speak were also received from neighboring communities.

The approach to each group required consideration. For example, the members of a Lion's Club would be interested in the cost and value of technical assistance. The Farm Bureau would ask questions about the FAO. Women's organizations were interested in peace and the future of their children. And what could one say at a tri-county Hobby Club meeting where the interests ranged from collecting buttons to raising cocker spaniels? The answer of this teacher was that one must start with peoples' interests. For example, collecting flags, or stamps, or making a study of songs of the United Nations, might become a hobby. Here were opportunities also for giving information concerning United Nations broadcasts, telecasts and indicate the sources for films and United Nations publications.

While community interest in the United Nations was developing, this teacher's social studies classes were studying world affairs and school projects were also being initiated. For United Nations Day, the librarian assisted in collecting pamphlets for student use and materials for bulletin board displays. Celebration of United Nations Day spread from the school to the community. One minister preached a sermon relating to the United Nations. A merchant had a display of United Nations pamphlets, posters, and flags in his show window.

The United Nations annual contest, sponsored by the American Association for the United Nations and the Education Committee for School and College Activities, was introduced as a school project. Since there is no award, at the state level, in Indiana, the American

Legion Post and the Lion's Club gave awards to the two winners of those participating from Morocco High School. Each of the above organizations furnished a judge to assist in selecting the top papers. This gave the local organizations the feeling that they had a share in the education of children in world understanding.

In connection with the United Nations contest, a unit on the United Nations was prepared for study by all pupils in the social studies classes. Teachers are now considering sponsoring a model United Nations Assembly in which all of the high schools of the county may participate. At this Assembly each school would be assigned to represent a given nation of the world.

Another activity of Morocco High School is the annual, model Student Legislative Assembly in which all social studies pupils in the tenth, eleventh, and twelfth grades participate. One half-day is devoted to committee meetings.

Of the five committees into which the pupils are divided, the Foreign Affairs Committee is the one that reports out a bill pertaining to world relations, or possible resolutions relating to the United Nations. After time has been allowed for the printing and study of the bills, they are presented by their spokesmen in the Senate and House of Representatives, which are in session for one day. This project ties in with the community. Adults serve as parliamentarians and many parents and community leaders visit the sessions which are open to the public.

Another means of interesting Morocco High School students in world affairs is through guided tours to the United Nations. Although Morocco is a long distance from New York, the seniors, accompanied by their sponsor, principal and a school trustee, have visited the United Nations twice on what have become annual trips East. These student trips have stimulated adult interest and when local citizens go to New York they make an effort to visit the United Nations.

A local summer institute for Methodist youth of high school age included a daily class taught by a teacher from Morocco High School on "The UN: How and When It Works." The institute attracted teenagers from every section of northwest Indiana. The course seemed to open new vistas of understanding for some of the students coming from high schools where there had been no study of the United Nations.

Experimentation with a Global Relations Course

With the end of World War II hostilities in 1945, came an end to "indoctrination" pressures. But one thing stood out very clearly in the minds of teachers in the Overbrook High School in Philadelphia. The wartime course in Contemporary History had left a fine residue in the minds of students which paid splendid dividends in their pursuit of standard courses in the social studies. At the same time, the new United Nations Organization and the new air-age problems thrust the global picture into the classroom.

In order to meet the needs of those students whose interests and aims were closely identified with international problems, a major course called Global Relations was developed. This was inaugurated during the period when Philadelphia was being considered as the permanent seat of the United Nations. Social studies teachers planned to work closely with the Department of Foreign Languages and thus be in a position, eventually, to supply employees for the international body. The sudden decision to establish the seat of the United Nations in New York vitiated the more pragmatic features of these plans. A major course on Global Relations was developed, however. It has been offered continuously since 1946.

The areas of study in this new course have undergone several adjustments. At first it was planned to concentrate rather heavily upon such units as: Air Geography, Cartography, Current United Nations Matters, International Exchange, and the Global Scene. The most valuable results seemed to come from the study of physical geography and the history of parts of the world which ordinarily are not dealt with in courses in European or World History.

By 1950 teachers were building the course around Air Age Geography, Cartography, Latin America, The Pacific Rim (Korea, Indo-China, etc.), Asia. A recent switch of emphasis resulted in less concern about Latin American History, with more for Pan-American problems, and an added unit on Western Europe, as its history and present problems impinge upon American history and current world leadership.

The Global Relations course has not yet emerged from the experimental stage. It is doubtful whether it can ever become static or formalized. Textbooks cannot be selected with a view to comprehensive coverage. The teachers have used a small library of supplementary materials, such as pamphlets, abstracts, outline maps, atlases, and current journals. A fairly even distribution of time is devoted to research, discussion, reading, and map-making.

An interesting feature has been the establishment of one of the classrooms as the "International Room." The wall decorations, the room library, and all arrangements are designed with a cosmopolitan motif. The school also conducts a "Good Neighbors Club," an organization devoted to learning more about the peoples in the world beyond the boundaries of the United States. This club is under the direction of the Department of Foreign Languages.

Individual Research in an International Problems Course

Hunter College High School in New York City offers to its intellectually gifted girls a senior elective course in International Problems. One of the major requirements is the successful completion of an individual piece of research on some international problem. A research paper is first written. This is followed by an oral report to the entire class at which time each student must "stand for questioning" from both classmates and teacher.

In a recent term four students were especially interested in the relation of the United States to the United Nations. Two chose to work on the problem, "How the United States Mission to the UN Functions." They immediately went to the Mission offices at 2 Park Avenue. There they talked to people in the Press Division, collected all of their background materials on the work of the United Nations (with special emphasis on "positions" taken on important questions), were placed on the Press Release list, and arranged to attend a few of the Press Division's meetings.

These students were amazed to find that a steady stream of groups from all over the country are constantly being briefed before going to the United Nations. These groups constituted a cross section of the interests of the country. From briefings they learned how our policy is determined, the relationship between the Mission and the State Department, how the United States functions within the various Commissions and Committees of the United Nations, as well as about consultative processes with other delegations.

In order to get some first-hand knowledge of actual work within a Commission, the girls sought an interview with Mrs. Eleanor Roosevelt who had been a member of our first Mission to the United Nations and who had represented the United States on the Human Rights Commission. Here they were also made aware of the work of the American Association for the United Nations, which is expanding its program in order to keep the American people informed.

Senator Wiley, the Chairman of the Foreign Affairs Committee, was questioned as to the relationship between that Committee and the United States Mission. It was discovered that "open hearings" were being held throughout the country on the question of the revision of the United Nations Charter which comes up in 1955. Fortunately for the girls, Mrs. Oswald B. Lord, a member of our present Mission to the United Nations, spoke at one of the Hunter High School assembly programs. She described at some length the attempt which the Mission is constantly making to inform the country of its work and problems, as well as to sound out public opinion.

The problem of atomic energy and its control was taken by another student who did extensive research in the work of the Atomic Energy Commission. She attended its sessions, interviewed one of its members and explored our "position" on that Commission.

UNESCO goals and accomplishments, with particular emphasis upon the relation of the United States to it, was the concern of a third student. In addition to the voluminous materials on UNESCO available for study, she was able to obtain two interviews with people who either had been, or were directly concerned with, our United States National Commission for UNESCO. This Commission was established by law to advise the Department of State in UNESCO's fields of interest. The culmination of it all, however, was this girl's interview with the Chairman of the National Commission, Dr. George N. Shuster, President of Hunter College.

These research papers all dealt with a different aspect of the same problem. All represented individual research and conferences with some authority in the field. All were presented to the class orally and subjected to the most searching discussion. These students learned to organize, to anotate, and to defend ideas and materials in a scholarly way.

Part II

ALL-SCHOOL AND
OUT-OF-CLASS ACTIVITIES

CHAPTER 4

Clubs, Forums, and Youth Conferences

FEW educators now question the value of student activities. Those who conceive education in terms of personality development place a high value on such activities. Where education is largely viewed as the acquisition of knowledge, there is less enthusiasm but often acknowledgement that solid and worth-while content can sometimes be found in out-of-class school activities.

Proponents and sceptics may find activities to commend and to criticize in this chapter. Few, if any, can doubt, however, that the examples cited are serious attempts by students and teachers to achieve major purposes in American education. Respect for the individual person, cooperation for common ends, careful research, and the acquisition of knowledge are here to be found in varying degree. In addition, there is present the high idealism of youth for achieving a better world for all peoples through conscious human effort. The world will surely be a better place in which to live as boys and girls strive to make it so.

A Junior UNESCO Club's First Year

In 1952 a Junior UNESCO Club was organized in one of the elementary schools of San Mateo, California. The first task the club undertook was that of preparing a mimeographed manual which was given the title, *You Can Help Build a Peaceful World,* and the subtitle, *Here's How.* This little paper contained seven suggestions for boys and girls:

1. Sell UNESCO Gift Coupon Stamps.
2. Write "Pen Pal" Letters Abroad.
3. Read about the United Nations.
4. Read about people whose ways are different from ours.
5. Make a United Nations Flag.
6. Write Articles for School Paper about UNESCO and the UN.
7. Organize a UNESCO Club in your School.

The purpose of each suggested activity was explained and various specific plans were offered for carrying out each purpose. Line drawings by the pupils enlivened the text and pointed up the argument. Finally, addresses were supplied of persons or associations from whom additional information or materials are obtainable. Readers were admonished: "The Success of Junior UNESCO Depends on YOU!!"

Copies of this little manual were sent to teachers in nearby schools who were known to be interested. Out of the resulting contacts, the first Junior UNESCO Conference was held to explore the question, "What Can We Do to Promote International Understanding?"

Pupil delegates from the fifth through eighth grades in schools of three adjoining cities met for half a day to view the film, *Brotherhood of Man;* to listen to an address by a locally prominent educator; to see an original play written and enacted by a fifth-grade group, *En route to the UN;* and to report on activities in the several schools represented. Perhaps the most unusual report given concerned the "adoption" of an orphan in faraway Italy by the children of an intermediate school. This adoption was carried out through the facilities of the Foster Parents' Plan for War Children Inc., of New York City.

Following the conference UNESCO club members decided to issue a small newspaper three times a year. The first issue was printed in October. In it appeared this editorial by a sixth-grade boy:

Dear Friends:

This is *United Nations Week*. We are happy that we can present the first issue of our paper to you during this week. . . .

Grown-ups don't realize that children can help the United Nations, but our club is proving that we can help.

After explaining other activities of the club, he added,

We are going to have a United Nations birthday party and invite some students from foreign countries who are here attending the local college as our guests of honor. . . . You can help, too! Why don't you start a UNESCO Club? Send us news about what your clubs or classes are doing. The Junior UNESCO News will be delivered to your school. . . . It's your paper—Contribute to it.

The girls of the club made a United Nations flag. They sewed so industriously that soon the work was completed. It was agreed that the best way to get the flag more widely displayed would be to present

it to the Mayor for exhibition in the City Hall. Appropriate cere-
monies of the presentation took place, with a photograph of the
event appearing in the local evening press. A letter of appreciation
from the City Manager gave the children considerable satisfaction.

In January the second issue of *Junior UNESCO News* made its
appearance. It showed that the appeal to other schools for contributions had not been in vain. Two girls sent poems. There was a letter
from Hawaii.

The second annual conference of Junior UNESCO was announced
in the April issue of the *News*. A review of the accomplishments of
the year that had intervened was set forth also.

1. Forty-five schools are receiving the *Junior UNESCO News* regularly.

2. Pen pals are corresponding with children in Japan, Philippines,
Hawaii, and Canada.

3. Pupils in India and the Philippines are being helped to get needed
school supplies through the sale of UNESCO Gift Coupon Stamps.

A report describing the third of the listed activities stated:

Last year our Junior UNESCO raised $81.75 through the sale of UNESCO
Gift Coupon Stamps. $10.00 was used to buy a braille watch for a blind
class in Bandung, India. $71.75 was used as part of a $150.00 project to
buy an eight-inch circular saw for the boys of Boys' Town, Manila,
Philippines. These boys will now be able to build desks and tables for
their school.

Again in October, *Junior UNESCO News* went to press to celebrate its own first birthday as well as the eighth anniversary of the
founding of the United Nations. In this issue a seventh-grade girl
described how her school had once celebrated United Nations Week.
"We set up a model of a United Nations Assembly Meeting," she
explained, "by using little dolls dressed in the costumes of the 60 different member nations. . . . By planning and building this model assembly we were able to learn a lot about this great organization, the
United Nations."

The concrete accomplishments of this Junior UNESCO Club only
suggest the attitudes and outlooks of the participating children.
Teachers and administrators are convinced, however, that these
children have gained immeasurably in appreciation of the brotherhood of all mankind and in a better understanding of some of the

problems human beings must solve before peace and happiness can come to the whole world.

A World Friendship Club Promotes International Understanding

At the beginning of the school year in Chaffey Union High School, Ontario, California, a survey is made of all foreign-born students attending the school. These students are given a special invitation to join the Chaffey World Friendship Club.

The school paper always makes this survey a major topic in one of its issues. This is followed up by write-ups on particular students, usually those who have recently come to the United States or have an unusual foreign background. The closeness of the world to the student body is revealing and paves the way to better understanding. Students are asked to share their foreign experiences. There is a great carry-over of this survey throughout the year.

Although the club has many guests and world travelers speak at its meetings, the discussion which follows the speeches is considered the most essential part of each meeting. Often the World Friendship Club shares its meetings with other club groups within the school. The language clubs have especially helped to broaden the interests of members.

Working with the California State Federation of High School World Friendship Clubs has also been stimulating. This gives an opportunity for Chaffey students to meet with students from other schools and to discuss mutual problems pertaining to the promotion of world understanding. These meetings with large groups of young people are truly inspiring and provide for further exchange of ideas. Foreign students from neighboring colleges are invited to attend club meetings. Some have even been made honorary members. Exchange students seem to enjoy a chance to meet with American high school groups.

Club activities have encouraged some students to apply for participation in World Affairs Institutes, Seminars, and Work Projects. The American Friends Service Committee particularly offers many splendid opportunities to high school pupils. Students returning from these experiences do much to promote international understanding in both the Chaffey high school and in the local community.

An ideal opportunity to promote the objectives of the club is afforded when an exchange student is brought by the club group to the community. The American Field Service sponsors a very fine program of this type.

One of the best ways of promoting international understanding and friendship has been found to be the "pen pals." Nearly every member of the World Friendship Club has one. The foreign language clubs have been very successful in this project.

The Chaffey World Friendship Club tries to broaden the meaning and significance of Valentine's Day by making it a World Friendship day. Valentine collections have been very successful. Projects, such as aid to a French School through Save the Children Federation, care of a Korean orphan through Foster Parents' Plan, and CARE packages for India, have been sponsored by the club and the student body during the postwar years.

The Christmas season is always a time of good will. All clubs— student government, language clubs, and World Friendship Clubs— either by their gifts, or various welfare projects, emphasize international understanding at this time. They do not stop here, however, believing that a gift, or a letter, fulfills the mission of promoting international relations. The students all feel that along with welfare activities there must be study, reading, and discussions on an informed basis concerning the problems of the world. They know that gifts alone will not bring about international good will.

An International Relations Club
Accomplishes Many Purposes

The International Relations Club of Bristol High School, Bristol, Connecticut, has been a continuous organization since 1934. The purpose as stated in the constitution is "to develop an appreciation and an understanding of the people in other lands by a study of their customs and of their activities past and present, and by contacts made with people of other lands."

The club functions through the regular officers and the following committees: Program, Bank, Foreign Correspondence, Book (for library purchase), Bulletin Board and Displays, Publicity, Refreshments, and special committees as the need arises. Each committee writes an annual report which is filed with the secretary. The dues for a membership of 85 to 100 are fifty cents a year. These are used largely for philanthropic purposes, such as CARE packages. Meetings are held twice a month. One meeting is frequently used as a workshop in which the club meets in groups to do research for coming club programs or assemblies.

Activities consist largely of programs, parties, and an occasional school assembly. One year the club members broadcast a series of panel discussions on the United Nations over the local station. Members have at times presented programs for organizations such as the local League of Women Voters. Last year the club met with a neighboring International Relations Club for a panel discussion on "Foreign Correspondence."

In October each year the club has a program on the United Nations and prepares classroom, school library, and corridor United Nations exhibits. The art classes and the Library Club cooperate. Another meeting each year is devoted to foreign correspondence. A map on the bulletin board shows the location of pen pals.

At the beginning of the school year each member proposes an area for study. These suggestions are discussed by the program committee which submits two or three choices to the club adviser for approval. The club is divided into as many groups as there are topics. In a study of China the topics were: geography, history, past leaders, present leaders, music, education, religion, and current activities. Each group was responsible for a meeting. The program committee secured two films on China and invited a Chinese student from a nearby college to talk. At this meeting Chinese food, prepared by the Home Economics Department, was served. The speaker supplied chopsticks and these were used with varying success.

One year the club studied "Internationalism in Bristol Industries." This involved interviews and visits to factories. The year the club studied Mexico a guest soloist presented a program during which she taught the members *La Cucaracha*. At another meeting a Spanish teacher talked on Mexican dances and, with a group of club members, performed in fiesta costumes. Another year it was decided to study the lands of the members' own national origins—the emphasis to be on contributions to the United States. Students were urged to obtain first-hand information from friends and relatives. At the first meeting a teacher interested in genealogy helped the club members begin a genealogy chart. At the end of the year a tea was given in honor of the friends and relatives who helped with the study.

Africa was recently studied; this was a huge order, as the club discovered. It was decided to concentrate on a few sections, such as Egypt and the Union of South Africa. The inspiration for this area was an issue of the *Saturday Review*. The fact that a member of the school had lived for several years in Angola added interest to the choice.

Various types of school assemblies have been planned and produced, usually in cooperation with other clubs. "Christmas Carols and Christmas Customs in Many Lands" was done in cooperation with the language clubs and the music clubs. A pageant, *Around the World Cruise of the Peace Crusaders,* was written and produced by the club.

Parties are of a varied nature. One very successful party featured the folk dance, during which the physical education teachers taught some of the simpler folk dances of England, Holland, and Italy. Every year the club has a Christmas party with the French, German, Latin, and Spanish clubs.

The success of the International Relations Club has been made possible by the generous aid and cooperation of the various school departments and other clubs, plus the enthusiasm of its members. The students in a recent poll expressed their own evaluations by such statements as: "This club helps us to defeat prejudices"; "Through international correspondence we get a really personal look at people in other countries"; "This club is generous with its treasury and makes you want to help people in this country and in other countries"; and "The International Relations Club makes us realize international influences in our own lives and international influences in our nation."

Stamps Tell the Story of Cultures

Marshall High School of Chicago, through its Stamp Club, acquaints students with the culture of other peoples, fosters friendship, and leads students to become aware of the bonds which unite peoples in distant parts of the world. During Red Cross week students collect and display stamps from many countries which honor the Red Cross. They study the history of that organization and the role it has played in world affairs.

"A Salute to Aviation," on the fiftieth anniversary of aviation,

featured a collection of stamps from various nations honoring aviation and aviators. This was followed by a discussion of the impact of
aviation upon world affairs and the problems it has created, as well
as the problems it has solved.

On St. Patrick's Day students display the stamps of Ireland, discussing their legends. As the Jewish holidays approach, stamps from
Israel are studied and their meaning noted. Pan American Day is the
occasion for a display from Latin-American nations, with attention
drawn to the ideas and facts which these nations have publicized
through their stamps.

Columbus Day brings about an exhibit of stamps featuring epi-
sodes in the life of Columbus. Familiarizing students with the biography of Columbus, this collection from many countries shows the
number of nations with whom we share Columbus, thus strengthening the concept of the interdependence of nations.

Through these varied activities students become interested in the
colorful stories which stamps tell of different parts of the world and
develop attitudes of friendliness toward people of different regions
and cultures.

The Eagle Rock High School Helps
Education in Korea

In February, 1949, before there was any thought of war, five principals of girls' high schools in Seoul, Korea, came to the United States
to spend a year visiting the high schools of this country. They spent a
day at Eagle Rock High School of Los Angeles, California, accompanied by Mary Chum Lee, a long-time resident of Eagle Rock, who
acted as their interpreter.

With the help of their interpreter, an assembly was held and information concerning Korean schools was given by these Korean
principals. It was shocking and hard for American boys and girls to
realize that there could be a place in the world where a lead pencil
could cost six dollars or where a student would be allowed only one
and a half sheets of paper per month for his class work.

This assembly impressed the students so seriously that even before
the Korean teachers had left the grounds the wheels were set in motion by two eighth-grade boys to organize a club for the purpose of
raising money to send school supplies to Korea. On Friday morning

of that same week, fifteen boys met to organize and start the plans for Eagle Rock High School's Korean Club.

The group decided to put pint jars, with the insignia of the Korean flag on them and a slit in the lid for the pennies, in all classrooms where there was an interest in having one. They used for their slogan, "Give your pennies to help Korean school children." The giving increased after the war started and held constant over the entire period.

During this period of time there was quite a change in membership as the club was opened to girls after the first three semesters. It was surprising that the club has held the interest of the students, since they do not receive service points for their time and work. They belong simply because they want to do so, and for the thrill they get out of meeting and working with the Korean people in the Los Angeles community. There have been many of these contacts.

During the first three semesters $285.94 was taken in and one shipment of school supplies was sent to Korea in June, 1950. An interested retired doctor made a microscope available at a very reasonable price and the rest of the shipment was books, notebook paper, and pencils. Another shipment of $87.26 worth of paper, pencils, wall pencil sharpeners, and erasers was just ready to go when the war broke out. It could not be sent until August, 1953. During the war the money from the collections was allowed to accumulate in the bank until such a time as it would be possible to get money or supplies directly to the groups that Eagle Rock High School wanted to help.

The club was started with the idea of making friends as well as giving help. Before the war, quite a number of Eagle Rock students were corresponding with the students in the high school which received the first aid sent to Korea. This stopped, of course, when the war began.

In November, 1952, when the papers reported Mrs. Van Fleet's visit to her husband, General James Van Fleet, in Korea, the club's sponsor wrote to Mrs. Van Fleet, giving information concerning the club and asking if it would be possible to help the club find a school which it could adopt. Her reply and assistance led to the cooperation of the United States Army. The educational committee of First Corps, Eighth Army, made purchases for the school with the money forwarded to it. A special "presentation ceremony" was held on the Korean school grounds when the supplies were received. Pictures and a tape recording of the program were received by the club.

The Korean children have organized an Eagle Rock Club and individual letters have been exchanged between the members of both clubs. Since the hope of Korea, and of international understanding in all lands, lies in its young people, the students of Eagle Rock High School feel that they are helping to build future citizens for Korea through helping with their educational program.

Students Hold a Yearly Conference on International Affairs

At the Oak Park and River Forest High School, Oak Park, Illinois, one of the important activities in developing international understanding is the High School Conference on International Affairs. This conference meets annually for a week-end discussion of some area or problem which bears significantly on American foreign relations.

Now in its twenty-third year, the conference represents joint planning by the high school and the Oak Park Council on International Affairs. The Council, an adult organization in Oak Park, aids the students in securing speakers and in program planning. In the past, it has granted financial assistance, but during recent years, the venture has been financially self-supporting.

The Conference on International Affairs is self-governing. At each yearly session, officers are elected for the coming year. They choose the speakers, make up the program, sell tickets, and conduct publicity with a minimum of adult help. As now constituted, the program consists of a Saturday evening dinner, followed by a program featuring a speaker. On Sunday afternoon there is a second speaker. Attendance runs from 450 to 600 students.

The 1954 program was devoted to the study of Africa, using the theme, "Light on the Dark Continent." Before and after this meeting the library and the history classes emphasized the conference theme in study, discussions, and displays.

The High School UNESCO Council in the City of New York

This High School UNESCO Council consists of three officers, an executive board, and representatives from the UNESCO Clubs or other cooperating social studies clubs from most of the academic and many of the vocational high schools in New York City. It meets four times yearly to plan programs, to elect officers and members of the executive board. The board meets as often as required to administer the program which involves four major activities.

1. The American Association for the United Nations conducts a Speakers' Workshop on Saturday mornings to help students run meetings, learn the issues involved in the topics the clubs have chosen for discussion and develop leadership techniques.

2. Monthly interviews of United Nations officials are held at the United Nations by Junior UNESCO club representatives and the High School Press Association with its 85 high school newspapers.

3. Visiting foreign college students are invited, with the aid of the Institute of International Education, to speak in assemblies, classrooms, and clubs.

4. Annual conferences are held in cooperation with the faculty advisors of the interscholastic Borough Discussion Conferences, the United Nations, and the Herald Tribune Youth Forum. The conference themes are suggested by the Junior UNESCO Council. The three themes used to date are:

1952.   "The Citizen and the United Nations" (Theme of the 3rd National Conference of the U.S. National Commission for UNESCO)

1953.   "The Role of the United States in the World Community"

1954.   "Youth Evaluates the United Nations Program"

In the 1952 conference the junior and senior high school groups both analyzed thirteen topics, as did the Senior Conference. Since these have formed much of the basis for club and assembly programs ever since, they are listed below:

1. Development toward an international legal order
2. Peaceful settlement and collective security
3. The fight against ignorance: Raising the world educational level
4. Pooling resources for the progress of underdeveloped areas
5. Food and people
6. International labor cooperation
7. Advancing human rights
8. Communications in the world community
9. Refugees and surplus population problems
10. Advancement of dependent peoples

11. International social welfare services
12. Meeting world health problems
13. Mutual advancement through world trade

In 1953 and 1954 five general areas of each theme were organized, with analytical discussions led by student leaders trained by the faculty advisors of the Borough Discussion Conferences. These topics in turn have been subdivided again into topics for round-table room discussion.

In addition to carrying on the discussion the five round-table groups vote on recommendations and resolutions to be presented to the General Assembly of the Junior UNESCO delegates meeting in the auditorium. The assembly program also featured the *Herald Tribune* Youth Forum delegates from foreign lands who presented the topic, "My Country and the United Nations."

Junior UNESCO Councils have received the very enthusiastic support of thousands of students ranging from New Haven, Connecticut to Allentown, Pennsylvania. Several serious difficulties militate against its achieving maximum results, nevertheless. They are:

1. Lack of any machinery for appropriating funds makes it a heavy burden on faculty coordinators who sometimes operate at a personal loss.

2. For the same reason physical facilities for meetings are seriously limited, both as to central location and as to time.

3. Continuous and careful faculty direction is required to keep the club meetings from distorting the aims of Junior UNESCO.

4. No special recognition is given faculty leaders conducting extracurricular programs.

5. There seems all too little protection against attack by biased members of any community.

Democracy Is Learned Through Membership in Junior Statesmen of America

One of the most productive out-of-class activities for the implementation of international understanding in the Carmel High School, Carmel, California, has been participation in the Junior Statesmen of America Organization. Local chapters are made up of students in grades nine through twelve. These chapters are self-governing. They are subject only to such over-all controls as are voted by all members, at state or regional legislative sessions, by the elected delegates of the members themselves. The organization tries to exemplify the democratic process.

The Junior Statesmen program is designed to give high school students a working knowledge of, and practical sharing in, the democratic system. The basic premise underlying the organization is that democracy can continue successfully only through the participation of well-informed citizens.

The local chapters meet regularly at their high schools or in homes of members. Twice a year, or oftener, there are regional meetings which are attended by large numbers of students. Twice a year there are general legislative sessions. One of these is usually held in the State of California Assembly Chamber at the State Capitol in Sacramento. All meetings are administered strictly under Robert's rules of order.

Before students attend chapter meetings, regional or state conventions, they write up bills, resolutions, constitutional amendments, and statutes. At the various legislative sessions the students present, debate in detail, and vote upon the various measures and proposals. Copies of the bills, including action taken, are then sent to officials interested, including the President of the United States, various congressmen, governors, and others.

The following list includes the titles of resolutions actually written and debated before legislative sessions of Junior Statesmen of America:

Junior Statesmen of America:

A Resolution Pertaining to the Limitation of the Veto in the United Nations

A Resolution Pertaining to the Korean Armistice

A Resolution Pertaining to the Lowering of Trade Tariffs and Other Barriers to International Trade in the United States.

A Resolution Pertaining to the Bricker Amendment.

A Resolution Pertaining to the Complete Repeal of the McCarran Immigration Law

A Resolution Pertaining to the Settlement of Deficits and Credits Incurred in World Trade

A Resolution Pertaining to the Strengthening of the United Nations Charter

A Resolution Pertaining to the Admission of Red China to the United Nations

The following resolution was introduced at Sacramento by two students of Glendale High School, November 14, 1953:

A Resolution Pertaining to the Disposition of Trieste

WHEREAS: Trieste was ceded to Italy under the treaty of Saint Germain in 1919; and

WHEREAS: In 1945, Tito's Yugoslav troops entered Trieste, but were prevented from taking full control by British and United States forces; and

WHEREAS: On June 20, 1945 a compromise agreement was reached for the joint occupation of Trieste by Great Britain and the United States in Zone A and Yugoslavia in Zone B; and

WHEREAS: The United States and Great Britain have recently turned their control of Zone A over to Italy, and strong objections have been raised by the Yugoslavs; be it

RESOLVED: That the JUNIOR STATESMEN OF AMERICA go on record as favoring permanent control of Zone A, including the city of Trieste, by Italy and retention of Zone B by Yugoslavia; be it further

RESOLVED: That copies of this RESOLUTION be sent to: The President of the United States of America, The Secretary of State of the United States of America, The Delegates of the United States of America to the United Nations.

DISPOSITION RECORD:

Vote of the legislature 80 to 48
Carried   X   defeated
Verified by the Secretary of State
Date

Intense and lasting interest is stimulated within each student as he debates and resolves each issue. It is felt that the understanding of complex international problems is brought into meaningful focus through participation in the Junior Statesmen of America Organization.

Junior Councils of the Cleveland Council on World Affairs

In the greater Cleveland area there are at present 30 Junior Councils, with an additional number from outlying areas joining them for outstanding programs during the year. Membership in individual clubs varies from 4 to 110 students. The program in the high schools has been in operation since 1937.

It is important to note that in most groups the student members themselves make all plans and carry them out. The World Affairs Council, through its youth director, usually acts only as a service agent and administrator for these clubs. The director furnishes the councils with speakers, films, and programming ideas.

Most groups find that variety in programming is extremely important. Panel programs, discussion groups, film forums, debates, symposia, and guest speakers are among the various program devices used. Sometimes councils in two or three schools get together for joint meetings and occasionally there are student conferences to which each Junior Council will send representatives.

The outstanding program of the year for the Junior Councils in Cleveland is the Model General Assembly held each spring in cooperation with Western Reserve University. Approximately 400 students take part in this annual event. Each school is assigned two countries to represent and at least six weeks is spent on research and preparation of position papers on the various countries. The success of this preparatory work results in no small measure from the cooperation of the Cleveland Public Library and its branches.

A plenary meeting opens the Assembly, with an address by a member of the Political Science Department of Western Reserve University. He introduces and gives background on the topics to be considered. The groups are then broken up into six committees and meet for two-hour discussions, both in the morning and the afternoon. A short time is allowed for caucasing before the final resolutions are introduced and a vote taken at a plenary session which closes the Assembly.

Many of the Junior Councils plan observances for special occasions —United Nations Week, World Health Day, Pan-American Week, World Trade Week, and Human Rights Day. There are other special projects, such as collecting items for Korean Relief packages or raising money to buy UNESCO Gift Coupons. And, on an individual basis, Council members carry on correspondence with young people in many countries throughout the world.

The Junior Council program as a whole has a varying degree of success and is usually dependent upon the amount of variety put into the year's program. It is generally agreed however, that these Councils afford an excellent opportunity to students who want to explore current developments in world affairs.

High Schools in Ohio Hold Conferences on Public Affairs

In the fall of 1947 the director of the Ohio High School Speech League, which has its headquarters in the Speech Department of the Ohio State University, approached the University School with a proposal for a noncompetitive interschool discussion conference. The first experimental conference was held at the school during the morning, afternoon, and evening of a school day in early December, with about 100 students from some twenty high schools in central Ohio in attendance. While details and procedures are constantly being modified in the light of experience, the general pattern was rated as highly successful by both students and teachers and the conference has now become an annual affair.

A list of the subjects year by year will give an idea of the kind of issues with which these young people are dealing.

1947.   Taft-Hartley Act
1948.   Shall we press now for federal world government?
1949.   How much socialized medicine do we want in the United States?
1950.   How can the United States best prepare to defend itself in the present world crisis?
1951.   Is world peace possible?
1952.   How can we raise the ethical and moral standards of the nation?
1953.   Are we losing our freedoms?

The mechanics of the conference have changed very little since the beginning. The discussion subject is usually broken down into five issues. These are sent to the schools in advance of the conference as a guide to students in their preparation. For example, the following issues were selected as major areas under the topic, "Is World Peace Possible?"

1. What is the threat of Communism to the free world?
2. Can the United Nations keep the peace?
3. Will the North Atlantic Pact keep the peace in Europe?

4. Would a similar system of collective security keep peace in Asia?
5. What kind of role should the United States play?
Sub-issues were suggested for each of the major issues.

Each conference begins with a general session at which the plans and working techniques are explained. It then breaks up into small discussion groups of eight to ten students, all of whom are from different schools. Each group has a moderator, usually a university student from a discussion class, who is supposed to see to it that each member participates and that the particular issue is explored during the hour session. A student messenger can be sent to summon an expert in case there is a wrangle over the facts, but the adult tries only to help the students think together, not to tell them what to think.

At the end of the hour each group chooses a reporter, and all students reassemble in general session, with the reporters from all groups forming a panel which is led by an adult moderator. The professor who teaches the classes in discussion on the Ohio State University campus has always performed this function. Each group reports in turn and then the moderator summarizes the agreements and disagreements, and picks out some of the major disagreements for general discussion.

This process is repeated for each issue. At the final session, if the subject has any implications for legislation, the conference usually votes to send a summary of its conclusions to Ohio representatives and senators in Washington.

During recent years the conference has been held on Thursday afternoon and all day on Friday. This arrangement is understandably popular with the students, especially since it provides a social evening Thursday. At this time there is a dinner, a talent show to which all schools are invited to contribute, and a social hour afterward. The students have learned that they must plan ice-breakers, but that with a little effort the social contacts are valuable reinforcements for other conference activities. The discussions the second day warm up considerably, participation is freer, and students are more confident and at ease.

Students have been playing an increasing part in the planning of the conference as techniques have slowly been developed for bringing them into it. Each school is now asked to include at least some juniors in its delegation. At the final sessions there are nominations and elections from the students below the senior level for the next year's planning committee. The faculty adviser for an elected student is automatically considered elected to the planning committee also. This committee meets in late April or early May to select the subject and date for the next fall, to evaluate the experiences of the previous conference, and to divide responsibilities for preparing for the next one.

If students have anything to say about it, the public affairs discussion conference is here to stay. Their enthusiasm for such an intellectual, noncompetitive event is so encouraging to teachers that they are willing to take the time and put forth the effort which such an enterprise entails.

Twenty Years of International Relations
Conferences in Colorado

The first state-wide International Relations Conference for high school pupils of Colorado was held twenty years ago under the leadership of the World Citizenship Committee of the Colorado Education Association and the Social Science Foundation of the University of Denver. There were a number of newly formed Internation Relations Clubs in high schools at that time and representatives from these clubs constituted most of the enrollment for this first conference. Two decades later, having weathered hard times, a war, changes in school organization, and purposes of education and curriculum, the Colorado International Relations Conference for high schools is a strong, active institution with well-defined objectives to promote world understanding at the community level.

Colorado's schools are scattered far and wide over her broad plains and rugged mountains. Programs for world understanding in these schools vary all the way from definite feelings against anything that seems foreign, to active International Relations Clubs, enthusiastic Pen Pal Clubs, well-organized UNESCO programs, panels by high school students before civic groups, and classroom instruction in world understanding.

The conference plan provides ways by which contacts may be made easily to encourage each community to develop its own program in world understanding in the school and related organizations. It opens the way to offer assistance if the community asks for and needs a boost to get started. The plan helps to keep teachers and pupils informed on new materials and new approaches to the subject. It helps to bring Colorado's widely scattered schools and communities closer together to promote the common cause of world understanding.

The appointment of committees is one of the duties of the co-sponsors. The Conference Planning Committee consists of ten or more high school pupils and four or more sponsors who represent various schools in different parts of the state. The committee meets for one all-day session and, if possible, oftener. At the all-day session pupils and teachers talk over the kind of conferences pupils find profitable and select topics for exploration.

Equipped with first-hand information from pupils and teachers, the chairman of the Conference Planning Committee and the director of the Social Science Foundation select a timely theme and appropriate topics for round-table discussions. Available material relating to the topics is assembled from many sources and in quantities of fifty copies or more. An experienced teacher usually writes a study guide which contains:

1. Background papers for each topic
2. Questions to bring out different sides of the topic
3. The controversial aspects of each topic
4. A bibliography
5. A tentative program for the conference
6. The date on which the conference will be held
7. Other information which schools will need to know if they anticipate attending

In early September, a complementary copy of the study guide and a letter of invitation to participate are mailed to a carefully selected list of teachers in 100 or more schools. Some schools are grateful for the study guide and want to keep in touch but will be unable to attend. Others know at once that they will attend. Whatever the reply may be, communication between the planning committee and schools continues by letter and by telephone, until the day of the conference.

Students and teachers have about three months to prepare for the conference. Each group works out plans for study so that each pupil will be informed on the theme and the topic which he expects to discuss with other students. Sometimes this preparation is done in the classroom. Frequently it is done in night sessions. During the first week of December the two-day conference is held on the University of Denver campus.

New features of this conference type of study have developed in the past few years. A small publication called the *I R C Exchange* is written by students, edited by a sponsor, and circulated to forty-seven schools in the state about six times during the year. Regional conferences are being held more frequently in different parts of the state and each club is now working on the idea of helping to organize a club in a neighboring school.

CHAPTER 5

Assemblies and Other All-School Activities

THERE seems to be a close correlation between meaningful assemblies and other all-school activities, and the insights and resourcefulness of administrators and teachers. Real understanding of other peoples goes deeper than tolerance, or even knowledge. It is dependent upon experiences which stir the emotions in sympathetic perception.

In this chapter descriptions are presented of a number of ways in which international understanding is sought through student organizations, a library, special programs, music and the arts, as well as through visual aids. The skills of many people are involved. Ideals of the human brotherhood of all men are clearly apparent.

Student Organizations Are Utilized to Welcome Pupils with Foreign Backgrounds

Lowell High School is situated near the heart of the cosmopolitan city of San Francisco. Every semester sees a relatively large number of foreign students enter this academic school. They represent most of the nations of the world and often have difficulty in adjusting to their new situation. Many times they are confused and have a definite feeling of being alone in a strange school world. The best method of orienting these newcomers seems to be through the activities of existing student organizations.

Two organizations of the school welcome all new students. The Big Sisters welcome all new girl students and the Big Brothers do the same for the boys. Both assign a member to each new student. A number of activities are used to welcome newcomers. Activities include dances, group luncheons, and intramural athletics. Each sponsor assumes responsibility for the scholastic, as well as the social, orientation of his neophyte.

Additional activities are added in the case of foreign students. The

Big Brothers maintain a "Speakers Bureau." When a class has need of information about a particular country the instructor calls upon the bureau to provide a foreign student who represents that country. The resulting informal talk helps the foreign-born student to be recognized, appreciated, and accepted. He performs a valuable service to the class and at the same time serves as an unofficial ambassador of his country. Class interest is usually stimulated by these talks and the speaker finds the students are eager to know him better.

The school newspaper utilizes the story value of foreign students and the countries of their origin. Articles are written and the resulting publicity gives a tremendous boost in morale. Newcomers are all encouraged to participate in a variety of group activities. They have a choice of athletics, music, art, and varied clubs. The school also serves as an information center for a number of outside agencies interested in the foreign born.

The success of the Lowell High School in working with foreign students has been the result of planned utilization of existing school facilities and organizations. The result of this program is a better understanding by both foreign and American students of the world in which they live.

Seeing Is Believing

The librarian of the Oak Ridge High School, Oak Ridge, Tennessee, was given the sum of $100.00 to spend while she was traveling in Europe for anything she wished that would enrich the school program.

This librarian attended the Institute for English Speaking Teachers at the University of Oslo in Norway. After reviewing carefully the purpose of the Institute, which is essentially to explain Norwegian life and culture to students and teachers from other countries, it occurred to her that perhaps the best way she could bring back some of the everyday things dear to the hearts of the Norwegians would be to purchase their school books, history, geography, readers, picture books, fairy tales, and even comic books. She also collected Norwegian clothes for festive occasions and as many pictures as possible. She saved candy wrappers, parcel papers, string, tickets—railroad, streetcar, and play tickets—as well as business letters, telegrams, and, of course, newspapers. Later, these items were pasted on large sheets of brown wrapping paper and as a collection were called a scrapbook on contemporary life. The newspapers subsequently proved especially interesting to a group of sophomores studying European countries. They were not only amused at the Norwegian comics but they found format as well as the arrangement of news very similar to our own.

Book Week in November seemed the most logical time to display, in and around the library, the wares from faraway places. It provided the incentive to invite other teachers and students who had traveled abroad to share in carrying the theme, "Reading Is Fun All Over the World," to the entire school. All contributed generously. Student curiosity in the things displayed was heightened by printed signs in the language of the books displayed. For example, the sign SNAKKE NORSK asked our boys and girls if they spoke Norwegian so that they might read Norwegian books.

A bulletin board was devoted to a display of catalog cards, reading lists, borrower's card, membership cards, and other everyday library paraphernalia gleaned from Norwegian, Danish, Swedish, and Austrian libraries. These further emphasized the book week theme which was changed to read, BOOK WEEK ALL OVER THE WORLD.

Students were impressed with the great similarity between libraries abroad and their own. The correspondence school in Oslo sent a complete library course for library assistants. Although the text could not be read, illustrations were understood. There was much surprise to find that Norwegian books were classified with the Dewey decimal system, just as in the high school library.

Another incident concerned the correspondence school which this librarian visited while she was in Oslo. When she, with other visiting teachers, had gone to see this school and hear about its work, they were given sample lessons from some of the courses. One on child care and development especially interested the teachers of Oak Ridge High School. They were pleased to find that similar ways, clearly illustrated, were used in Norway for baby bathing and choice of toys.

A piece-by-piece model, built to scale, of the Kon-Tiki raft was one of the foreign purchases, along with a Norwegian edition of the story *Kon Tiki*. It was no trouble at all to find a boy in the Oak Ridge school whose hobby was model building. This builder assembled the raft for display.

There followed a big demand on the part of pupils for the story. This also brought a need to see the pictures of the raft which are now on display in Bygody in Oslo. One girl asked if she might take home the Norwegian publication for her mother to read. She loaned the library in exchange a book of Danish recipes written in Danish.

Later, a group of boys reviewed the story, *Kon-Tiki*, on a Teen-Agers Bookshelf radio broadcast. In order to do this it was necessary to examine the model carefully, and to note the conditions confronting the men who dared the perils of the sea on balsa wood. One of the most interesting comments from one of the boys was, "Golly, those six men had to be intelligent as well as strong to stand an ocean trip on a raft." The boys seemed to feel the strength of the Norwegians as a people.

Perhaps one of the most satisfying experiences of using the materials from overseas was that of being invited by several fourth grades in two local schools to tell them about Norway. Letters of invitation, written by the pupils, expressed the wish to know how the Norwegians lived, what food they eat, how they go to school, what clothes they wear, and what kind of houses they live in. Here again pictures and objects served to enlighten the telling. The textbooks, however, provided the greatest interest to these younger children. These were used by Norwegian boys and girls, as textbooks are by American boys and girls and led to such spontaneous comments as: "Why they dress like we do?" "They learn stories as we do about the same things—mother, father, sister, brother—"; and "They sing songs as we do, and they even sing *our* songs." This was just the right time to teach a little Grieg song which is known by nearly all Norwegians. It is *Fola, Fola Blaaken*.

Perhaps the most happy and rewarding feeling came to this librarian-teacher when she received over 100 thank you letters from her young friends in the local elementary schools. Many of these were illustrated with some of the ideas that had been talked about during her school visits. One class sent a packet of charmingly drawn messages in pictures, including flags and witches and many flowers.

The materials purchased with the money which the Oak Ridge High School alloted has thus served in numerous ways. It would seem that this good-will collection from across the seas has planted an insatiable curiosity for ideas and concepts of neighbors abroad which, like the proverbial mustard seed, will continue to grow and spread.

A School-Community Project on Africa

During the school year 1952–53 vast and varied Africa was considerably in the news. From press, microphone, and by word-of-mouth came clear evidence that the peoples of that once "dark continent" were reaching toward a brighter horizon and more favorable days. The story of the struggle of the peoples of Africa to achieve freedom reached the Vaux Junior High School of Philadelphia and moved pupils, teachers, and and parents into a school project that involved everyone, one way or another, in a study of African backgrounds, problems, purposes, cultures, and aspirations.

From a humble start with news clippings brought in for current-events discussions, the study grew into individual class projects. Soon grade groups were visiting other classrooms to share information and a pleasant rivalry developed.

The beauty of Africa described photographically in *Life* magazine captured the imagination of many. Rooms and corridors became resplendent with African scenes and portraits. African music was heard and reproduced. Songs and stories were written and dance interpretations developed.

A team of teachers, working with parents and students, endeavored together to assemble books, pamphlets, pictures, and countless artifacts in the school library. They took turns as curators and librarians, explaining to visiting class groups the significance of each item, as well as the over-all theme. Classes from neighboring schools were invited to Vaux and welcomed when they appeared. Visual aids from the Division of Visual Education were used extensively.

Visitors from Africa were invited to the school to speak—in assemblies, in the library, and in the classrooms. They told stories illustrating the African's well-developed ethical concepts. They sang songs that revealed how tender mother-love is everywhere. They recounted experiences that revealed the dignity prevailing among our African brothers.

One teacher traveled to New York to do special research in literature not yet translated from the French and German, as well as in books published in England which are not widely known in America.

Through the efforts of the Student Council, faithful plaster replicas of ceremonial masks were purchased from the University of Pennsylvania museum. These masks were attached to specially devised frames, made in the wood shops and painted in the art rooms. They were hung in the corridors. The entire second floor of the building was so decorated.

Bibliographies grew apace. Art work abounded. Assembly programs increased in number as well as in beauty. The school dietician surprised everyone by her research into African dishes, which made possible especially prepared African desserts.

Trips were arranged with the metropolitan museums and to central libraries. Correspondence with Africans developed. Personal films taken by missionaries where shown in the auditorium. A traveling exhibit was developed.

The project culminated with an invitation to the community to come to the school, to view the art work, to sense the appreciations pupils and teachers had developed, and to share the knowledge that had been acquired.

All had grown measurably, had developed in wisdom. Although our culture has no calibration for such growth, participants cherish the hope that henceforward their approach to the problems and aspirations of Africa's millions will be made in terms of the developing wisdom that has come through sincere and earnest study.

International Day in a Senior High School

The proximity of Edina-Morningside High School of Minneapolis, Minnesota, to the University of Minnesota has presented both an opportunity and a challenge. How should the school utilize the resources represented by the many foreign students at the university? One answer to this question was to invite a group of foreign students to spend a day in an American school.

International Day at Edina-Morningside High School has now become an annual event. It is not merely a social occasion, although the complete naturalness of high-school students on such occasions promotes an almost festive air. Students spend the larger part of the day in a series of informal seminars, meeting each of the guests, hearing about his country, and answering questions about the United States.

Junior and senior classes are divided into groups of approximately fifty students, who rotate on schedule from room to room, spending almost a half-hour with each foreign visitor. This permits a more personal, intimate contact with foreign students and has tended to ensure discussion through students' questioning.

Having guests from every corner of the globe, representing different racial groups, different religious beliefs, different cultures—having them all come together at one time in face-to-face relationships with small groups of students—is impressive. Information is gained, of course, but, more significantly, the basic sameness of peoples, their problems and hopes for the future, is revealed. When students become aware of this common bond, they are on their way to achieving a realistic approach to world understanding.

The guests are not completely exploited. Since two are assigned to each classroom, the seminar periods are alternated with periods of free time, when they can rest, have coffee, or visit classes that are operating regularly. Most of the visitors have never had an opportunity to visit an American high school or to talk with American boys and girls of this age. Many express the belief that these high school students have offered them something their university courses could not.

Preparation for International Day is always a serious affair. Classes in world problems, world literature, and languages become resource spots for information to be used in conversation with the anticipated guests. Students are in complete charge during the day. They direct the seminars. They take their guests to lunch in the cafeteria. They arrange the opening and closing assembly programs. They plan and print the programs. Faculty members may attend but they are strictly supernumerary.

The first International Day was so successful that its annual repetition has since been taken for granted. Each year the program has been improved, providing greater variety in the day's activities through the use of films, general assembly speakers, and musical numbers by the school choir.

The pleasure with which International Day has been received by students has led them to wonder if other high schools, even though they may not be so conveniently close to a university, might not consider sponsoring such an activity. In smaller communities, civic organizations might assist. International Day might be planned to center in the school but include a cross section of the hospitality and friendship of an American small town or city.

There are approximately 700 foreign students at the University of Minnesota. International Day in which only a small number of this total group participate may seem to be an insignificant gesture. Teachers and pupils are convinced, however, that it has a profound effect each year on the thinking and attitudes of some 350 high school students. In the four years the program has been in existence, the school has made friends who have returned, or will return, to twenty-five different countries of the world. And the world has changed for the students. Japan, for instance, will never be so far away as it once was. It is now Dr. Takano's home, a friend they met when he was studying medicine at the University of Minnesota.

A Festival of Friendship

A dramatization of international understanding occurs each year in the Lakewood Junior High School in Long Beach, California. Conceived originally as a culmination of the Latin-American unit of the ninth-grade social living course of study, the project has developed into a school-wide Festival of Friendship which is held annually during or near the week of Pan-American Day. After the first year the Festival became not only school-wide but community-wide as well. It has even drawn some attendance from other nearby areas.

Although the participation of the community has varied from year to year, the activities of the school have remained constant. On Friday, a festival of dances is held in nearby Pan-American Park. This is an afternoon of folk dancing, using both indigenous and Latin-American dances, with the dancers in early American or Latin-American costume. The entire student body joins in many of these dances and all students and teachers participate in the costuming which accompanies the Festival.

On Saturday, all members of the Latin-American consular association from Los Angeles and their families are guests of the community. They are entertained in the homes of the residents and are conducted on a tour of the surrounding area. Several times a street parade has been held in which the consuls and their families rode in open cars, each car bearing placards and the national flag of the country represented.

Early in the afternoon, the audience gathers in the park for the final dramatization of the school's activities, the exchange of flags. Each year, a Latin-American neighbor is selected as the particular country to be honored. The final assembly embodies an exchange of national flags by the consul or other representative, acting for a designated school in his own country, and an official of the Long Beach Board of Education for the Lakewood School. A display of all the flags of participating countries and a formal processional of students in costume furnish the backdrop for this dramatic portrayal of mutual good will and respect. Music for the formal march is furnished by the school band. Consuls, officials, students, townspeople, and guests form the audience.

Two selected members of the student body bring the two gifts—the United States flag and the one from the selected Latin-American country—to the platform, through an aisle formed by students carrying the flags of all Latin-American countries. The flags are exchanged on the platform, each flag becoming the property of the other school. The spoken good wishes of each school accompany the giving of the national flag.

At the conclusion of the ceremony the Lakewood glee clubs sing the American national anthem and that of the honored country in its native language. In the eyes of the visiting consuls the singing of their national anthem is an item of honor second only to the exchange of the flags.

The festival is given considerable publicity in the Latin-American country so honored, as well as in the local press. Clippings from newspapers and letters from the participating school frequently follow the festival. In almost every instance, a comparable ceremony takes place when our gift flag is received abroad. In Brazil, through the good offices of the consul-general, an exact duplicate of the Festival of friendship took place on the Fourth of July.

Eight American flags now hang in as many schools in widely scattered schools among our neighbors. Long Beach young people and their parents have met in person the official representatives of twenty friendly nations and have found them to be courteous, cultured, and eager for our friendship and understanding. The consuls have, in the words of one of them, "talked to Americans without stiff shirts." They have visited in American homes and schools. They have eaten American food and shared in songs and dances.

Each of these nations, however small, has been presented to our young people with the same dignity and respect which is due our own nation. Their flags have flown with ours, and our children have learned that a flag is a symbol of a living people, to be cherished and honored. Participation in the festival, particulaly in the exchange ceremony, has become a valued reward for worthy citizenship and a long-remembered experience for many hundreds of our students. The school and its community have been more tightly welded. The eyes of thousands of young Americans have lifted to horizons of peaceful cooperation and mutual respect among peoples of differing cultures which have common aspirations for freedom and self-fulfillment.

The Acceptance of All Kinds of People Through Music and Drama

The entire area of intercultural and international relations is so complex and has so many facets that teaching within it is apt to be superficial. Children may repeat parrot-wise many concepts that sound good but, in reality, have neither meaning nor feeling behind or within them. Because our emotions are so deeply involved in the development of a concept about human relations, the arts should be extensively used to reach our children, for inherent in song, dance, drama, and the graphic arts lies the essence of mankind's emotions and feelings.

Music is so much a part of people, it matters not from which area of the globe we come, what color our skins, how we worship our God or gods, nor what work we do. Ever since the beginning of time, man has expressed his feelings in singing, dancing, acting, and playing on instruments. His sorrows and joys, desires, longings, frustrations, humor, and accomplishments have all found their outlet in the music he has made for himself.

When the third grade of the Falk School in Pittsburgh discusses the countries from which their parents and grandparents came, the songs and dances of these countries are used. A seventh-grade study of the Latin-American countries presents a fascinating opportunity for a blending of the old and new in the musical contributions of these countries. Children learn the steps of an ancient Peruvian Harvest Dance and sing the powerful Bolivian chant, *From the*

White Earth. They learn how to dance the rhumba and samba. They listen to *Tico-Tico* played on the Hammond organ by Ethel Smith, or they enjoy the exciting rhythms in Xavier Cugat's orchestrations.

During these activities children should also be making some drums, maracas, claves, and guiros for their own orchestra. They should not miss hearing the recording of Andres Segovia's guitar playing, the delightful folk songs of the charming Brazilian, Olga Coelho, and the unusual voice of the Inca Princess, Yma Sumac, who has toured the United States. They should have the opportunity to become familiar with such names as Albeniz, da Falla, Lecuona, Chavez, and the Iturbis. All the information gleaned from the classroom study and music periods can be put into a program consisting of a series of speeches and some musical numbers. One may, for instance, stage a market place in any Latin-American city, creating characters, dialogue, and action around a tortilla vendor, a strolling band of musicians, a group of workers returning from the fields, a humorous rhythmic dramatization of a bull fight or a fiesta.

St. Patrick's day is a wonderful time to add Irish songs to the repertoire. Children at the Falk School sing the rollicking good song, *Pat on the Railway*. The contributions of the Irish to the building of great railroads are discussed. They learn how to dance *The Galway Piper,* in which the people of the little coastal town of Donegal created the steps of the dance to represent the patterns and designs of the sea, which was so much a part of them. The Irish lullaby, *Too Ral Loo Ral,* made famous by Bing Crosby, is sung, as are: the little South American lullaby, *The Mockin' Bird;* the German *Guten Abend, Gute Nacht;* the Russian *Bayushki Bayu;* and the Chinese *Bamboo Flute.* It is easy to discover that a lullaby knows no geographic or racial barriers.

In the month of March there is a holiday, *Purim,* or *The Feast of Esther,* which is celebrated by the Jewish people all over the world. This is a joyous commemoration of the bravery and courage of a very beautiful young woman who was willing to give her life to save her people from extinction. There have been many other brave women in history since Esther's time—Joan of Arc, Edith Cavell, Madame Marie Curie, Molly Pitcher, Amelia Earhart. The story of Purim is a good story to tell, for it has a beautiful heroine, a good king as its hero, a wise man, and a wicked villain. It can be told in an assembly program, with large poster-size portraits of the characters held by four children, who expose the picture of the character as it is mentioned and flip up the blank side of the card when the picture isn't needed.

The entire school can sing some of the Purim songs. *Oh, Haman Was a Wicked, Wicked Man* is the favorite at the Falk School. They can also try writing their own songs. The words come easily. And if the children aren't accustomed to composing music, they can try using a familiar tune as a beginning. Such a story as that of Purim also provides an excellent opportunity for dramatization.

Humor isn't the property of any country or people. To laugh is as natural as to breathe. There are songs like the English *Tree in the Wood,* the South African *Tante Koba,* the Australian *Waltzing Mathilda,* or the American *Comin' Round the Mountain.* There are humorous instrument songs, such as the Czech *Shusti Fidli,* the German *Musikanter,* or the Archie Bleyer–Julius La Rosa version of the Italian *Eh Cumpari.*

Stephen Foster expressed humor in his song, *Some Folks Do,* as did Luigi Denza in *Funiculi, Funicula.* Girls like to create a funny dance sequence to the Shostakovich *Polka* from the *Golden Age Ballet.* A group of boys at the Falk School developed a rhythmic dramatization to Stephen Foster's humorous song, *The Camptown Races.*

The dramatization of one of Richard Chase's humorous *Jack Tales* and a choral reading of Edward Lear's *Owl and the Pussycat,* with a narrator to talk about humor expressed in words and through musical tones, provide the ingredients for an assembly program.

Something is added to the enjoyment of songs from other peoples if children can learn to sing these in their native languages. Children like to twist their tongues around new sounds. This isn't difficult, especially if the verses are sung in English first, with only the refrains in the foreign language, before both parts of a short song are attempted. Here are a few examples of songs that are fun to learn: *Frere Jacques,* in French, Spanish, and German; *Mia Chacra,* the Spanish equivalent of *Old MacDonald Had a Farm;* the French-Canadian *Alouette;* the Czech *Cerveny* (Little Red Handkerchief); and *Zum Gali Gali,* a modern Palestinian round with very easy Hebrew words. It is fun, too, to sing some of the Christmas carols in German, French, Spanish, Italian, or Polish!

Many learnings have come to an eighth grade from collecting, singing, and studying the contexts of national anthems and patriotic songs of countries around the world. It was amazing to teachers and children to note how similar were the expressions of the strivings, goals, and love of country. They relearned how much alike people are in spite of different geographic locations, varying climates, divergent religious beliefs and customs, and diversified industries. They became conscious of the tremendous task before the representatives of the United Nations and decided to weigh their criticisms more carefully.

Some of these anthems and patriotic songs can be incorporated into an assembly for United Nations Week. A group of United Nations representatives may decide to have a party, entertaining each other with songs and dances and informal conversation to bring out the customs, needs, and problems of their countries. Refreshments can represent choice confections and special delicacies! The party may end with a chorus of voices singing the words of *A Song of Peace* to the music of the chorale from *Finlandia* by the Finnish composer Sibelius.

Dedication to high ideals can become meaningful when boys and girls read in unison the Greek prayer:

May I be no man's enemy, and may I be the friend of that which is eternal and abides. May I never devise evil against any man: if any devises evil against me, may I escape uninjured and without the need of hurting him. May I love, seek, and attain only that which is good. May I wish for all men's happiness and envy none. May I never rejoice in the ill-fortune of one who has wronged me. When I have done or said what is wrong may I never wait for the rebuke of others, but always rebuke myself until I make amends. May I win no victory that harms either me or my opponent. May I never fail a friend in danger. May I respect myself. May I always keep tame that which rages within me. May I accustom myself to be gentle and never be angry because of circumstances.

Teachers of the Falk School have found invaluable source material for special kinds of programs in a little magazine called *American Unity,* published by the Council Against Intolerance in America in New York; in *Newsletter for Boys and Girls,* sent out by American Friends Service Committee of Philadelphia; in publications of the Anti-Defamation League of the B'nai B'rith of Philadelphia, and of the Civic Education Foundation of Cambridge, Massachusetts. Public libraries also have endless suggestions for stories of the holidays and special days of people around the world.

Assembly Film Program on the Universal
Declaration of Human Rights

Audio-visual aid programs to develop worth-while attitudes and to foster world understanding are systematically used at the James Fenimore Cooper Junior High School in New York City. The following auditorium program themes reveal the sustained nature of this work since the Charter of the United Nations was signed.

1945. Building the Peace
1946. Clarifying the Concepts of the Preamble of the Charter of the United Nations
1947. Our American Heritage
1948. The Democratic Way of Life
1949. The Earth and Its People
1950. A Better World Through the United Nations
1951. World Freedom Through the Declaration of Human Rights
1952. What Can We Learn from America's Great Men and Women?
1953. What Can We Learn from Our World Neighbors?

The theme of 1950, "A Better World Through the United Nations," represented the culmination of the previous "concept-development" topics. This program started with the building of the new home of the United Nations in New York City, reviewed the founding of the organization, discussed its structure, its problems, its various agencies and commissions, and concluded with a consideration of the goals toward which the countries of the United Nations are striving. Through the cooperation of the Film Division of the United Nations, the program included not only all the films of the division at that time, but also teachers' guides for use by the discussion leaders and still photographs to stimulate pupil curiosity on the films. Twenty-one films were used, the last being *Of Human Rights*. This film marked the termination of the 1950 auditorium film program and formed the connecting link between that program and the theme for September, 1951—"World Freedom Through the Declaration of Human Rights."

The eighteen films in the Human Rights Program came from many sources and represented a variety of experiences, in contrast to the preceding program which had used the films of the United Nations exclusively. Since no films had been created to illuminate specifically the articles of the Declaration, each one that was chosen had to contain some point which could serve as a springboard for discussion of the particular article in the Declaration which it was to illustrate.

Six examples of films used in studying the Human Rights program, along with a brief explanation, will illustrate the nature of this series.

ARTICLE 1

Answer for Anne   Religious Film Association

Anne, a High School student, assigned an essay on "Should our Town Take in Displaced Persons?" finds community hostility towards their admission. This feeling within the community negates the spirit of Article 1 of the Declaration which states: "All human beings are born free and equal in dignity and rights. They . . . should act towards one another in a spirit or brotherhood."

ARTICLE 2

It Happened in Springfield   Anti-Defamation League

This film shows how the school system of one community, in an effort to eradicate intolerance, geared its curriculum to the teaching of respect for the contributions of the various national groups to the American way of life. This "Springfield Plan" is in harmony with Article 2 which states in part:

"Everyone is entitled to all the rights and freedoms set forth in this Declaration, without distinction of any kind. . . ."

ARTICLE 3

A Chance to Live   March of Time

Article 3 says: "Everyone has the right to life, liberty and security of person." This film depicts the work of two priests in Italy who attempt to restore "security" to a group of post-war orphans through the establishment of a self-governing Boys' Republic. This film is based on a true event.

ARTICLE 5

Les Miserables   Teaching Film Custodians

In this film, based on the novel by Victor Hugo and set in early 19th Century France, a man is sentenced to ten years as a galley slave for stealing a loaf of bread. This film served to illustrate the meaning of Article 5: "No one shall be subjected to torture or to cruel, inhuman or degrading treatment or punishment."

ARTICLE 7

The Challenge   Anti-Defamation League

Assigned to do a series of articles based on the report of the President's
Committee on Civil Rights, a photographer-writer team interview religious, business and labor leaders for their views and observe civil rights
programs in action in various parts of the country. Article 6 states: "Everyone has the right to recognition everywhere as a person before the law."
Article 7 says in part: "All are equal before the law. . . ."

ARTICLE 29

Make Way for Youth   Association Films

Article 29 contains three sections. Section 1 states: "Everyone has duties
to the community in which alone the free and full development of his
personality is possible." The film tells the story of how one community,
stimulated to action by tragedy, gets together on a constructive youth
program, and breaks down the "fences" between neighborhoods, races
and religions.

Bringing the program to a close, this last film emphasized the responsibility and the obligation of the individual to the community.
It ended the program on a positive note of participation.

A distinctive feature of the auditorium film program at the James
Fenimore Cooper Junior High School is that each series is related to
the various subjects of the curriculum. Teacher guides are worked
out suggesting materials which might be used in the special fields of
science, music, language, and the social sciences. Activities are also
proposed which might help in the integration of a series, such as the
one on Human Rights, with school subjects and student organizations.

CHAPTER 6

Contacts Abroad

ANYONE who has corresponded at some length with individuals living in another culture knows what a stimulating experience this can be. When such contacts are supplemented by extensive face-to-face relations, the resulting learning can be intensified.

The democratic values of belief in people and the intellectual joy in exploring differences are of paramount importance. For unless they exist to some degree, contacts abroad may intensify the belief that one's own way of life is so superior as to lead to condemnation of those who fail to emulate them. An excess of feeling may, on the other hand, lead one to the conviction that anything found abroad is better than what one has at home. There is considerable truth in the statement that one sees what one wants to see and believes what one wants to believe. Intellectual honesty and impartial inquiry must be present, if the truth is to be known and maximum long-time benefit to result.

In this chapter are rather sustained descriptions of schools which have developed contacts abroad. Many other examples appear, however, throughout the study. In all examples the boys and girls, teachers, and citizens of all the countries involved show good will toward each other. They discover more likenesses than differences and seek to be mutually helpful. These seem to be essential elements for building a sound basis for international relations.

Christmas for San Sae Ni-e

It was two weeks before Halloween. The boys and girls at Shoemaker Junior High School of Philadelphia anticipated mischief—air to be let out of tires, walls to be decorated, teachers to be plagued, glass and cars to be soaped. These things they had done on other Halloweens. These things they would do again.

Then came the letter from Korea. It was signed by the major and countersigned by a young private who had graduated from Shoemaker some years before. The letter asked for help with a Christmas party the regiment was planning for a Korean community. It said,

The purpose of this letter is to acquaint you with a Christmas Gift Program which this battalion is undertaking in order to make the holiday season a little happier for a Korean community. We, as do many other American citizens, feel a deep sense of responsibility in re-establishing this country. . . . In this connection we have selected a small community nearby which is called San Sae Ni-e. The population is approximately 600. Of this number 187 are children, ages one to ten. We plan to collect old clothing, material that can be converted to clothing, shoes, canned foods, toys, candy and other items that can be put to use in order to make this a real and joyous Christmas for these people.

Here was a made-to-order Halloween project. The students knew about Korea. Their brothers and friends had fought there. Some had died there. The letter was read in assembly. The Student Council was approached. A flier was prepared and distributed to every pupil. Advisers talked with classes about the need in Korea. The principal said she would pay the postage. Before it was over she thought she might have to mortgage her home to meet the obligation, but it was worth it!

The packages came in! Clothing! Canned goods! Toys! Candy! Pounds of things! Student Council members sorted and packed. The big boys did the carrying and weighing. The deadline for mailing Christmas parcels to Korea and Mischief Night happily coincided. The parcels went to the post office. Just before dismissal, the principal sent a notice to all classrooms which said, "Congratulations everybody; we have just sent approximately 100 pounds of gifts to the post office for our friends in Korea."

Nobody said anything about Mischief Night. Nobody mentioned vandalism. But the gleam in the eyes of the pupils at dismissal was the gleam of justifiable pride. And the gleam in the eyes of the faculty was one of satisfaction. Not a single instance of vandalism was reported. The air stayed in the tires. The walls remained clean. Soap was used to scrub grubby hands and Korea was suddenly closer than it had been before.

Golden Rule Peace Crusaders

This is the story of a crusade begun by a teacher and her pupils in a fourth-grade class at McKinley School, Youngstown, Ohio. All had become greatly disturbed, when they saw fathers leaving their wives and children to go to war, and they decided to do something about it. A "Golden Rule" organization was formed with a prayer, motto, aim, and wish.

OUR PRAYER

Our dear Heavenly Father we pray for peace for children and their families all over the world. Help us to live the Golden Rule—so there will be no more war.

OUR MOTTO

The Golden Rule: "Do unto others as you wish they would do unto you."

OUR AIM

Write to one child in America. Write to one child abroad.

OUR WISH

Freedom of Religion
  Freedom of Speech
    Freedom of Work
      Freedom to live Happily
        For the Whole World

The sixth-grade class at Bancroft School in Youngstown wrote a *Crusader Song,* the first stanza of which is:

> We're the Golden Rule Crusaders
> For the coming of World Peace;
> We're working and we're praying
> That all war forever cease.
> We're writing, writing, writing
> To our friends both near and far;
> Our message must go on!

Local school administrators, as well as members of the press, radio, and television, became interested. McKinley school began the publication of *World Peace Crusaders.* A United States Army Captain in Berlin, Germany, read about the children's crusade. He wrote for information and through him four Berlin newspapers carried the message of friendship and understanding from American children. And so a rather remarkable campaign was launched.

Berlin children joined the movement. One McKinley pupil wrote to family friends in Zonguldak, Turkey, about the children's crusade. As a result teachers and pupils in Zonguldak, Istanbul, and Denizli were enrolled. Word of the movement spread to Japan, Formosa, and India. Children from these, and other lands, now correspond with many American children located in twenty-four different states. They exchange pictures and tokens of friendship. But most of all they feel bound together through prayer, love, and understanding.

An Eighth-Grade Class Corresponds with German Children

Members of an eighth-grade class of the Malaga Cove School, Palo Verdes Estates, Los Angeles County, California, have recently had a most vital experience. They have been exchanging letters with twenty children in Bremen, Germany, all of whom are in ninth-grade classes and live close to the Russian zone. A number of the German children have even briefly lived under the Soviet rule in East Germany.

This project was made possible by the County Coordinator of Instruction who recently returned from a summer's travel in Europe. She brought back the names of the German children and, also, colored slides that showed the school to which these children go and street scenes from the city of Bremen.

In addition to personal correspondence, members of this eighth-grade class prepared a scrapbook which they sent as a gift to the German children. Appearing in the book were articles written by pupils on such subjects as school activities, games played, and descriptions of other American customs. Each article was written by a pupil committee and was approved by the class before it was included in the book. Numerous snapshots of the school, of classes at work and at play, of various members of the school staff, and of representative community buildings were also included.

The spontaneous interest of Malaga Cove School pupils in writing to German children has served as a strong motivation in many of the learning activities in the school. It has stimulated reading in the eighth grade and has given added impetus to the study of foreign countries and their governments. Map reading has become more meaningful, as has the study of geographical factors and their effect on social and economic activities. Pupils appraise their own hand-writing and composition more carefully as the result of foreign correspondence. There has been an increased awareness of vocabulary weaknesses and greater interest in more exact use of words. This has intensified the use of dictionaries during writing periods.

Students have also become more observant of their own community as they have looked about them for interesting subjects on which to write. Perspective was sharpened as Palos Verdes youngsters examined what they have and enjoy as Americans and compared those benefits with present European standards of living, as described by their newly acquired friends in Bremen.

Adoption of a High School in the Philippines

"When the Americans shelled the town of Pasig in an attempt to drive away the Japanese, the buildings of the Rizal High School were among those destroyed. Before that time the Japanese had occupied the school, destroyed all the equipment, and burned all the books. The 3000 students we have are sadly in need of reference books, novels, and magazines."

An English teacher in the Decatur High School of Decatur, Illinois, and her classes responded to the appeal contained in this letter from Manila. Three of her groups were remedial in nature and she felt that these boys and girls needed some school activity to give them prestige and a sense of belonging to the school.

Students and teacher listed topics about the school, the city, and the state that might interest their new Philippine friends. Then each chose a topic and wrote a letter so that the complete set of letters, when read to a class overseas, would give a background for friendship. In return, Decatur received similar letters from the Rizal High School. Throughout the year topical letters were written in answer to specific inquiries and for special holidays. For example, American ways of celebrating Christmas and their origin provided almost thirty topics, enough for each pupil to write a different letter. The replies taught the Decatur pupils much about Philippine customs.

After the first letters were on their way, the pupils of these English classes bought enough used current textbooks to fill twelve boxes, of not over 22 pounds, for the Philippines. Many of the pupils had never packed, wrapped, and addressed a box for mailing, so the experience was educative on this score. The name of the pupil chairman in charge of each box was placed on it. Later each chairman received a letter of appreciation from the president of the student government in Rizal High School.

Then a letter came from Miss Licsi that revealed there were almost twice as many students in Rizal High School as in Decatur High School. This aroused both faculty and students. The Student Council decided that the whole school should have a Philippine book collection drive.

A Salesmanship Club volunteered to make announcements in all home rooms, to furnish tags to students who donated books or money and to weigh the books as they came in. Student Council representatives in each home room made arrangements for the collection of books. The French Club volunteered to keep the records and to make out tags. The Latin Club offered to sort the books. So a week of book collection began.

A ton and a half of books were received. Pupils picked out badly worn and obsolete books and the school librarian evaluated books of fiction. Books discarded were sold for paper and the money used to buy new reference books. Most of the English classes had a day's lesson on preparing boxes for mailing. School clubs devoted one meeting to packing and wrapping boxes of books.

One hundred nineteen packages were dispatched to the Rizal High School in the Philippines. The school there had had advance notice that the books were coming, for the Associated Press had become interested and had forwarded the news to Manila. Also, a citizen from Decatur received a letter about the project, while she was in Manila, and made a trip out to Pasig to take movies to show at the Decatur High School.

Grateful Philippine students wanted to show their appreciation. At the suggestions of one of the Decatur teachers they sent used stamps from Asiatic countries to the Decatur High School. The two schools were now exchanging school newspapers and souvenirs of various activities and Decatur students were excited to discover the similarities between school life in the two communities.

The Home Economics Club sent boxes of pencils with the Decatur school's name on them to the Philippines and received in return a hand-made luncheon set which they now use when they serve lunches and dinners. Framed pictures of Philippine scenes arrived. Beautiful hand-made gifts came for pupils and teachers who wrote to their new friends across the Pacific. Twice the trophy case in Decatur High School was filled with a Philippine exhibit. Pictures taken of these exhibits were mailed to Pasig where they were printed in the high school paper.

The Decatur Branch of the American Association of University Women had as speaker a Moro princess, who was in the United States on an AAUW fellowship. When she heard of the books sent to Pasig, she appealed for elementary school books for the schools of Mindanao. Decatur pupils throughout the city responded generously.

The principal of Rizal High School, Mr. Bandong, later came as a student to the University of Minnesota, and the Business and Professional Women's Club brought him as a guest speaker to Decatur. Thus the high school was able to have a Philippine assembly and hear Mr. Bandong, as well as a charming Philippine student from Northwestern University. Mr. Bandong, who was especially interested in vocational education, visited the industrial education classes and talked with the pupils.

It seems that such a project can never be over. Philippine students and visitors to America find understanding friends in Decatur. Decatur travelers and servicemen find in the Philippines people who have a friendly feeling toward Decatur. Packages and letters still travel back and forth and news of happenings in the Pacific islands is read with sympathy and understanding in many Decatur homes.

International Understanding Through School Affiliation

For several years the students and teachers of the Whittier Union High School District have been in close touch with the students and teachers of Freiburg, Germany, through an affiliation made possible by the American Friends Service Committee. Correspondence between individuals of the two communities started after the Second World War when the Whittier Community sent material aid for the rehabilitation of Freiburg residents whose homes had been bombed during the war. The students started their affiliation at the same time. In addition to the individual correspondence, many classes began to exchange class work of different types and special projects. This exchange is now being carried on by two of the high schools in the district, California High School and Whittier High School.

Gifts received from Germany have included student art work, notebooks with photographs and descriptions of life in Germany, and projects which portray their holidays and festivals. Freiberg students and teachers have sent booklets describing their school activities and the culture of Germany, and have also presented character dolls dressed in the native costume of the Black Forest.

Whittier students have sent copies of their school newspapers, yearbooks, colored slides, and photographs which depict different phases of school life. Recordings of musical and dramatic activities, and a typical school dress made by Home Economics girls have been sent. Other classes have provided subscriptions to American magazines, such as *Life* and *National Geographic,* as well as notebooks which describe the community of Whittier, life in California and the United States.

Each year members of the art classes have designed Christmas cards which are hand blocked and printed in the shops. Other students have submitted Christmas verses, to be printed on the cards which each student signs and sends to a student in Freiburg. This activity has greatly stimulated individual correspondence.

One of the Whittier staff administrators visited the Freiburg schools during a summer. He was invited to extend the greetings of the Whittier School district at the Freiburg graduation exercises and to address the students of a second school. Two other faculty members have also visited in Freiburg.

In 1953 one of the Freiburg teachers, in the German teacher exchange program, spent a month visiting the high schools in the Whittier area. During her visit teachers and pupils became interested in making plans for a Freiburg student to spend a year at Whittier High School. With the aid of the American Friends Service Committee and the American Field Service, applications of Freiburg students were received and a seventeen-year-old girl was chosn to come to Whittier.

A committee composed of students, teachers, and community representatives made plans to raise the necessary funds, to find a home for the student, and to arrange for all the details in connection with her visit. Different organizations in the school, including the Student Body, the Girls League, and the language clubs, assisted the Freiburg Club in raising money. The community members of the committee secured financial aid from the service clubs, the women's clubs, and the churches. Since all students and many persons had taken an active part in planning for the German student, there was great enthusiasm about her arrival.

After the guest student had had an opportunity to become oriented, she entered freely into the activities and life of the school and community. She became a member of the student government group, so that she might learn about the operations of self-government. She participated in the student talent shows, assisted with student committee work, and was featured in the community United Nations parade. She also spoke before many community organizations.

In order to present the guest student to other schools in Southern California, the high school Freiburg Club sponsored the annual conference of all the schools in the area which, through the American Friends Service Committee, are in affiliation with foreign schools. Other schools also presented their foreign exchange students at the conference. All the participating schools displayed the projects they had received from their affiliated schools in Europe and Asia. Ideas were exchanged for improving affiliation. All had the opportunity to see colored slides of life in Europe.

On another occasion the Freiburg Club put on an *Around the World Carnival* for the student body. Foreign language clubs and other groups, interested in world affairs, assisted with the activity. The program portrayed dances and skits from many countries, and refreshments typical of many lands were served.

Recently, a second exchange teacher from Germany spent a month visiting the three high schools of the district. Many other visitors outside of the schools, both from Freiburg and Whittier, have visited in each other's communities. These adults, both from the schools and community, have given much of their time to inform the students in both countries about their experiences.

International High School Work Camps

Making peace is much harder than making war. The nations of the world have been experiencing the truth of this statement over the last few years. We face the important question of whether or not we are going to be able to hold off the onrush of armed conflict long enough to recruit and train those who can bring real peace.

The manpower needed in the struggle for peace is to be found among men and women with a world spirit, armed with the weapons of understanding, and dedicated to a peaceful way of life. The George School, in Bucks County, Pennsylvania, seeks to help develop this type of citizen through the schools affiliation program which started shortly after the end of World War II.

A boys' school in Duesseldorf and a girls' school in Berlin were selected as affiliates. The early months of this program were spent in sending food and clothing and in exchanging correspondence. This soon led to the exchange of class projects and for several years has resulted in an exchange of students. Some have gone from George School to the German schools for a year of study and some have come from the German schools to George School for a comparable period of time. An exchange of teachers between these affiliated schools has also been helpful. But one of the most valuable experiences has been the overseas work camps which George School and its affiliated schools have operated for six summers.

Work camps have given teen-agers from different countries an opportunity for getting acquainted by working together at carefully selected tasks. The first camp, carried out with the affiliated school in Duesseldorf, was established during the summer of 1949. The work program was to clear away rubble so that the affiliated school, which had been destroyed, could be rebuilt. The camp included nine boys and one teacher from George School and a similar group selected by the German school. It was financed in part by the parents of the boys who participated. Additional funds were raised by the student body through the school community chest. Other money has been contributed by interested persons and by a foundation. The cost to the boys was about $600 each. This included all group expenses, though not personal expenses for souvenirs, gifts, and possible post-camp travel.

The second camp was coeducational, with American boys and girls working with German boys from the school in Duesseldorf and German girls from our affiliated school in Berlin. Most of these students were sixteen or seventeen years old and were underclassmen. George School students were selected by a Student-Faculty Committee, with the assistance of the American Friends Service Committee. The Student-Faculty Committee first set up the specific criteria for the selection of work campers and then interviewed each candidate. Recommendations of the committee were reviewed by a small group of the faculty, at which time final selections were made. Selectees went through a three-month orientation program. This included some language training, information regarding the country in which they would work, and a clear understanding of the purposes of the camp.

The site selected was in the small community of Dorlar in Westphalia, where a Protestant pastor was doing much of needed work with refugees. The work campers helped with the construction of a reservoir, the laying of pipes to bring running water into buildings, and assisted in improving the sanitary facilities. They also helped with the care of the young children.

The work camp the following summer, 1951, was also located at Dorlar. It included some students from the Germantown Friends School in Philadelphia and members of their affiliated school from Falaise in France. The camp was coeducational, trinational and trilingual.

The camp in 1952 was at the College Cevenol at LeChambon, France, with the same schools represented. Work campers here assisted in the repair of old structures and also in the construction of new buildings. The new environment brought new problems. These were solved democratically and the camp was counted successful in all of its human relations.

In 1953 the work camp was at Schloss Annaberg, not far from the city of Bonn. The work again was with refugees. The participating schools were George School and its two affiliates. The reasons for the change in the camp personnel were several. It was thought to be somewhat easier to conduct a bilingual rather than a trilingual camp. The number of students wanting to participate was so great that Germantown Friends School worked out its own program and George School returned to its earlier plan.

The camp in 1954 was at Kuehhude, near Berleburg, Westphalia, Germany. Again George School and its two affiliated schools were the participants. The project was again selected because of its significance and the possibility of students of this age making a valuable contribution through work.

Appraisals of the work camp experience all point to its great value as an educational method in bringing about international understanding and in building bonds of friendship which help to establish peace. George School administrators and teachers recognize that time is short, that progress is slow, and that there are numerous difficulties to be overcome. They feel that they have through these overseas work camps supplied a number of idealistic youth with an opportunity for significant work in an area where much work is to be done. At a time when so many factors tend to pull nations and peoples apart, it is a source of genuine satisfaction to see the overseas work camps assisting so effectively in preparing young people to live together in one world. The whole school shares vicariously in the educational values involved in conducting the program.

An Exchange of Teen-Age Art Among
Thirty-Three Countries

The International School Art Program was developed in 1947 by the Eastern Arts Association in cooperation with the American Junior Red Cross. The objective was to stimulate international interest among young people throughout the world. Later the National Art Education Association replaced the regional Eastern Arts group. In the beginning only the United States, Sweden, France, Czechoslovakia, and Venezuela participated in the project. There are now thirty-one countries taking part but the total has reached thirty-three.

The program has been described as a plan where "youth speaks to youth" in a sincere and friendly manner. Students from grades 7–12 are encouraged to interpret their way of life pictorially in a vivid and free manner. A glance at some of the labels attached to the paintings from Pittsburgh shows the nature of these first-hand experiences.

One boy wrote: "I am watching a man in the window. He is making doughnuts in a doughnut machine. Doughnuts are tasty cookies or cakes. Many people who are passing by stop to watch the doughnut man." Another student had this to say about his painting: "This is our gym. We wear tennis shoes and gym suits when we do stunts such as this. We use mats so we do not get hurt. Between classes we keep our suits in the green lockers." Other subjects have included: *My Easter Haircut, First Aid Class, Big Sister Has a Date, Working in the Woodshop at School, Our Cafeteria Crowds, Our Girl Scouts Entertain the Cub Scouts,* and *The Big Snow.*

Each chairman of the Greater Pittsburgh International School Art Program has used a different approach to stimulate interest in the project. On occasion, art teachers and small groups of students from each school have attended a meeting at which both kodachrome slides and an exhibit of work from the United States and other countries have been used to encourage worth-while participation in the program. At two of these meetings, foreign-born students told about their first impressions of the United States. Then they suggested the kind of ideas they thought would interest their former classmates. At another time, a large committee of teachers took over the job of making frequent contacts with their fellow workers and of distributing material related to the project.

Local radio stations have always cooperated by offering time for students to present the idea to the public. Station KDKA School of the Air has been especially cooperative. At the end of some of the dramatizations in a series entitled, *At Home Around the World,* children from the countries visited have compared life in the United States with that in their native lands. Recently, the International School Art Program was the subject for one of the half-hour art programs prepared by the Pittsburgh Public Schools for television.

Before the paintings from the Greater Pittsburgh Area are submitted to a national committee for screening, the work of the teenagers is exhibited so that all of the students and the public have an opportunity to see the pictures before they are sent abroad. A selection of student work from the United States and a number of other countries is always included, along with a large marked map and other explanatory material.

On one occasion, 300 of the paintings from the Greater Pittsburgh Area were on display in the auditorium of a large department store. Since Pittsburghers of today represent almost fifty different national heritages, it seemed logical that the Saturday afternoon opening should feature students of various nationality backgrounds in a program of folk songs and dances. Hostesses that afternoon wore costumes borrowed from members of their families. The following Saturday, students actually worked on paintings for the International School Art Program in the auditorium of the store.

On another occasion the exhibit was hung in the halls and various rooms at the main branch of the Carnegie Library of Pittsburgh. A collection of books on related subjects and sixty-three authentic costume dolls, collected in sixteen different countries, added interest to the display.

An exhibit of student work has been held at the Arts and Crafts Center in Pittsburgh. Contemporary craft work, created by professional artists in many of the countries in the exchange program, supplemented the work of the teen-agers. At the opening, a panel of boys and girls from grades 7–12 in the Pittsburgh schools, and students from other countries who are attending local colleges and universities, discussed the subject, "Friends Around the World."

Since the International School Art Program should contribute to world understanding, each student is asked to evaluate his work by following a list of questions set up as a guide. This self-evaluation emphasizes the importance of presenting in a creative manner a friendly message that has grown out of a personal experience.

Sharing experiences in a pictorial way promotes friendship among teen-agers throughout the world. It is because of the firm belief of the National Art Education Association and the Junior Red Cross in the value of this program in developing understanding among young people that both organizations have endorsed the continuation of the International School Art Program.

Paintings and Ideas Are Exchanged Between Pittsburgh and Yahata, the Pittsburgh of Japan

The mayor of Yahata City, Japan, and his secretary visited Pittsburgh, Pennsylvania, in the summer of 1952 and made the acquaintance of the superintendent of schools. The visitors were impressed by the similarity of the two industrial cities and became interested in Pittsburgh's art offerings, especially in its Arts and Crafts Center. Letters were later received from the mayor's secretary asking for information about the Center and requesting an exhibit of the art of Pittsburgh school children.

Accordingly, an exhibit of thirty-one paintings by children from kindergarten through high school was shipped to Yahata. Because it seemed impractical to send three-dimensional art, twenty-two glossies of children and their puppets, masks, papier-mâché, clay, and metalcrafts were included in the shipment. A carefully illustrated statement of the philosophy of art education was added to explain the childlike quality of the paintings by young children.

Yahata reciprocated by sending a set of children's paintings and very attractively enameled pins, bearing the names of the two cities. This was the beginning of an exchange that gains momentum and breadth year after year.

The first Pittsburgh consignment gave impetus to formation of a committee to establish a "Students' Arts and Crafts Center of Yahata City." In turn, three exhibits of Japanese children's work was circulated in the Pittsburgh schools. Students have collected gifts and toys from Japan and displayed them with these paintings. School libraries have prepared exhibits of books about Japan. A junior high school student writing about his appreciation of the paintings from Yahata City concludes, "All I can say is I hope they enjoy our art exhibit at least half as much as we enjoy theirs."

The Japanese formulators of the cooperative exchange plan have embarrassed Pittsburgh friends by their generosity. Not only the pins, but gifts of cups and scarfs and a large collection of high school crafts, including hand puppets, kites, block prints, embroidery, masks, dolls, model houses, tea cups and wall decorations, have arrived.

In Japan, newspapers have carried colored reproductions of the Pittsburgh paintings. The first exhibit was held in a large department store in Yahata City. According to Mr. Shiokawa, secretary to the mayor, "It was one of the most attended exhibits we ever had in this part of the country."

The exchange of paintings has stimulated an exchange of ideas on art education. Japanese teachers are interested not only in the philosophy of art but in art supplies, textbooks, and classroom furniture. A set of kodachrome slides of the art and crafts work in the Pittsburgh schools will be circulated in Japanese schools. This whole program has attracted the attention of the cultural attaché at the American Embassy in Japan.

One important outcome of the exchange has been the establishment of the Students' Art and Crafts Center of Yahata. Young people of that city have become eager to come to the United States to learn more about us. The success of the exchange can be attributed to the enthusiasm and energetic leadership of the secretary to the mayor of Yahata, Mr. Kazuo Shiokawa. The invitation to exchange children's paintings originated with the mayor of Yahata.

Though such exchanges are more difficult to carry on than the International School Art Program, in which the Red Cross assumes responsibility for shipping and distributing, this type of exchange has great value, since it is direct and reactions are not delayed or indefinite. For this same reason, both parties to the exchange accept a serious responsibility for its success. This voluntary exchange of ideas and paintings is broadening outlooks and shaping attitudes which should lead to friendly relations between the young people of Yahata, Japan, and Pittsburgh, United States of America.

Part III

SYSTEMWIDE SCHOOL AND COMMUNITY SERVICES

CHAPTER 7

Inservice Teacher Education and Services

THERE are many ways of judging the effectiveness of a program of education for world affairs. But perhaps as rewarding a type of evaluation as any is to seek to determine the quality and extent of Inservice Teacher Education and Services in a school system.

Democratic social and educational values require that abundant opportunity be given to many people in a system to set goals, experiment with materials and methods, evaluate results, and seek further improvements. The respect for personality, which is sought in relation to the peoples of other nations, begins at home in the relationships which are fostered among teachers, pupils, and parents. Widespread use of the experimental method of inquiry, of conscious problem-solving, should everywhere be apparent. Teachers strive to improve their problem-solving techniques as they work together to improve the curriculum. In turn, the more effective use of these techniques is apparent in schools and classrooms.

Even in small systems, where resources are meagre, working committees of teachers and administrators can be established to work at various problems involved in education for world affairs. Pupils can be involved in these tasks. Individual citizens and representatives of citizen groups can be invited to participate in the process. Indeed, if this is not done, the impression may be gained that the schools are too international in outlook, when as a matter of fact, they may be seeking only to explore the ways in which a great nation, such as ours, may seek to follow enlightened self-interest at home and abroad.

In larger school systems, which have more personnel and resources, system-wide services can be established to aid teachers in the frontier task of seeking ways of promoting international understanding. Teachers can be released periodically to engage full time in system-wide plans. New units and courses of study can be developed and tried out. Resources already available can be more extensively used.

155

Of major importance in such activities is the systematic continuation and extension of these efforts over the years. The job to be done is too large and too all pervasive to be achieved through fragmentary efforts.

Perhaps the most significant criteria to use in the evaluation of the quality of such inservice programs are suggested by such questions as these: "Does participation release the creative imagination of all those engaged?" "Are people inspired to give extra energy and time because the task of education for world affairs is so important to our nation and the world that it must be well done?" "Do teachers, pupils and lay citizens see themselves as active participants in the world-wide task of striving for democracy, prosperity and peace for all peoples and nations?"

The following examples have been submitted by people engaged in such tasks. Some programs are more extensive than others. Some doubtless show more insight and creativeness than others. But all demonstrate a sustained concern for system-wide, cooperative effort.

A Utah County School District Utilizes Foreign Students

Iron County is in southwestern Utah. The population is homogeneous. For the most part, the inhabitants are descendants of Nordic people. A dominant religion tends to unify life within the small communities. Cleavages resulting from wide variation in economic and social position are noticeably lacking. Six years ago in these sequestered hamlets the concept of world understanding was principally at the verbal level. Newscasts, state newspapers, and textbooks did not seem to school officials to lead either children or adults to feel deeply about world affairs.

The Iron County School District set for itself the goal of coming to know its world neighbors in the intimate, friendly, concerned way that next-door neighbors were known. The plan of action was simple. The State University enrolled many students from other lands. The Extension Division of the University was first approached. A request was made for cooperation in inviting foreign students to visit in the homes and schools of the county. The result was that five students from Asiatic countries and a coordinator from the Extension Division traveled 265 miles to spend three days in Iron County.

A threefold purpose motivated this venture. The hosts wanted to know their guests as people. They wanted to share some of the traditions, customs, and history that accounted, in part, for their guests being the kind of people they were. And they wanted to deepen and extend, at all age levels, the concept of world understanding.

The students lived in family homes during their visit. For these students, and those who came in later years, this was their first opportunity to live with an American family. Members of the welcoming committee, who had familiarized themselves with the name of each student and the country from which he came, met the group, took the students to the homes where they were to stay, made the introductions, and lingered a while to smooth the way in those first awkward minutes which follow the meetings of "strangers." One of the truly satisfying two-way experiences has been this housing of the guests-from-other-lands in homes.

All of the contacts in the schools were designed to enable the visitor to meet students and teachers in small groups. Only those who saw Mr. Schow take a tiny first-grade, blond-haired girl on his knee, while the other children sat at his feet, and heard him sing to them the Chinese lullaby that he sings to his own children, can really know the feeling of oneness that emerged. In these small-sized groups in the secondary schools there were opportunities not only for the extension of factual information and the clarification of ideas, but also for the assessment of feelings and the reasons underlying them.

At an evening get-together the hosts shared with these guests a bit of their cultural heritage. The guests heard the story of pioneer beginnings in this desert land, of struggles to cope with the relentless forces of nature, and the strains which accompany the merging of different cultures. It was then their turn to ask questions. There were also many relaxing and gay moments when all sang and square-danced.

The departure of this first group of foreign students was carefully planned. The final impression might well be a long-lasting one. Students, teachers, and some townspeople gathered for the good-bye. The new friends told their hosts how they felt about their visit. The hosts gave each guest a tiny souvenir selected by students and purchased with the students' contributions. The feeling tone of this last meeting was something that no one has ever been able to reduce to words or record on paper. No one was ashamed that moist eyes accompanied final handclasps and softly spoken well-wishes.

In the ensuing five years similar visits of foreign students have been arranged with the University of Utah, the Brigham Young University, and the Utah State Agricultural College. Each year pupils, teachers, and parents feel that the experience has been more worth while than the last. Recently seventeen educators from eleven countries visited Iron County.

The values inherent in this program may not be quantitatively measured. But the people who have had such experiences can now subscribe more realistically and sincerely to this bit of Chinese wisdom, "In the seven seas all men are brothers."

A Music Program in a Desert Region

In the Barstow Area, in the County of San Bernardino, California, distances do not matter for children who sleep the desert-miles away while twelve huge busses transport them over the roads that run like spider webs anchored in the homes and schools of a vast space.

Desert children see so far, hear so well, dream so much, and respond so quickly to opportunities. When the county education office staff first proposed the music festival idea, which would be devoted to understanding the peoples of the world, it was received with enthusiasm. Planned in the fall and performed in the spring, it proved to be a central theme throughout the year in all school activities.

Invitations were sent east to Daggett, Newberry, Ludlow, and fifty-two miles to Amboy; northeast to Yermo, Baker, Kelso, Cima, and 160 miles to Nipton; northwest 65 miles to Kramer and Red Mountain; southwest to Hodge and 16 miles to the Helendale boundary; across the underground Mojave River 13 miles to Hinkley and 37 miles past the fertile fields and rolling desert hills to Camp Irwin.

Comprehensive plans were made for a five-year music program. The suggested themes were:

1. *First year.* Folk songs and dances of America
2. *Second year.* Folk songs and dances of our Latin American neighbors
3. *Third year.* Folk songs and dances of the Eastern Hemisphere
4. *Fourth year.* Folk songs and dances of the world
5. *Fifth year.* Folk songs and dances of American ethnic groups

Representatives were called together from all schools. Songs were selected. It was agreed that each school would decide on the dance it would present at the Festival in the spring. Pupil and teacher goals were determined as follows:

To Grow in World Understanding Through Music Participation

Goals for Children

1. To have fun
2. To understand and know the children of the area
3. To become a part of the world and the world a part of them
4. To make the melodies of songs and dances their own
5. To recognize themes, rhythmic patterns, forms, harmonies while listening, singing, dancing to music of many lands
6. To develop a cooperative spirit
7. To enjoy beauty of tone, melody, harmony, mood
8. To make a life richer in experience by participating
9. To combine with solo instruments of orchestra and band and ensemble groups

Goals for Teachers

1. To set up a plan to accomplish world understanding
2. To bring teachers and parents together for better understanding
3. To bring children of sixth grades together to know each other and play together before entering Junior High School
4. To use as much as possible the social studies in presenting the songs and dances
5. To meet informally
6. To emphasize the social aspects
7. To preserve the heritage of the people of the United States
8. To promote better understanding of all peoples and their cultural backgrounds through the study of music
9. To develop music as an outcome of social studies, language arts and physical education
10. To stimulate interest and desire to participate in the music festival using song books, simple instruments, solo instruments, recordings, broadcasts and pictures

The success of the music festival given the first year grew out of the fifth-grade social studies unit on the Westward Movement and its colorful songs and dances. Teachers were enthusiastic and helpful. There were so many children participating that it was democratic education for all.

The next year's theme of "Songs and Dances South of the Border" was called a "May Fiesta." The theme was based on the unit study of

South America. The songs and dances were from Mexico, Panama, Venezuela, Argentina, Peru, and Chile.

Understanding of peoples resulted from the varied national and racial backgrounds of the participants. Children from Mexican and Negro, Chinese and English backgrounds sang, danced, and reflected joy and satisfaction. Teachers of English, Chinese, Japanese, and Mexican backgrounds have planned and guided the activity. Parents from these varied backgrounds have enjoyed the festivals with their children and the teachers. One cannot know what dreams of democracy in the minds and hearts of youth and adults have been initiated or satisfied.

New Insights Result from Intelligent
Use of Human Resources

In the public schools of Ithaca, New York, there is a systematic attempt to make maximum use of both children and adults who have lived abroad. A survey of the Ithaca community revealed that in September, 1952, of those pupils entering the system for the first time 117 children were of foreign-born parentage. Of these, 42 had themselves been born and had lived abroad. All continents and thirty-one countries were represented.

Personal interviews indicated that many of these people were willing and able to share their knowledge and experiences with pupils and teachers in the schools. Add to that the native-born American children who had lived abroad with their parents, the foreign students at Cornell University, business men with experience abroad, and foreign visitors, and it was evident that the human resources available in Ithaca were considerable.

A mother of two boys from Brazil helped her own sons to adjust themselves to American life, and also assisted Ithaca children in their relationships to her boys by giving generously of her time to school activities. She worked closely with the class on a unit focused on living in Brazil. Her active participation in the culminating activity, A Rio Carnival, made a strong contribution to a new appreciation of the culture of our largest neighbor "to the South."

In one elementary school, a student-teacher from Pakistan cooperated with teachers and parents to provide the first train ride for many American youngsters in her group. The children learned that, in spite of differences in appearance, language, and clothing, people from Asia may have many interests and traits in common with themselves. The respect of the young teacher from Pakistan for scholarship, for a job well done, for the "mastery" of learning in the fields of history, geography, and the language arts, stimulated the boys and girls to more than customary effort and aggressive drive in the learning tasks she developed with them.

A young woman from the University of Hiroshima did much to overcome misconceptions and prejudices about her people during her internship. As she demonstrated techniques of Oriental flower arrangement, she tactfully corrected a report by an American boy in the class who had lived in Japan that "the Japanese all hate flowers and that's why they don't grow any near their houses." She guided the children to deeper understandings of some of the relationships between the density of population of an area, and the amount, character, and wise utilization of arable land. Probably the most important outcome of the close association of the children with their Japanese student-teacher was in the area of feelings. Before the end of the four-week period of internship with this particular class, the Japanese student-teacher had been a primary factor in the transformation of merely emotional responses and surface rationalizations into reasoned, value-judgments.

On the second day of her period of service, the young woman from Hiroshima was greeted by one of the children with the remark: "My mother doesn't want me to have a Japanese teacher. My brother was killed by one of your soldiers." How this pupil, her parents, and her classmates, learned to like and respect the graduate student from across the Pacific, whose hearing had been seriously impaired by the atomic bombing of her people and native city, is a stirring example of the ability of people to become so sensitized and responsive to the feelings and the total personality of others that their attitudes and actions are positively altered.

Following this incident the children and their elders did some serious thinking about the differences which may exist among individuals within a country, about group standards and relationships, and about governmental systems which sometimes control the destinies and behaviors of citizens. A note, written by the children and signed by all members of the class—"Please come back to our grade soon. We love you."—was presented to the Japanese teacher at the close of her internship. It did much to ease the hurt of the early days of the term and indicated in a personal way how living and working in close daily association can contribute to an understanding of, and a liking and respect for, people of one's own and other cultures.

Other aspects of the systematic use of all community resources in the development of international backgrounds and desirable attitudes, in this school system, might be given. But perhaps the essential requirement is this: Only the continued support and united efforts of school personnel, board of education, and the total community of citizens make possible such a program.

A City System Establishes a Commission on International Understanding and World Peace

The Minneapolis, Minnesota, school system has established many curriculum committees and three commissions. One of these is the Commission on International Understanding and World Peace, which was organized in 1947.

The membership for the Commission is drawn from elementary and secondary teachers. It also includes one elementary principal, one secondary principal, and one member from the central office staff. The chairman of the Commission is a junior high school principal. Each year also several citizens whose work furthers international understanding are invited to serve. Membership is for three years. It is staggered so that approximately one third of those participating are replaced each year.

Commission committees include those on Evaluation and Distribution of Literature, Utilizing Students of Other Lands in School Activities, International Correspondence, Inservice Training, and United Nations Recognition Days.

The Committee on Evaluation of Literature secures and evaluates literature and other material that will aid teachers to do a better job in furthering international understandings. Two or three times during the school year, literature found to be suitable is combined in special kits and sent to the schools.

Several hundred students from other lands are enrolled at the various colleges and universities within the metropolitan area. Members of the committee devoted to utilizing students from abroad devise methods and procedures, in cooperation with foreign student advisors, to aid teachers and students in the utilization of these people in the schools.

One of the major projects the Commission undertakes each year is its United Nations Recognition Day. This program is held each fall, usually during the latter part of September. It is the responsibility of one of the committees within the Commission to plan and present a day of activities for sixth-grade representatives and their teachers from each of the seventy-five elementary buildings in the system. The following is a brief description of such a recent program.

The meeting was held at Coffman Memorial Student Union on the University of Minnesota Campus. Most of the program was presented in the large central ballroom of the Union. As the representatives arrived they were invited to tour the various exhibits set up by the Save the Children Federation, the American Junior Red Cross, the Children's Plea for Peace, and the Minnesota World Affairs Center. These displays were designed to stimulate interest in the organizations, to announce coming events and activities in which the children could take part, and to provide free and inexpensive materials as aids in furthering international understandings.

The program was opened by singing the National Anthem and repeating the Pledge of Allegiance to our Flag. This was followed by the presentation of 54 handmade flags of the member nations of the United Nations by a citizen from one of the suburban communities, who thus shared her most interesting and informative hobby with the children.

One group of sixth-graders from a Minneapolis elementary school demonstrated three favorite folk dances of children in other lands. These dances were selected for their interest qualities and the ease with which they could be taught to children in the schools represented by the observers.

After a short recess period the children adjourned to the banquet room where they lunched with college students from other lands. The tables were arranged so that each group of eight children were seated with one student. Parent and teacher guests were served luncheon in an adjacent dining room where they listened to a panel of speakers. This panel presented various ways and methods of stimulating international understanding in the classroom and in an entire school. After lunch the children met in informal groups with the foreign students where information about their respective lands was exchanged.

A panel discussion was carried on later by a group of Junior High School boys. This highlighted some of the purposes and achievements of the United Nations. The boys represented the Junior United Nations Association of the city. Much of the resource material that they used in their discussion was provided by their advisor, a teacher in the city system. The material was gathered while she was on a special summer assignment for the United Nations.

An evaluation session ended the program in which members of the Commission answered questions. The representatives then returned to their respective schools. Through later evaluation and informal interviews with many of the school personnel, the committee learned that the ideas gained by those attending had been used to good advantage in furthering international understandings among boys and girls in the system.

Providing Materials on World Affairs Through a Curriculum Periodical

Strengthening Democracy is a curriculum periodical which is issued six times a year to every teacher in the New York City school system. It is designed to promote the understanding, teaching, and practice of our American democratic heritage. In carrying out these objectives, extensive materials are published having to do with international democratic movements, as well as Communism and Fascism. Although the periodical is by no means devoted exclusively to world affairs, the latter comprise a considerable proportion of its contents and help to place its purpose in clearer focus.

A number of purposes are served by *Strengthening Democracy* in education for world affairs.

1. It furnishes resource units and materials useful for classroom teaching and describes practices found effective in school-wide activities and school-community programs.
2. It publishes interpretive articles on movements and developments on the world scene that are advancing or challenging democratic ideals and understanding among peoples.
3. It provides a forum for the exchange of points of view on approaches to the teaching of controversial topics in the area of world affairs.

To aid classroom teaching, schools are encouraged to develop and share, through the pages of the publication, resource units not ordinarily found in sources available to teachers. Resource units have been published on the land, peoples, culture, and educational system of the Soviet Union and on the nature and techniques of Communist and Fascist regimes. Units have also been prepared to stimulate the study of international developments, such as the Universal Declaration of Human Rights.

To serve as background information for the teacher, and as a basis for class discussion, the periodical contains brief reviews of pamphlets, books, and other current materials on world affairs. It makes available selections from resource materials not in common use. These include teaching aids, recent scholarly research, and specialized studies by government agencies and private organizations that come within the scope of the publication. Examples of items falling within these categories are recent collections of cartoons by Herblock and Fitzpatrick, the findings of the series of UNESCO publications on the race question, and the studies made by the Legislative Reference Service of the Library of Congress on such subjects as "Tensions Within the Soviet Union" and "Fascism, a Definition and an Analysis."

Special articles may include topics as varied as the implications of the outbreak of the war in Korea for American schools, misconceptions of American life held by people abroad, the relationships between our domestic policies with respect to civil rights and the success of our foreign policy, the international ramifications of the Fascist movement, the close parallels between Communist and Fascist totalitarianism, the bankruptcy of Soviet racial and nationalities policy, and the efficiency of the democratic system.

When honest criticisms are directed against the content of *Strengthening Democracy,* or against topics whose study the publication has encouraged, the editorial staff has an obligation to answer them. When there are unjustified attacks involving a perversion of the facts, the editors have an equally strong obligation to expose them. Such responses are essential to clarify the facts and to strengthen the security of teachers who may fear becoming the targets of criticism in teaching controversial subjects.

An article in *Strengthening Democracy* which analyzed the attacks on UNESCO evoked a particularly enthusiastic response from teachers, colleges, libraries, churches, and professional organizations. It was widely distributed by the Department of State.

A valuable service which can be performed by a curriculum periodical operating in the area of world affairs is that of providing a forum for the exchange of opinions on subjects that often arouse controversy. For a considerable period, a spirited interchange of contrasting points of view on approaches to teaching about Communism, the Soviet Union, and the methods of handling Communist propaganda was carried on. Debates of this type not only stimulate teacher interest and clarify concepts but also help to counteract existing fears of discussing controversial issues.

An asset of the curriculum periodical in communicating with teachers is the editorial staffs' ability to swing into action immediately and to afford a means of sharing materials that teachers and schools have developed to meet emergency situations. For example, when teachers returned from their summer vacations in 1950, the country was already deeply involved in the Korean war. During September, schools prepared mimeographed materials to acquaint pupils with the issues at stake. In the October issue, *Strengthening Democracy* stressed the implications of the Korean war for the schools and followed in November with a sampling of the materials prepared by high schools indicating the ways in which they were used. Special events can be stressed, such as United Nations Day and Brotherhood Week.

The periodical is edited by a committee. The give-and-take of the group process makes possible a pooling of skills and information, provides diversity of points of view, and encourages a more critical evaluation of contributions than would be the case if the decision were left to one person. The committee, which includes members from each level of the school system, must be constantly on the alert to provide materials of current interest and to anticipate what may be needed by the classroom teacher. Articles are appraised for their suitability to various grade levels. The committee decides what controversial materials are likely to be acceptable to teachers in the schools.

Collective responsibility transfers the burden from an individual to a committee when emotion-laden issues arouse adverse reactions. If, indeed, the extremists are never provoked to criticism, it is wise to re-evaluate one's materials. They may be ineffective. School authorities should have sufficient resoluteness to support an editorial committee against unjustified attacks and permit it to answer criticisms in its own way. The committee has been fortunate in having such understanding supervision.

For maximum effectiveness, an editorial committee requires freedom of choice in its selection and preparation of materials. When these responsibilities are ably executed, the confidence that is generated will frequently yield increased editorial freedom.

Developing World Understanding
Grades K Through 3*

When we think of ourselves not in terms of groups such as races or creeds but as members of the human race, our goal in developing world understanding is at hand. The fact that this thinking is not widespread in the world today indicates the important role the teacher has to play, especially the teacher of kindergarten-primary youngsters. Psychologists have discovered that attitudes about self and fellow man are almost wholly developed in the early years.

We see the responsibility of the teacher in combating prejudice and developing attitudes concerning the dignity and worth of the individual as that of furnishing children with carefully planned firsthand experience with people. These experiences can begin in the kindergarten with the family and expand to the neighborhood and the community in the first, second, and third grades. Suggested categories and experiences follow:

Conversation

1. Develop standards of conversation with children.
   Do I give the other person a turn to talk?
   Do I talk about subjects that are of interest to others?
   Do I keep my voice low enough so I will not disturb anyone working around me?
   Do I speak clearly so that people want to listen to me?
   Do I listen to what others have to say?
   Do I look for ideas in others' conversations that will help me?
2. Allow the children to engage in conversation while working.

* Two teachers in the Belding Elementary School of Richmond, California, here give their ideas for teaching world understanding in the primary grades. This statement has been distributed to other teachers in the system.

3. Encourage informal conversation while entering and leaving the room, getting ready for a movie, at play time.
4. Have a seating arrangement conducive to conversation (tables facing each other or in a horseshoe, for instance).

Free Activity Time

1. This is the time of day when the child has freedom of choice and a time he can call his own with no demands on him for producing anything. The teacher has the responsibility of having stimulating materials available for the child.
2. Have an evaluation at the close of the period raising such questions as:
   Do I share tools? Materials?
   Do I stop on time?
   Do I do my own clean-up job?
   Do I put books back on the shelf when through?
   Do I help others when asked to?
   Do I speak plainly if I wish to report on what I did?
   Do I listen carefully while others report?
   Do I cooperate with others in my work?

Free Play Time

1. The child has the opportunity to engage in self-activity of a play type.
2. Have an evaluation at the close of the period raising such questions as:
   Do I share equipment and take turns?
   Do I speak kindly to people at all times?
   Do I play with someone who doesn't have anyone to play with?
   Am I a good team player?

Storytelling

1. Tell a story about a picture.
   a. Show a picture and encourage the children to tell a story about it. The stories may be put on charts and a collection made. Discussion may be started by asking such questions as:
   How does this picture make you feel?
   Why does it make you feel this way?
   What do you think of when you look at this picture?
   How do you think the people in the picture feel?
   b. Sources for storytelling pictures include magazines, both secular and religious, and calendars.
   c. Some criteria for selection of pictures might be:
   Do the pictures help children to see the sameness in the needs of people?
   Do they help to show that there are many kinds of people?
   Do they show that there are many ways of doing things?

Do they avoid stereotypes?

(Such stereotypes as non-white being shown in native dress, Negroes as porters on a train or engaged in picking cotton, homes as comfortably middle class, Father in his office—all giving the impression that important people are white.)

    d. The picture collection may be grouped according to:

How people work together.

How people play together.

How people worship.

Where people live.

Where people go to school.

Where people get food and clothing.

Dramatizations

1. Prepare for a trip by:
   a. Acting out appropriate social behavior enroute, at destination.
   b. Acting out responsibilities at destination by starting a game, passing refreshments, etc. This gives the child security because he knows what is expected of him and what is going to happen.
2. Act out the work of each member of the family.
   a. Teacher should point out the worth of the contribution each member of the family makes to the community.
3. Act out the work of someone observed in the community. This might be made into a guessing game where the other children try to guess the kind of work that is being acted out.
4. Act out what the children can do to help the community. (At play, at school, in the parks.)
5. Act out a family going to church.
6. Use puppets to act out the suggestions in 1 to 5.

Interviews

1. Invite a person to school to talk to children about his occupation, his religion, or a hobby or special interest. (Include guests of various racial groups.)
2. Prepare for the interview by guiding the children to answer such questions as:

   What do I want to find out?

   How will I greet the guest when he arrives?

   How will I ask my questions of him?

   How will I make him feel at home and what will I tell him when he leaves?
3. The teacher has the responsibility for indicating to the children his friendliness to and appreciation of the guest.

Trips

1. Take a trip to a plant where many workers are working at different jobs. This is a good opportunity to observe the dependence of one worker upon another.

   a. The teacher can prepare for the trip by guiding the children to answer such questions as:

   What do I want to find out?

   What social behavior will be appropriate on the bus? on the walk? while there?

   How will I greet the workers?

   When will I ask my questions?

   How much time will we take? (Learning to have respect for people's time and work.)

   b. The teacher encourages the children to be friendly by the way he greets and talks with people. He also calls attention to all workers so that children will not assume that some workers are more important than others.

2. Take a trip to another school to see an activity, a film or attend a party. Make plans to include the parents. Seeing the parents friendly helps the children to be friendly too. Both classes should take part in the get-together to plan for refreshments, decorations, program or games. This will make every person feel that he has an important part to play in the venture. (This would be fine experience for children where one of the classes is interracial.)

   a. The teacher can lead the children to answer the following questions beforehand:

   What people will I greet at the party?

   What social behavior will be appropriate at games? while eating? while viewing a film or program?

   Who am I going to play or work with?

   Will I take turns in games and conversation?

3. Take a trip to see a religious observance. This may be in a home, in a church or synagogue, or out of doors. The trip may also be for the purpose of interviewing a Catholic Sister, a Protestant minister, a Jewish Rabbi or other church worker at a place of worship.

   a. The teacher encourages the children to be friendly by his own friendliness.

   b. Preparation for a trip such as this can be handled as for other trips.

Map-Making

1. Make a floor map of the neighborhood or community. The map should be of as large dimensions as space allows. This will give each child space to include his home and *all* of the other places he knows

in the community. "All" is emphasized because every place where a human being lives or works is important. The map will be a concrete way of sharing with others what each child knows about the neighborhood or community. The children can play they are helicopters and fly from place to place on the map. This gives them the idea that a map is a picture of places seen from above.
2. Make a products map showing the things we send to other countries and communities and the things we receive. Paste samples of the products on the map.

A Citizen-Teacher Committee Revises a Unit on the United Nations

Recently the California County, in which Daly City is located, revised the eighth-grade social studies unit on the United Nations. Because of the difficulties encountered by other districts with regard to the teaching of this particular subject, it was considered very desirable to have laymen represented on the committee. The county office asked five organizations, constituting a cross section in the county, to send representatives to be on this committee.

The five laymen represented the following groups: the 17th District P.T.A., Pro-America, UNESCO, League of Women Voters, and the American Legion. On the committee also were five classroom teachers, two principals, and three members from the county office, with one serving as chairman.

The committee met a total of seven days. The first two meetings were spent getting acquainted, establishing group rapport, discussing the social studies framework from the kindergarten to the eighth grade, and setting common goals and objectives. The next five meetings were devoted to evaluating and deleting material from the old unit, setting up objectives for the new one, getting material organized, selecting the proper words (since certain words had different connotations for each member), and the screening of instructional materials. The latter task involved the text to be used, supplementary texts, library or reference books, audio-visual material, and miscellaneous free or inexpensive material from outside agencies.

Educators are often so engrossed in techniques and the proper educational jargon that they fail, in such situations, to locate important current social problems and needs. Laymen help by stating how they feel on some of the problems of today. They act as the pulse of the community. In this cooperative revision, each layman reported back to his respective group on the progress of the unit. At one of the school P.T.A. meetings a member of the 17th District P.T.A. spoke before the group and told of the part he had had in working on this unit. One committee representative stated that the work of the group was a "vivid example of democracy in action."

The committee did not disband after the completion of the unit on the United Nations. It remained a standing committee, to be called together from time to time to evaluate and screen additional material.

Before the new unit was used, an orientation meeting was held for all teachers in the school district. This was done to acquaint them with the unit and to answer questions. At this inservice meeting, the need was expressed for a study group in which teachers and members of the P.T.A. could participate. Such a group was organized with the title of "World Communication and United Nations Instruction."

Teachers from all grade levels had been encouraged to come to the inservice meeting, where it was stressed that teaching world understanding does not begin in the eighth grade. Children form likes and dislikes early which affect their attitudes and opinions. It is the job of the entire elementary school to guide these attitudes and opinions into channels which will make for more flexible and versatile individuals.

Junior High School Teachers Plan in Advance

A number of years ago the junior high schools of Denver, Colorado, set up a "World Understanding Committee." Its purpose was to stimulate the teaching of world understanding among junior high school pupils. This included an evaluation and an understanding of the United Nations program. Membership includes not only social science and English teachers, as one might expect, but also teachers of mathematics, science, art, dramatics, music, and the vocations. A representative is chosen from each school. Members elect their own chairmen and secretary and the Department of Instruction assigns one or two advisors. This group has great freedom to make curricula suggestions.

A unique feature of the program is that meetings may be called twice each semester on school time. The World Understanding Committee uses this alloted time and usually schedules one or two meetings during the school year in addition. At the close of school a session is held to see that individual names have been placed on mailing lists. Sources for materials are also exchanged. It has become customary for the committee to have a meeting in August to pre-plan for the fall teaching, to exchange materials and sources, and to make recommendations for activities for United Nations week. It seems apparent that the activity must have value when busy teachers give all this planning time and are not only willing to meet but do so gladly. The subjects under discussion have become a vivid, meaningful, portion of the junior high school program.

Here is a sample of the type of activities which can be recommended.

1. At the beginning of the year, notice surnames. You will see some very interesting ones with definite implications. Before a week has passed you will find a United Nations group within your classroom.

2. Look at newspapers. Make a note of two foreign countries you see mentioned. Now follow through with the news for ten days, and see how many times each is repeated. At the end of the two weeks, compile a class list. This is a possible starting place in the study of world understanding, which is synonymous with world friendship.

3. Try "pop-ups"! As soon as roll is taken those who have prepared a news item "pop-up" out of their seats and in turn report to the class. No clippings are allowed in the class room. Preparations must have been made. The idea of a "pop-up" eliminates the unprepared. This has been found to be very stimulating for seventh and eighth graders—low, medium, or high groups.

4. Here is a way to begin the study of world geography. Graphs showing the size of countries are made in the 8th grade. The member nations of the United Nations may be taken. The area of each is graphed by individuals. Then this is displayed in the room and all are amazed at the definite and lasting picture that is gained regarding the comparative size.

5. The work of the Junior Red Cross should be widely used.

6. Children love rôle playing. They can assume the rôle of an American family and one of some other country. Try it and see what you learn.

7. Assembly programs, which bring out the need and function of the United Nations will be well received.

8. The central art department can design a post card which can be used for "birthday greetings."

Along with such activities which create a desirable atmosphere the many materials on the United Nations can be used. Thus, *every day* can be United Nations Day.

Developing a Unit on International Relations: Design for Peace

In making the course of study in civics in the Chicago Public Schools a large committee was assembled, consisting of teachers, pupils, principals, district superintendents, parents, and community resource persons. At the outset of the work, a forum was held at Wright Junior College, featuring speeches by a professor from a nearby university and a reporter for the *Chicago Tribune*. There followed an open discussion by the audience, which consisted of university professors, civic leaders, teachers, and students. A recording was made of this meeting and played back to the members of the committee at their next meeting.

The committee first determined upon general objectives and defined the scope of the course. Upon completion of this task, subcommittees were set up, each one assuming responsibility for one unit. The unit on International Peace was assigned to a subcommittee consisting of one principal, one classroom teacher, and two research teachers from the Division of Curriculum Development. This subcommittee proceeded as follows:

1. They solicited units from various classroom teachers in Chicago. These were carefully examined and the best features from each pooled.

2. They examined the available material, consulting with the librarians of the various public and private libraries in the city, as well as the Division of Visual Education, the Division of Radio, and the Pamphlet Shop of the Council of Foreign Relations.

3. They drew up a tentative unit, which they sent to schools for classroom experimental work. Comments of both teachers and pupils were carefully studied by the committee.

4. The unit was revised in the light of the comments and submitted to the entire committee. After discussion by the committee of the whole, several changes were proposed and the unit was referred to the research teachers of the Division of Curriculum for further revision and editing.

5. It was later approved by the committee and a copy sent to every civics teacher.

The nature of the unit, INTERNATIONAL RELATIONS: DE-SIGNS FOR PEACE, is here suggested.

THE CHALLENGE: THROUGH WHAT PEACEFUL PROGRAMS CAN
PEOPLE HOPE TO SETTLE INTERNATIONAL DISPUTES?

1. The causes of international wars
   a. The role of fear, frustration, and hostile attitudes on the part of leaders and their peoples, in international disagreements
   b. Types of situations in which such disagreements tend to arise
2. A historical survey of men's attempts to resolve disagreements by peaceful measures
   a. Types of devices used, ranging from diplomacy to collective security
   b. An appraisal of each type
3. Recent designs for peace that recognize causes of war
   a. Education in world understanding
   b. International cooperation for economic improvement of less prosperous countries
   c. Progressive integration, by consent, of larger areas under a political system of enforceable law

Curriculum Revision—Kindergarten
Through Grade XII

When the social studies teachers of Milford, Connecticut, sat down together in 1950 to plan an over-all curriculum revision, they talked about the needs of young people in relation to the society and the world in which they were to live. What were important skills, attitudes, and understandings for a young American to possess in the mid-twentieth century? How could young people be helped to learn the necessary information for living in this complex, interdependent world?

It was recognized that the development of skills, understandings, and attitudes cannot be the result of a single learning situation. Meaningful learning is as slow as growing up. It requires time, and many different kinds of experience, before the desired goals become as "second nature" to the child. Attention in Milford, Connecticut, has been given therefore to providing recurring experiences of increasing complexity, while avoiding deadening repetition in educating for citizenship from Kindergarten through Grade XII.

The Foreword of the Elementary Social Studies Guide

Two questions constantly before us in working with children:

How can we best serve our children in preparing them to live in the here-and-now world?

How can we help them to understand and assume their responsibilities in the shaping of a better world?

The focus in the primary grades is upon:

1. Learning to get along with others.
2. Assuming responsibility in school, at home, and in the community.
3. Developing a feeling of interdependence in one's own community as a prerequisite to acknowledge similar world ties.

In these early grades the study of various holidays is used as a means of gaining a greater understanding and respect for the religious and nationality backgrounds that combine to make up each community. There is a warm feeling for all concerned when the Hebrew *Succoth* and the *Festival of the Lights* are celebrated at the time of Thanksgiving and Christmas where both Jewish and Christian groups are in the same classroom.

In the intermediate grades attention is centered upon an understanding of the people, resources, conditions, and ways of life in other lands. In the fourth grade they compare how people live in different regions of the United States with similar regions in other parts of the world. Major concepts to be developed at this level are listed in the curriculum grade as follows:

1. People in foreign lands live as they do because of their environment.
2. We learn from the experience of others.
3. People must provide themselves with food, clothing, and shelter.
4. Man shares responsibilities and cooperates in work, play, maintenance of health, religion, and government. Cooperative effort is often necessary in order to control the forces of nature and to utilize our natural resources.
5. Customs and ways of living are determined by natural, geographic, and climatic conditions of the earth. Man's control of fire, air, water, and other elements of his natural environment has made him increasingly powerful.
6. People migrate to other places in search of improved living conditions.
7. People govern themselves according to their local needs. We appreciate the government of other people, but we believe in our own democratic form of government.

Sixth-graders have their introduction to the influence of historical events upon our world neighbors. This is not just the "Old World Backgrounds" recommended by the Committee of Eight in 1905, although there is a unit contrasting early civilization with Egypt and the Near East today. The history of the European countries, including the Balkans and the Soviet Union, is studied in relation to the present problems of these nations. The focus is upon our nation's present situation, each nation's contributions to us, and its role in the United Nations. In the introduction to the work of the sixth grade, teachers are asked to "give pupils the opportunity to realize clearly the smallness of the modern world, the ever-increasing interdependence of nations and the need for understanding and open-mindedness." Stories, songs, films, and speakers who know of these lands help boys and girls to understand and appreciate all peoples of the world.

Here is the first part of the guide to a study of the Soviet Union:

1. *Significance of Topic*

   In a comparatively short time the U.S.S.R. has not only become the most powerful nation in the Eastern Hemisphere, but is also exerting increasing influence in world affairs. A knowledge of the history, the people, the land and the way of life in the U.S.S.R. will aid today's children in understanding the effect that the growth of this particular nation has had upon the peace of the world. Since world harmony can only be secured and maintained through the understanding and application of democratic principles, it is essential that we continually foster and strengthen those desirable attitudes and understandings which will insure the preservation of the democratic way of life.

2. *Brief Outline of the Topic*

   To learn about the life of the Russian people today it is necessary to study the following topics:

   a. Russia's topography
   b. Russia's climate
   c. Russia's natural resources
   d. Russia's history
      1) Contrast of conditions before and after the Revolution of 1917
      2) Similarities and differences between life in U.S.A. and U.S.S.R.
   e. Cause and background of her planned government
   f. Russian folklore
   g. Russian art
   h. Russians who contributed to our American way of life and culture; for example Alexander de Seversky, Igor Sikorsky, Prokofieff, and Tchaikowsky

3. *Possible Outcomes*
   a. Better understanding of what makes Russians act as they do
   b. Realization and appreciation of our way of life in the U.S.A.
   c. Knowledge of the vastness of the area and population of U.S.S.R.
   d. An appreciation and understanding of the UN and its role in world peace

Constant mention is made of the fact that many people share the earth with the pupil and that it is their world as well as his own. This results in a recognition of the need for world friendship and world organization for peace.

For Grades VII to IX, the over-all theme is "The Interdependence of Man and Society." In the seventh grade, there is an emphasis upon the effect of environmental factors upon ways of living, beginning with Connecticut and branching out to other regions of the United States and to Canada and Latin America. The eighth grade is devoted to how our American culture influences the way we live and think, with emphasis upon the four factors of our being a nation of many peoples, a democracy, a nation with high productivity, and a world power. In Grade IX, how the individual becomes a participating member of a school and community, is the area for study. This is especially appropriate because this grade is the first year of high school in Milford's school system at present.

The theme for Grades X to XII is "How Cultural Change Creates Adaptations in Man's Behavior." In Grade X, World Civilization, students are helped to see the importance of the Asian peoples in our modern world. Topics which are studied include the history and culture of India, China, and Japan, the influence of Western imperialism, and the force of the present Asian revolution. World-minded Americans must understand that although Asian people may seem "backward" in their ways of living, they are by no means backward in their desires. Education, health, and better economic conditions are as important to a family in Indonesia as in the United States.

An important unit of Grade XI, United States History, is the one entitled, "How Our Country Has Emerged As a Great World Power with World Responsibilities." This unit extends in time from 1865 until the present day. It includes the relations of the United States with Latin America and the Far East, World War I, attempts to avoid entangling agreements in the period following the first World War, World War II, and our active participation in world affairs since 1945. "Desired learnings" for this unit were established with the aid of a student committee.

Students in Grade XII, Modern Problems, begin their work with a study of the problems of emotional adjustment, the need for emotional and intellectual maturity, and for a satisfactory philosophy of life in our world of rapid cultural change. They see that aggression is an infantile reaction and that the best way to solve a problem is to be objective, to study all related data, and to examine the effects of any decision upon all parties concerned before making a decision. They discover that the mature individual knows how to meet conflicts between himself and his environment, avoids worry and anxiety, considers others, has the ability to cooperate, is able to adjust to various situations, and, in a crisis, keeps cool, doesn't blame others, and doesn't run away. These concepts are applied to individuals and then their meaning is discussed for the entire nation, for a mature attitude is considered an important goal for world-minded Americans.

Later in their year's work twelfth-grade students spend eight to ten weeks in a careful study of the ideological basis for Communism, the differences among the "isms," the purposes of the Russian leaders, the problems of world Communism and of Communism in the United States. This is followed by a study of the implications of the use of atomic energy and of the hydrogen bomb for our "One World or None."

As a concluding problem for the senior year, the possible roads to peace are reexamined in the light of the student's cumulative international understandings from Kindergarten through Grade XII.

At the close of this twelve-year program most of the students do show evidence of a world point of view and of a willingness to work actively for world cooperation, while they accept the probability of a continued "cold war" throughout their lifetime, with all that this implies in terms of personal and national sacrifice. They would agree with Oliver Wendell Holmes that "a man should share the action and passion of his time at peril of being judged not to have lived."

CHAPTER 8

Community Groups Cooperate with the Schools

FOREIGN visitors to the United States, as well as local observers, have often commented on the existence of innumerable civic organizations. For groups of citizens to see a social need is often tantamount to organizing to achieve it. This is a part of the dynamics of the American scene.

This chapter illustrates how citizens, in various ways, have sought to promote international understanding in cooperation with schools. The strength of these examples lies not only in the fact that vital learning situations were made possible for children and youth, but more important, that citizens, young and old, have worked together for the supreme ends of world peace and world understanding. In the process, through their joint efforts, all seemed to have learned more about problems inherent in seeking to live with other nations.

The reader is doubtless already aware that this is not the only chapter in which there are descriptions of cooperation of community groups with educational institutions. Clear cut examples are to be found in other sections, particularly in Part II, All-School and Out-of-Class Activities, and Part IV, College, Teacher, and Adult Education.

Teen-Age Diplomats Promote
International Understanding

In the fall of 1952 a group of fourteen students from seven European countries were brought to Rochester, New York, to attend the public schools and to live in Rochester homes. The value of this undertaking was so apparent that a second, and larger group, was sponsored during the school year 1953–54 and the program will be continued.

The initial screening of these teen-agers was done by the American Field Service. The arrangement for home and school placement was the work of the Association for Teen-Age Diplomats and the financing has been made a part of the regular budget of the Rochester Association for the United Nations.

The adjustments of these European youths to American schools have been relatively easy. The visitors have been surprised at, and have approved of, the friendly relationship between American teachers and pupils. The sincere interest taken in each pupil, concern for his future career as well as immediate success in his studies, free discussions of all kinds of questions, and the encouragement to challenge opinions—even those of the teacher—apparently make a deep impression on youth from foreign schools.

The visiting students eagerly participate in the extracurricular activities of their various schools. They join the foreign language clubs, help edit school newspapers, and try out for the senior play. One boy is credited with being the mainstay of his school's soccer team. Another visitor was one of twenty winners in a nation-wide contest sponsored by the Pakistan embassy in Washington, D.C. A third submitted a prize-winning poster in the United Nations poster contest sponsored by the Rochester Association for the United Nations.

Assimilation to new schools seems to offer fewer hazards than to foster families. Unquestionably the success of this experiment has largely resulted from the many sacrifices made by the "adopted parents," whose affectionate concern and wise counseling have been broad enough to include an extra son or daughter. The host family receives no financial remuneration and, in addition, generally finds the family car even more in demand to meet the social engagements of an extra teen-ager. Earning their own spending money becomes a common problem for the visitors. The newcomers in the family soon investigate the financial possibilities of baby sitting, grass cutting, or newspaper routes.

Comments of these Teen-Age Diplomats indicate considerable success for the project. A young girl from West Berlin says that she now fully realizes how wrong the Russian propaganda about American warmongering is, knowing now that the American people don't want war. She feels that upon her return she will be able to dispel, with facts, whatever false notions her home folks have about America. A boy from Austria says he hopes to improve his school student council and newspaper. He feels he has gained a valuable approach from the way these activities are run in Rochester schools.

A brisk exchange of correspondence between those who have returned to Europe and their adopted families and friends in Rochester keeps alive the interest sparked by these young diplomats. Magazines, school publications, and pictures are thus directed into European communities in a way that ensures their being used to the best advantage. One of the German students reported that he had talked to a meeting of parents, teachers, and pupils on the subject, "The American and His Education," and had illustrated his remarks with slides depicting school life in the Rochester High School where he had been a pupil.

Any effective exchange program must be reciprocal and, accordingly, the summer of 1953 found eight Rochester High School students outward bound for a taste of internationalism. Like their European counterparts, each of these young people was "adopted" by a family. Six went to Germany, one to Greece, and one to Belgium. As in the case of the Europeans coming to America, so in this reverse program, the screening was done by the American Field Service. Fifteen Rochester students had the opportunity of visiting in Europe in the summer of 1954.

It is impossible to estimate with any degree of accuracy the accomplishments of the Teen-Age Diplomats program, but it does represent a sincere effort to create greater understanding between the peoples of Europe and the United States and to break down barriers of ignorance and prejudice. It is a concrete expression of the belief in the Sanskrit quotation:

Walk together, talk together, Oh Ye Peoples of the Earth; then shall ye know one another and have peace.

How the World Affairs Council of Philadelphia Works with Local Schools

For years Bartram High School has been one of the many schools which has been privileged to work in close harmony with the World Affairs Council of Philadelphia. The earliest contact came when the teachers desired to take a class to the United Nations at Lake Success. From that beginning has developed the annual fall trip to the United Nations in New York. The World Affairs Council always arranges a date and plans for the reception of the students by the proper authorities. Teachers have been able to avail themselves, also, of trips planned by the Council to the State Department in Washington, D.C.

Students of the school are members of the Interscholastic Student Council, which is sponsored by the World Affairs Council. Moreover, one of the members of the faculty serves on the Council's Senior High School Faculty Committee which suggests activities, services, and plans agenda.

United Nations Day at Bartram High School is celebrated by a special assembly program. One year the *Story of Interdependence* served as the theme for a pageant in which filmstrips supplied by the World Affairs Council were utilized. On another occasion, the pupils wrote and performed a program on the work of the United Nations. Research was done through the library at the Council, where excellent material for enriching studies of various lands and cultures and current affairs is available. As one student wrote, "In the Senior year at Bartram, all students do a research paper on a topic of their choice. The World Affairs Council library has proved invaluable. The pamphlets and splendid bibliographies that the Council sends to the school have been very helpful to us."

The Council provides exhibits for classroom use to local schools which help students to gain a better understanding of world affairs. Each month it sponsors a senior high school forum attended by pupils from many schools. Speakers from foreign lands are sent by the Council to schools that request them and this helps increase understanding of the peoples and their countries.

Each year a Model United Nations is sponsored to which schools send pupil delegates and faculty group advisors. The pupils choose the country they wish to represent and prepare papers for the agenda. To quote another pupil: "We are getting ready for the Model United Nations. We have sent delegates to most of the briefing sessions, and have discussed issues in class that will be brought before the Model United Nations. We have enjoyed excellent outside speakers who have been giving us background material."

The boys and girls of Philadelphia enjoy going to the headquarters of the Council and often return with tales of meeting "strange peoples from other lands." No request seems too large or too small for fulfillment by the World Affairs Council.

A School Resource: The International Red Cross

Today's children mature in a 36-hour world. A plane can land in any world capital within 36 hours after leaving the United States. In our world, disease, ideas, and war spread but so do happiness, understanding, and peace. Today's children must learn how to live *in* a 36-hour world and how to live *with* it.

Living with others successfully is a key idea of Red Cross. All schools through their membership in the Junior Red Cross can take advantage of the resources of this international organization. There are, for example, the well-known Junior Red Cross Gift Boxes, on the outside of which a school's name and address may be placed. To a child far away, the soap, toothbrush, comb, pencils, notepad, and toy spell useful gestures of friendship from America. For the givers they signify that all youth are neighbors. For teachers they are tangible teaching tools.

The gift box may serve as motivation or a culminating activity in the study of other lands. Study of maps and globes becomes more purposeful when the route of a gift box can be followed. The friendly letter of appreciation placed in the box may be returned with news of the recipient, his life, how he happened to receive the box, and what it means to him. These letters furnish good material for class discussion. When bound together, they form a source of stimulating material for all classes to utilize. One or more letters from children in the same school may be the beginning of the preparation of a Red Cross Correspondence Album.

Direct contact with foreign schools, and the exchange of classroom work, can be effected through Correspondence Albums. They include letters, snapshots, original drawings, school work examples, descriptions of student activities like sports, music, student government, Red Cross projects, the story of your own community, the story of the government, customs, geography and history of our country.

There seems no end to class study which can be included in or stimulated by an album. In one situation field trips, with the help of the local chamber of commerce, formed the basis of one album. The unit of work being carried on was built around business and industry. Pupils and teachers both found satisfaction in the goals achieved, with the added advantage that the album was of value in interpreting a community.

Seven Korean high school boys, aged sixteen and seventeen, have recently sent friendly and inquiring letters to one high school in Minneapolis, Minnesota. The letters came through the American Red Cross, the Internatonal Red Cross having provided them with food and clothing in time of need. These boys in a large high school of 2500 students, situated but a few blocks from Syngman Rhee's home, are now writing to unknown friends. They say: "We have many friends in Korea but none in other lands." "I like to skate and study. What do you like to do?" "We go to school six days a week." "We want to learn about your country." These are typical statements and questions posed by world-minded Korean youths.

The school fortunate enough to receive such letters has the opportunity to share the great story of its own community, Minnesota and the United States, in an album of letters, essays, school papers, original drawings, snapshots, maps, charts, and pictures. One page may contain questions students want answered by the Koreans. It will take careful planning and organizing to decide from the wealth of material available what should be included or deleted from the first album. Thirty-six countries exchange albums with American schools.

Junior Red Cross International School Art and International School Music programs promote international understanding. The art program aims to tell the world of life in a student's own home town: the school cafeteria, the football game, watering horses on the family's farm, the ski slide in winter, a day at the beach in summer. Through their recorded music, the band or orchestra, chorus or choir tell how American youth take part in music at school and how much music means to them. The classics, spirituals, and American folk songs and jazz may all be recorded. Music and art can play a vital role in making world understanding and friendship a reality.

The two national Junior Red Cross magazines are useful sources of teaching material. Many elementary teachers are familiar with the news stories and pictures of children in other lands and the interesting ways the news provides motivation for study of other lands. Most high school teachers have not discovered, however, the usefulness of the *Junior Red Cross Journal,* the secondary school magazine. Student interest and classroom study needs find satisfying articles and excellent pictures on the United Nations, vocations in the American

Red Cross, the problems and needs of youth in other lands, and the daily life in other countries. The *Journal's* human interest stories are a rich resource for both written and oral reports. A school's membership in the Junior Red Cross will assure it of copies of this magazine each month.

Red Cross programs may be effective tools in helping young people plan together with their teachers, assume responsibilities in small working groups, and help to relate speaking, writing, music, and art to international projects. Working cooperatively with a local Red Cross Chapter may tie the school and community together. The chapter can provide schools with complete descriptive and helpful free material on the Junior Red Cross programs—Gift Boxes, Correspondence Albums, art and music programs. Source materials— films showing the Red Cross in action at home and abroad; "Introduction to the Red Cross," a short history and description of services of the American Red Cross—are available from local Red Cross chapters.

The Junior Red Cross is well known for its assistance to young people caught in emergencies, flood, and war. It teaches today's child how to share with and understand others, a double-barreled answer to the questions posed by a 36-hour world.

Community Ambassadors Represent
the United States Abroad

In Manhasset, New York, a Community Ambassador program was implemented through the efforts of the School Community Association, an organization of parents and teachers whose work is similar to that of a P.T.A. The money for the ambassadorship program was raised in the same manner as the rest of their scholarship money, through the operation of a "turnover shop." Outgrown, but not outworn, children's clothing is brought to the shop for sale on a 50–50 basis, 50 per cent to the donor and 50 per cent to the School Community Association.

Members of the Association became convinced that the Community Ambassador program was an effective means for developing international understanding. They did a great deal of public relations work in getting community support for the project. School personnel were equally convinced of its value and cooperated fully.

Faculty members met to discuss organizational plans with School Community members. When the funds were available, several of the faculty were on a committee to select a student ambassador. The faculty also helped prepare the student ambassador by giving him additional help in the language and background of the country to which he was going. Community members helped by giving further orientation on local, state, and municipal affairs.

When the selection of the member of the junior class to receive the School Community Ambassador Scholarship was announced, the students expressed their point of view in the following article in their high school newspaper.

They Shall Know the Truth

Manhasset High is indeed fortunate that Dave Dantzscher will be sent abroad next summer. Of course, for him the trip will be a marvelous experience but more important he will be an ambassador of good will from Manhasset and the United States.

Dave will be able to tell those he meets about the true America and its people. Many Europeans base their opinions of us on second-rate movies which make the United States look like a cross between a place where bloody crimes are committed on every street corner and where there are Indian massacres on the unsettled Western frontier. Many of them have the idea that all Americans are rich and have no worries, cares, or responsibilities. Our Manhasset ambassador will be able to clear up these misconceptions.

Dave will be learning, at the same time, about the lives of the people in the country where he is staying. By learning the problems that are confronting these people, he will thus understand them more fully. The letters that he writes home and the talks he gives afterwards will interpret their problems and views to us.

Only by mutual understanding can countries and peoples hope to achieve friendlier relationships and peace in the world. This is essential. It is up to us, the younger generation, to help make this a reality instead of an ideal.

The Manhasset local papers carried David Dantzscher's letters which kept the community abreast of his on-the-spot reactions to this enlightening experience. When David returned, the entire student body and the community benefited from his talks with individuals, as well as before small groups and large assemblies. The value of the experience was so great, both for David and the community, that there was no hesitation on the part of School Community in providing funds to send another such ambassador abroad. The second time a girl, Emilie True, was selected.

Community interest in the Ambassador Program has become so great that a group of women undertook to raise funds through organized clubs and civic groups and individual contributions in order to send a Community Ambassador from the young adult age group abroad in the following summer. The citizen who has given the leadership in this extension of the program states:

When a community sponsors an Ambassador, it is actually buying a share in international understanding. It takes a constructive step toward world peace by obtaining a first-hand, direct education on conditions abroad not through so-called "experts" but through one of its own neighbors. It demonstrates that American communities can step forward into international education.

A Local Foreign Policy Association Group Helps
High Schools Present a United Nations Assembly

For the third year the Foreign Policy Association of Hartford, Connecticut, has sponsored and organized a model meeting of the General Assembly of the United Nations. Nineteen public, private, and parochial high schools from the area take part with over 150 students participating. Each school selects eight delegates to represent eight nations and its students speak as those nations would speak. Meetings of the four committees are held prior to the plenary session of the Assembly.

About a month before the conference the student delegates are sent on a day's trip to New York, with expenses paid by local service clubs, parent, or alumni associations. These trips are made to see the United Nations and to speak with representatives of those nations whose part the students will take.

In the actual meeting each committee is led by a student chairman with the help of an adult adviser. The plenary session has a student president and an adult "Secretary-General." Four agenda questions, one for each committee, are chosen in advance from the actual United Nations agenda. Recently, the questions were:

1. The admission of new members to the United Nations
2. The expansion of technical assistance programs

3. The problem of prisoners of war
4. The problem of self-determination in the trust areas

The plenary session is set up to imitate that of the United Nations General Assembly. The President and the Secretary-General sit in front with the flags and the seal of the United Nations in the background. The nations are seated as they are in the United Nations. And just as the Assembly does, committee reports are given, including, when appropriate, a minority report. A final vote is taken.

Any evaluation of this program must consider how much is learned by the students and how much interest is aroused. The Model Assembly has become the focal point around which most foreign affairs studies and international relations clubs center their work during the entire spring term. The agenda questions, covering problems in all parts of the globe, give a world-wide emphasis while study is concentrated on specific countries.

Questions are admittedly difficult. The students may not be able to bring out the ramifications of all of them. But in the process of finding out another nation's attitude toward the questions students must delve into world opinion and the reasons for such opinions. They come to the realization that ideals for the world can be a goal to work toward, but these cannot be forced on other nations.

The Assembly arouses tremendous interest among the students. The New York trips are inspiring and usually supply specific information for each student participating. The community interest in the trips provides another incentive. Students are often asked to speak before the organization which has financed their trip. The model meeting itself is the culmination of their efforts. They have with few exceptions been well prepared and are able to carry on lively discussions in the committees. Since each one is playing a part, the part of another nation, each delegate must stick to facts as these are interpreted by those people he represents. The U.S.S.R. delegation, for instance, has walked out and has used parliamentary procedure to delay proceedings. This role playing is coupled, of course, with serious discussion.

Finally, as concrete proof of student and faculty support, every teacher involved in the program has expressed enthusiastic approval. It is of some significance to note that the student membership in the Foreign Policy Association has jumped from 156 in 1951 to more than 400 in 1954.

A School-Community Council Sponsors Neighborhood United Nations Workshops

The Riverside Neighborhood Assembly, a large school-community council in District 8, New York City, has dedicated itself to the idea of promoting a "curbstone interest" in the United Nations by involving every section of the community in its program. To implement this purpose, all-day conferences on "The UN At Our Door" were planned and held at the beginning of United Nations Week.

To stimulate interest in all sections of the community before the Conference, parent workshops were organized. A related two-week community art exhibit was planned, and miniature United Nations sessions were conducted in the schools. The clergy of all denominations promised to preach about the meaning of international co-operation from the pulpits the week before the conference. The Foreign Policy Association agreed to co-sponsor the conference with the Riverside Neighborhood Assembly and to regard this undertaking as a pilot project, with a view to extending it to other communities.

In preparing for parent workshops the planning group faced many problems. There was much apathy among community residents for the whole theme of the conference. How to choose subject matter for the workshops and how to dramatize the role of the American citizen in assuming his responsibility to the United Nations became paramount.

Leaders of the Riverside Neighborhood Assembly, therefore, met with a consultant. They asked for help in making the United Nations easily explicable and for help in finding ways to relate international issues to community concerns, such as the call to military service of 18-year-old boys, the increase in juvenile delinquency, and existing prejudices toward minority groups living in the community.

A member of the Church Peace Union became the workshop leader. He provided the "know-how" in setting up the workshops. Five different schools became hosts, each for one workshop session. Each school was charged with providing a social committee, an arrangements committee, and a publicity committee. Community leaders became panel members.

The West Side News, the community newspaper, was utilized to inform the community of the results of each workshop. Parent Association bulletins were utilized to create interest in the sessions. The parent presidents of each of the eleven schools in the district were invited to the workshops. One result of these sessions was that four more of the better organized schools of the district set up similar workshops, and three others planned trips to the United Nations.

In evaluating the workshops it was concluded that:

1. They furnished a learning situation for many community leaders.
2. They were a tool for integration, since Spanish-speaking citizens as well as old-time residents, were involved.
3. They involved religious and civic leaders as well as parent participation.
4. They stimulated thought and interest in the United Nations.
5. Many materials on the United Nations were distributed throughout the schools.

There was, however, a general feeling that the impact of the Neighborhood United Nations Workshops was not community-wide. It was realized that many on-going projects would have to be planned in the future to involve more people.

A City Newspaper Cooperates with Schools

How can dramatic news happenings all over the globe be related to the curriculum? Teachers in the Upper Midwest area of Minnesota, North and South Dakota, and Wisconsin have found one answer. More than 1,600 of them are using a unique study program designed to bridge the gap between textbooks and the day's headlines —the Program of Information on World Affairs.

This program, developed by Minnesota educators and the *Minneapolis Star,* is a year-long study and quiz plan for use in grades 7 through 12. It departs from the traditional chronological study of history by shifting the emphasis from the past to the present. The major current issues in our world are listed. Then background material is presented which is essential to an understanding of each problem.

The center of the program is a 48-page guidebook with study outlines on 26 major world issues. Augmenting the booklet are weekly study aids and multiple-choice quizzes. The plan was worked out seven years ago by the late Dean Peik of the University of Minnesota College of Education and the editors of the *Minneapolis Star.* Educators have helped determine policies over the years by service on the program's Advisory Board.

The *Star* offers this service without charge and without any circulation subscription tie-up whatsoever. Each year 26 new issues for study are suggested. Covered in the current series are such topics as The United Nations: A Place to Promote Peace; Russia's Role in World Affairs; The Communist World; The Two Germanys; Southeast Asia: Red Terror in Jungle Lands; The Free World's Defense System; Japan: Cinderella of the Orient; and The Foreign Policy of the United States. The guidebook can be used as the basis for an entire course in world affairs or as a supplement to other materials.

In the fall teachers are sent the new program with ready-to-use study outlines and suggested reading materials on the 26 topics of study. Each week during the year they receive an up-to-date background article on the current topic and a multiple-choice quiz. Teachers then give the multiple-choice quiz on the day of their choosing. At various times during the school year the *Minnesota Star* also publishes a four-page tabloid-sized publication, *World Affairs Teacher,* in which teachers share teaching experiences.

Many schools make extensive use of resources in their community. Pupils hold International Days with foreign students from nearby universities. They take field trips to local government offices. In many instances they stage a weekly panel discussion on the topic of study at meetings of community organizations or over the local radio station.

One seventh- and eighth-grade class in a rural area developed a weekly "Assembly of Nations." Pupils represented foreign countries prominent in the week's news and answered questions about their "homelands." At other schools students pretended they had been named to Congress or to the United Nations General Assembly. They then had to make decisions on problems and issues that would confront such persons.

Pupils also make use of documentary films and newsreels, bulletin boards, scrapbooks, and wire recordings. They evaluate newspapers and sponsor such events as a World Affairs Conference, attended by students from high schools of neighboring cities, and Crusade for Freedom drives. They form Junior United Nations clubs.

The World Affairs program is designed primarily for Upper Midwest teachers. The *Minneapolis Star,* however, makes the guidebook available, in limited quantity, to teachers outside this area. The booklet is free but there is a charge of $1.00 for the year's series of weekly materials.

Radio Station KDKA Develops an "At Home Around the World" Program

At Home Around the World is a Pittsburgh, Pennsylvania, social studies radio program which combines geography and intercultural understanding. It is a dramatic serial, each episode complete in itself, of two American teen-agers, brother and sister, who visit people in various countries of the world to learn their thinking and their ways of living. The program was first planned in cooperation with the Department of Curriculum Research of the Pittsburgh Board of Education and a committee of geography and social studies teachers in the area.

The subject matter for each script is chosen by a committee of teachers who plan it so that it will be most effective in connection with the geography studies of the children in both public and private schools. Scripts are prepared by a professional radio writer on the KDKA staff.

After the scripts for the series are finished, the teacher committee goes over them for factual subject matter and then prepares teachers' outlines for school use. KDKA prints and distributes these handbooks to all teachers who wish to use the series in their classrooms, as well as to schools and colleges outside the Pittsburgh listening area where there is interest in such material for teacher education.

The series was first presented in 1948. At that time the head of the Art Department of the Pittsburgh Board of Education was trying to promote an International Art Exchange between students in the United States and other countries. The station was asked if it would develop a series to serve as an incentive to interest young people in this project. This International Art Exchange was then sponsored by the Eastern Art Association, the Western Arts Association, and the Junior Red Cross. The Art groups handle the details of the subject matter and choice of paintings to be sent. The Junior Red Cross attends to the actual physical details of shipping and delivery.

The scripts on the Art Exchange program were made available to schools and radio stations in other parts of the country, to youth groups, such as the Girl Scouts and Camp Fire Girls, and to community agencies, such as the Community Radio Exchange of Buffalo, New York. The United States Office of Education also requested and distributed the scripts.

In 1953–54 many of the Pittsburgh area schools requested that the series be repeated. This was done, after being rewritten and brought up to date. In the revised series young people from abroad take a tour of this country to learn the many and varied ways of living here.

The Art Department of the Pittsburgh Board of Education has asked that the International Art Exchange be included. Each week it sends to the station a boy or girl who is either a native of the country being dramatized or one who has lived there. At the end of each program these young people describe briefly their impressions of the United States, contrasting it with countries abroad. Details are given of these contrasts, which are depicted in the paintings being produced or received in the Art Exchange program.

The series is scheduled to run through two years. It is planned that programs will cover countries of Europe, Asia, Africa, and South America. Events are dramatized in the homes of people, in their cities, countryside, and towns.

The series embraces simple production techniques. It uses an organist in the introduction, scene bridges, curtain, and sound. The two main characters, boy and girl, appear regularly. Each week one or more characters of the country in which the characters are traveling are added. A KDKA director casts the series from professional actors and is in full charge of the production from the KDKA studies. The program could be produced in a school workshop, if a school were interested in such a project.

Boulder, Colorado, Does Something About World Affairs

In 1947 many of the teachers and other community leaders of Boulder, Colorado, went to Denver to attend the Mountain-Plains Regional Conference on UNESCO. These delegates returned to Boulder with enthusiasm at a high pitch. They immediately launched a Boulder UNESCO program, designed to meet the interests of every age group.

Adults formed a community UNESCO group and invited representatives from every city club and organization to join. The aim was to promote a cultural exchange between the city of Boulder and an adopted city of Meppel in Holland. Mayors, business men, industrial workers, and housewives exchanged letters. School children exchanged essays, art work, and as pen pals, laid the basis for lasting friendships.

Teachers, administrators, and the Board of Education were represented on a UNESCO Council which was organized by the teachers. In order that a broad program for the Boulder public schools might be planned, it seemed advisable to delegate certain responsibilities to committees.

One committe was instructed to find the sources of all worthwhile materials on the United Nations and world affairs and to make these materials available to schools, teachers, committees, and community groups.

The purposes of a second committee included:

1. Working out plans which would offer teachers an opportunity to travel in foreign countries
2. Providing for the exchange of teachers
3. Considering possibilities for summer study or attendance at national or international conferences
4. Arranging for attendance at world affairs workshops
5. Bringing in noted speakers and leaders to discuss world affairs

A form letter which suggested possible opportunities in the above fields was sent to all teachers in order to ascertain their interests relative to participation in this program. The committee then met with the teachers who were interested. Teacher travel, education, and improvement thus began.

Since the inception of this program in 1947, Boulder public schools have engaged in the following activities:

1. Two teachers attended school in Norway.
2. Three exchange teachers went to England.
3. One exchange teacher went to Scotland.
4. Three teachers visited Hawaii.
5. One teacher studied in Mexico.
6. Five teachers toured Europe, Asia, and Africa.
7. Six teachers, two parents, and two students attended the national UNESCO meeting in New York City.

8. Many teachers attended meetings in Denver, Colorado Springs, and San Francisco.

As a means of stimulating participation, a part of the expense of each enterprise has been met by the teachers UNESCO Council. But each teacher has assumed a great portion of the expense and agreed to share experiences later with the schools and the community.

An Anti-United Nations Campaign Is Unsuccessful

Marin County, California, has been heralded as a community which has successfully handled an attack on the United Nations and UNESCO. The success was due to the prompt and intelligent action of individual citizens. People in Marin County became active agents in their own political life and thereby gained some control over their own destiny. Misinformation was met by facts, falsehoods were corrected by statements from prominent leaders, and doubts about the United Nations were alleviated by documented refutation of the claims of the critics.

A drive to compel the public schools in Marin to stop teaching about the United Nations started at the office of the County Superintendent of Schools. Two women, who asked that their names be withheld, appeared before the Superintendent and asked that the United Nations Handbook, prepared by the County Instructional Staff, be withdrawn from school use. The reasons for requesting the withdrawal were vague and general. "UNESCO is a corrupt plot to capture the minds of American children, and our schools shouldn't teach it," one woman stated.

As the campaign progressed, the bibliography contained in the handbook was attacked, first on the basis that the books were subversive, and later on the basis that some of the authors were "controversial." The tactics of quoting out of context, or misrepresenting facts, were difficult to meet. Cynics said that nothing could be done to stop the fearful reactionaries who were attempting to undermine public confidence in the world organization. Fortunately something could be done and was done.

The Board of Education appointed a citizen's committee to study the United Nations Handbook and to recommend appropriate action. The representatives on this committee were chosen carefully and wisely. They served as individuals, but they were well-known people active in the League of Women Voters, Parent-Teachers Association, Church Groups, Service Clubs, American Association of University Women, as well as members from the Daughters of the American Revolution and the American Legion. It was quickly apparent that the majority of the committee saw nothing harmful in the United Nations Handbook and that the main problem was to help the uninformed get the true facts.

Most of the people in Marin look with favor on the United Nations. A few have lost faith in it. They fear it, they are suspicious of it and, in their fear and suspicion, they would destroy it. It was the fearful few and their whispering campaign that had to be handled.

Outside the formal committee, a group of volunteers, determined that a smear campaign was not going to work in their community, met and formed a self-appointed watch-dog committee to rally the constructive, thinking people together. These volunteers recruited other volunteers in an all-out effort to get a cross section of Marin County alerted to the situation. Each volunteer was given a specific assignment. Personal liaison was established with the press and radio in Northern California. Letters were sent to the editors of Marin County and San Francisco newspapers. Radio programs were prepared, on which the critics discussed their opposition to the United Nations Handbook, along with the County Superintendent of Schools and members of the American Association for the United Nations. Study groups for PTA Presidents and International Relations Chairmen were initiated and held throughout the county. Pamphlets describing the methods and the people behind the anti-United Nations forces in the United States were widely circulated. Particularly noteworthy were the excellent news stories carried by two of the largest dailies in San Francisco, the *San Francisco Chronicle* and the *San Francisco News.*

By the time a well-known anti-United Nations speaker appeared in Marin, the people were prepared with facts to challenge any falsehoods. The speaker, who had successfully waged a war against teaching about UNESCO in Los Angeles, seemed totally unprepared for her critical reception.

The self-appointed United Nations committee worked day and night. The results made their work worth while. Following a thorough investigation of the facts, the special committee appointed by the Board of Education accepted the Handbook itself. Amendments which would have deleted mention of UNESCO from the Handbook were killed, as were several other suggestions by a minority member. A state senate hearing was called off, after the local senator discussed with members of the pro-United Nations volunteers the inherent danger of holding such a hearing where unjust and unsupported charges could be made. A Marin Committee For the Public Schools was formed to support teachers and administrators and to protect the schools from unwarranted attacks. This committee is now ready to alert the community when efforts are made to restrict freedom of education.

So the matter rests today. The issue is not a closed one. What the incidents so far have proved is that citizens believing in the United Nations can and should rally together to develop community understanding of the role of the United Nations. It takes time and thought, but a vocal and critical minority should not be permitted to spread distortions in any community. The American people will not follow the prophets of this kind of community confusion, provided they know the real situation, provided the distortions are not permitted to go unchallenged.

Part IV

COLLEGE, TEACHER, AND
ADULT EDUCATION

CHAPTER 9

Classroom Activities and Courses of Study

THE influx of students into United States colleges and universities in the aftermath of World War II continues into the present, and prospects for the future appear to indicate that the increase will continue. Moreover, thousands of foreign students now regularly attend American colleges ad universities, while an ever-increasing number of American youth, as well as adults, study abroad. We are nearer the old world of Europe and the older world of Asia than ever before.

This situation poses problems of curriculum reorganization which are reminiscent of those which obtained some years ago when enrollments at high school level moved sharply upward and changed in quality as well as amount. People began to realize that the function of secondary education was no longer largely a preparation for college. It was rather to prepare for a great diversity of situations at home and abroad. Indeed, it was to prepare for life itself.

As education at college level is today provided for a larger fraction of the total population, a realistic appraisal of the course offerings and educational experiences must similarly be undertaken. We are no longer training solely a small percentage of the population for the professions of law, medicine, and theology. The college population of today includes also the marginal "C" group, whose interest will not long be held by classroom lectures and readings of a factual nature alone. A larger variety of method and stimulus is needed. The student must be creatively involved and implicated in the activities of the classroom, and beyond the classroom, if the young adults who move into positions of responsibility in our world society are to be prepared to play a constructive role in the resolution of the problems of our day.

One of the areas in which curricular offerings need to be enriched, and approaches made challenging, is that of world understanding. In view of our position of leadership at world level it is necessary that college youth become acquainted with the large international problems which confront us. These include the struggle for the minds of men which is going on at so feverish a pace today.

The real meaning of democracy and, in turn, Communism must be determined and the skills requisite for the realization and expansion of freedom developed. We can learn to know the views of governments and peoples about world problems not only in Europe, but in Southeast Asia and other areas as well. Technical assistance can be seen as a creative endeavor on the part of free people to enlarge the prospect in life for underdeveloped countries and their people.

The role of the United Nations in building the peace must be understood as depending upon the people of the world and their governments, including the United States. Knowledge is needed, of course, but this knowledge should be coupled with the ability to transform it into constructive action. Growth on the part of students as they study in our colleges can in part be determined by their willingness to engage in activities concerned with building the peace in our world.

This chapter presents four descriptions of work done in colleges, five in teacher education institutions, and four by colleges and other educational agencies, particularly for the adult population of the community.

The diversity of approach is noteworthy, ranging as it does from the academic setting to participation in direct life experience. Even where instruction is offered through courses which, by name at least, have long been listed in college catalogs, the approach to international relations education is at once broad and direct. Effort is made to give concrete meaning to words and concepts. Thus, foreign language study becomes a bridge to an understanding of other cultures, and comparative education has its foundations laid not in the comparison of the structure of various educational systems abroad but in the broad areas of cultural development, and in the economic, social, and political trends of the past century.

The descriptions reveal a vital concern, moreover, for the development of an understanding of present problems. The locus of emphasis is frequently *the now*. This serves both to heighten the interest of the learner and also to bring home to him the fact that, in a limited way at least, he is a critical factor in his world.

The frequent use of students from abroad as resource people is reassuring. At present there are approximately 35,000 students from other lands in the United States and they constitute one of the really valuable assets for the study of international relations. Apparently some colleges are beginning to use this resource in a functional way.

Several descriptions set forth the values derived either from an exchange of people as between two countries, or direct study abroad. The continuation of this latter practice on the part of some of the leading colleges of the United States after an initial trial period is evidence of the fact that the experience has been found to be educationally both challenging and sound.

Finally, a reading of the descriptions which are concerned with courses designed for the adult population shows that some colleges have recognized a responsibility to bring educational leadership in international relations to the adult citizens of their communities. These adults are, after all, occupying positions in which decisions are being made, decisions which influence directly relations of the United States with other countries of the world and, indirectly at least, influence the character of education the colleges offer.

Orientation to American Life for Students from Abroad

Beginning in February, 1954, the foreign students at Western College for Women, Oxford, Ohio, have been enjoying a new course in Orientation to American Civilization, conducted by the Foreign Student Adviser. It is one hour in length, offers one academic credit per semester, is required of new foreign students and optional for those who were in college the preceding year.

The course consists of lectures and field trips. Various heads of departments have been invited to speak informally to the students on those phases of work which are uniquely American. The students enjoyed hearing a discussion of the teaching of art in grade schools, high schools, and colleges in the United States. Psychology, as applied to the problems of foreign students in the United States, was the subject of another lecture. Home economics, both from a practical and a professional point of view, is another subject with which our foreign students were unfamiliar. American music also is of special interest to students from other countries. While it is impossible to learn much about these subjects in one or two lectures, at least a beginning can be made which may lead to further study.

There has been great enthusiasm for the field trips. A visit to an American farm proved especially interesting. The students also attended a meeting of the Oxford Village Council where they had an opportunity to see democracy in action in a small town. They have accepted an invitation to visit the office of the *Middletown Journal* to see an American newspaper being made. A conducted tour through the Ft. Hamilton Hospital, Hamilton, Ohio, is another project planned for the future. The class will also visit the Cincinnati Art Museum and the Taft Museum accompanied by faculty members of the Western College Art Department. With biology students they will share a trip to the Cincinnati Zoo.

These projects have proved so interesting, and the friends of Western College have been so cooperative, that there have been more invitations than it has been possible to accept in a school year. Since the course did not begin until the second semester, with students already well adjusted to college life, lectures dealing with college affairs such as the use of the library, the College Government Association, or social customs were not given the first year. They will later be included as the course covers two semesters.

The privilege of making American customs and institutions better known to friends from other countries, and of hearing their impressions of various phases of American culture, is becoming of increasing importance in Western College's foreign student program.

Special Study in International Politics

Sacramento State College, California, offers a two-unit upper division course called International Politics. It is described as a "study of: current international tensions, the motivating forces influencing world politics, and the role of diplomacy and international organizations in resolving conflicts." Included as part of the course is a project which may be of use in teaching similar courses elsewhere.

During the first half of the semester the instructor surveys the United Nations, with emphasis upon its functions of alleviating international tension. In so doing he deals with the motivations of the major powers and their current diplomatic methods in securing political and economic goals. A textbook with content somewhat paralleling the course is used for this period.

In the fourth week the instructor gives three duplicated sheets to each one. The first contains a list of names of important countries in each of the three major areas of world tension today. Ten countries are listed from the Far East, twelve from the Middle and Near East, and twelve from Europe. From the list each student is asked to select two different countries, each from a different area.

The second sheet lists fifteen topics for each of the three areas. These serve as reference points in studying the relationship of the country selected to the general problems of the area. For example, the list for the Far East contains such items as: recognition of China; China in the United Nations; disposition of Formosa; unification of Korea; neutrality of India; exports and imports; political status and stability; and attitudes of the United States, the Union of Soviet Socialist Republics, and other major powers toward the United Nations. The third sheet gives the student an annotated list of twenty-five journals and periodicals as possible sources from which to obtain current information on the various countries.

Students are asked to become well informed on the countries which they have chosen and to be prepared to give a twenty-minute presentation on each country, using the reference points as the basis for organizing the talk. Presentations are as objective as possible, the emphasis being placed on an attempt to present the attitudes of the government and people in the country concerned rather than on the point of view of an American citizen. A five-minute question-discussion period follows each talk during which time both students and instructor contribute.

Prior to the student talks on each geographical area, the instructor gives a twenty-minute lecture, citing the major problems involved and developing a short historical background. Following the last student talk in the area he summarizes the important points presented. At the next class meeting a quiz covering the talks is given. Toward the end of the semester the instructor lectures on the interrelationship of the international problems discussed and attempts to show the contributions that diplomacy and international organizations can make toward acceptable solutions.

The class is usually made up from 18 to 25 juniors and seniors. It may be noted that in addition to the values attained by the use of the procedures outlined above, they serve to prepare students for participation in the West Coast Model United Nations Conference.

Junior Year in France

The Junior Year in France under the auspices of Sweet Briar College, Virginia, is open to men and women students in regular academic standing in any college or university recognized by the Junior Year in France. Students must be recommended by the chairman of the department of their major subject, the chairman of the French department, and the dean of the college, and must have had at least two years of pre-college French and two years of college French, or the equivalent. After a preliminary language session at Tours, students are enrolled at the University of Paris in a variety of courses.

The Sweet Briar Junior Year in France offers students a full academic year at the University of Paris where, with French classmates, they may broaden and deepen their comprehension of the language, customs, history, and culture of France, as well as specialize in such international subjects as art, government, history, international affairs, literature, philosophy, or political science. French is the exclusive language of communication in the classroom, in the French families with whom students live, and in informal conversation.

In France the American student becomes aware of the great emphasis placed on individual effort in the field of study selected. He is expected to accept the responsibility of greater academic freedom, as well as greater social freedom. He has to make his own way without the aid of the many extracurricular and social organizations of the American campus. He must adapt himself to the French university system and not expect a great university to adapt itself to him. Thus he attains an intellectual and social maturity of inestimable value in his senior year at home and throughout life. He returns, furthermore, with a greater understanding of world problems and a better perspective of those of his own country.

Eighty-five colleges and universities have been represented by 466 students in the first six years of Sweet Briar's administration of the Junior Year in France. Since Yale was one of the first colleges to recognize the Sweet Briar Junior Year in France, it is only fitting that it should head the list with 51 men. Yale's recognition of the plan was followed by recognition from Harvard and Princeton. No one of these three colleges had ever approved a junior year organization before. The fourteen colleges sending the largest number of students are Bryn Mawr, Carleton, Cornell, Dartmouth, Harvard, Middlebury, Mount Holyoke, Princeton, Radcliffe, Sweet Briar, Vassar, Wellesley, Wheaton, and Yale.

Major Area in Peace Studies

Manchester College in North Manchester, Indiana, undertook in 1948 a new academic venture. It established a program of peace studies. Several factors were responsible for this step. It was believed that a more thorough study of the war-peace problem is essential to the survival of civilization. Also the conviction was widespread that a college founded by one of the historic peace churches—The Church of the Brethren—has a special responsibility to undertake work in this area and to try to interest some of her most promising students in this field.

In the program an attempt has been made to coordinate the efforts of both the "pacifist" and the "nonpacifist" peacemaker. Since Manchester is a liberal arts college it is assumed that these objectives cannot be realized by any narrow types of specialization. Students who wish to work on the war-peace problem must have a balanced program because the purpose is to develop, first of all, well-rounded individuals. Their more specialized training will naturally be undertaken on the graduate level. A certain amount of background concentration is required of all students, however.

A major in peace studies has been set up that cuts across departmental lines. It is intended not only to meet the needs of the student who expects to do graduate work in this area, but also to foster attitudes conducive to peaceful human relations in those entering industry, business, the teaching profession, Brethren Volunteer Service, church work, or other forms of service in the local community. Peace studies is not a conventional major in political science. Manchester believes that a student well qualified for work in this area needs a broader base. He needs a rich background in all the social sciences, philosophy, religion, and ethics as well.

In the first two years students are concerned mainly with getting the basic courses usually required in the liberal arts. Students are urged to take a course in the history of civilization and one in language and thought which examines some of the reasons why language habits lead people into conflict, misunderstanding, and misevaluation.

The major itself calls for 80 hours in the social sciences, distributed as follows: 40 in history, 20 in political science, 16–20 in sociology, and 8 in economics. It is quite obvious that if a student is a well-integrated individual, adequately motivated, he will also need to draw upon the fields of philosophy and religion. For this reason 24 hours are scheduled in this area. This includes a study of some of the leading contemporary philosophers, their diagnoses of the crisis of our age, and a study of the contributions of the great religions of the world to the philosophy of peace, as well as a study of Christian thought on the war-peace question. To assist in the matter of self-integration a year's reading course is given in the great classics, the reading being orientated around the problem of the goal of life for the individual and the nature of the good society.

The requirement in political science includes a course in international relations, similar to that given in many colleges, e.g., a study of the causes of war, contemporary problems of international relations and international organization. Probably the more unique part of the program is a sequence of courses in which the emphasis is placed upon the principles and procedures of *peacemaking*. This includes a study of some of the contemporary peacemakers and their techniques and various approaches to the peace question. In this course outside lecturers who have had first-hand experience in the various fields have been brought in to give the student a better understanding of these approaches. Among the men who have spoken in classes are: Andrew Cordier of the United Nations; Kermit Eby of the University of Chicago; Douglas Steere, member of the Administrative Committee on the graduate curriculum in Social and Technical Assistance at Haverford; David Henly, dean of Earlham College; M. R. Zigler, director of the European branch of the Brethren Service Program; Ernest Lefever, secretary for the Department of Justice and Goodwill of the National Council of Churches and Dan West, founder of the Heifer Project.

Students are encouraged to undertake some field project in the summer of the junior year. This may be participation in a work camp, an interracial workshop, students-in-industry project, institutional service units, or international seminar. This work is taken under the supervision of the appropriate department and academic credit is granted.

To carry out the program successfully, it is believed that the efforts of the entire faculty are required, at least indirectly. An unusual feature of the program is a staff course designed to bring into focus the resources of a number of faculty members on the peace question. Each attempts to show the light his particular field throws on the problem. The departments which have collaborated in this course are: psychology, economics, sociology, history, political science, religion and philosophy, physics, and physical education.

Education for Social and Technical Assistance

Haverford College is offering qualified men and women a Graduate Curriculum in Social and Technical Assistance in the belief that the development of a peaceful world society depends on large-scale social, economic, and political reorganization in many regions and over a long period of time.

All who engage in assistance programs should be both emotionally and intellectually qualified for the task. As men and women of good will they should be able to work harmoniously with people of different races and possibly under difficult and primitive conditions. They should be able to appreciate the values of foreign cultures and understand the basis for variant economic and political theories.

Projects for the improvement of living conditions which are essentially technical in character make a profound impact on the social life of the people who are affected by the changes. Thus, professional competence of technicians is not sufficient of itself. They must be alert to the social implications of their work and prepared to help the affected population to adjust to a new economic-social order. Practically all of the technical and social assistance projects now in progress or envisaged by the intergovernmental, governmental, and private agencies are therefore as much problems of human engineering as they are a matter of putting technological principles into practice.

The Graduate Curriculum in Social and Technical Assistance offered by Haverford College presupposes a broad general education as basic preparation, preferably accompanied by some training or experience in a technical specialty. The course does not necessarily specialize in the needs of specified areas, on the principle that a graduate should be broadly prepared to serve wherever the opportunity offers. In the case of individuals who are planning to join specific assistance programs, however, opportunity is offered to apply course content and method to the problems of particular areas. The College places considerable emphasis on personal attributes, as well as upon the performance of academic requirements. For this reason the curriculum includes a ten-day pre-semester work camp in Philadelphia at which students become acquainted with each other and with the problems of urban society, and a mid-winter Work and Study Project of six weeks duration. The latter has been conducted on the reservation of the Cherokee Indians in North Carolina.

The academic program consists of the following required full-year courses: Case Study of Assistance Programs, Anthropology and Human Relations, and the Orientation Seminar which covers religious, political, and economic ideologies. Two additional semester courses are elected from the following: Community Development, Fiscal Management, International Relations, Social Research, and Modern Languages.

Although this curriculum has been given for only three years, many of the 48 students who have completed it are already finding positions of responsibility. Sixteen are serving in twelve different foreign countries, 5 are engaged in governmental service in the United States, 11 are with local agencies engaged in community development and social services, 9 are teaching, 3 are doing administrative work in educational or civic organizations, 2 are continuing their education to advance their technical competence, and 2 are in industrial or commercial work.

Total charges payable to the College, including room and board under a plan of cooperative housekeeping, are about $1400.00, plus the cost of the transportation to and from the site of the field project. Special scholarship funds are available for this program, including the substantial Christopher Reynolds Fellowships which are for persons who have had several years experience in technical work or with an assistance project.

Area Studies for World Understanding

The State Teachers College, Willimantic, Connecticut, emphasized study of foreign countries in its 1954 Sophomore Seminar on Contemporary Problems. This is a course for twelve points credit that enrolls all sophomores and integrates the natural sciences, social sciences, and literature. The theme this year was "Area Studies for World Understanding." A major expectation was that students would gain a clearer understanding of peoples and values of nations other than our own and, through comparison, a better appreciation for basic American values.

The Seminar included studies of Russia, India, the United Nations, and selected documents underlying American traditions of liberty. The staff included a natural scientist, two social scientists, and a literature specialist. The success of the Seminar depends, of course, largely on effective cooperation among the full-time staff. Time pressures, problems of communication, and training in different academic fields make for difficulties. Practical ability to work together improved this year during the semester. A student-faculty planning committee helped make plans and decisions in a number of areas and, also, helped the faculty consider student feelings and opinions.

The life and culture of Russia and India were studied by all students each week, from the approaches of the history, geography, literature, and current social problems of each country. In order to develop a fuller picture of the cultures, other faculty members were invited to give lectures on the music, art, and dance of the two countries.

Russia served as a case study in how a totalitarian nation attacks problems of advancing from a backward to an industrial state by use of authoritarian techniques, while rejecting past values. India, by contrast, illustrated the efforts of a recently freed colonial country to resolve similar problems by democratic procedures, while trying to conserve values inherited from the past.

America's documents of liberty were studied through three main topics: Problems of Discrimination, Education for Democracy, and Can America Afford Economic Aid to Other Countries? Students in small sections also discussed readings from Thoreau, Jefferson, Paine, and others. The United Nations included study of three problems: Issues Involved in Control of the Atom, The Role of the United Nations in Indo-China, and The Role of the United Nations in the Middle East.

A conference on World Affairs, with enrollment from eight high schools in the area, was sponsored by the Seminar. Speakers from Harvard University and Goddard College discussed methods for studying the Soviet Union today. They also analyzed the power potential of Russia and explored the philosophical values which India has to offer to world understanding. The sophomores, who led and participated in discussion groups with the high school students, found the experience an effective stimulus to review and to engage in additional learning.

Regional study tours, an annual feature planned for the Seminar, is to provide visits during which further information about areas already studied may be acquired. One group is to visit Russian and Indian Embassies, as well as the State Department, in Washington. A comparison is also to be made of the Tennessee Valley Authority, by actual observation, with similar resource developments in other countries. Another group will visit the International Civil Aeronautics Organizations headquarters in Montreal. A third will spend a day at the United Nations and meet with Indian, Pakistani, Syrian, and Israeli delegations as well as with experts on the Soviet Union in New York.

The faculty and students have had a number of difficult problems to overcome. Willimantic, a small teachers college, has a limited budget for books and this is a handicap to studies such as these. The staff also faced a challenging task in preparing themselves to teach adequately in unfamiliar areas. For students, the Seminar was an entirely new approach to college study. Understanding of Russian and Indian cultures, which were also strange and new, presented many problems.

It is too early in the experience of the Seminar to tell just what has been achieved, but the evaluations of students and faculty indicate that the Seminar has been a satisfying experience for all the staff and for most students. Many students say they are now keeping more closely in touch with world affairs, have learned much they did not know before, and have had raised in their minds new questions, not just about the areas studied, but about world affairs in general. They realize, too, that they have to observe future developments to find answers to their questions. As the program is repeated, some minor changes growing out of the initial experience will be made.

Student Teachers Develop International Understanding

In the belief that the teacher's attitudes are basic to all considerations of world understanding and human relationships, student teachers at the University of Redlands in California are given many opportunities to analyze their own feelings and to bring their own view of the world and its peoples into focus. Students are led to discover what they need to know about the other people of the world, of their own country, and of the community.

Acceptance of the families and the cultural backgrounds from which the children in American schools come leads beginning teachers into a growing awareness and understanding of children's attitudes and behavior in terms of causes. Belief that there is no insignificant member in any group, whether his minority springs from race, nationality, religion, economics, or native abilities is a basic philosophy which underlies each student teacher's activities in his practice situation.

It is believed that an understanding of the people of the world begins in American classrooms, in situations where the principles of democratic action are in complete acceptance. The climate of opinion of classrooms is observed, analyzed, and studied by students. A diagnosis of the elements of autocratic, democratic, and laissez-faire control is made in classes preceding student teaching. A great deal of discussion on actual experiences is carried on, also, in the problems courses which are taken concurrently with student teaching.

An overview of the dynamics of group action, suitable to both elementary and secondary classrooms, is an important phase of the background for students in the courses leading to student teaching. Problem-solving through role playing is studied. Elementary pre-student teaching classes observe demonstrations of role playing. Student teachers learn sociometric techniques, bring sociograms to the problems courses, and share the findings and analyze causes of poor relationships.

Prior to student teaching, the program recommended for the elementary schools of California by the State Framework for the Social Studies is carefully studied and each student prepares a unit of work for a chosen grade and area. "How man has worked together in developing his basic needs of living and of his need for government, both in America and throughout the world," comprise this program. In these ways the student is led to seek understanding of promising ways of leading children to learn about the people of other countries, their cultural differences, geographic conditions, and related problems.

UNESCO materials are available for study and analysis in the Curriculum Laboratory. Often the public attacks on UNESCO in the schools has led to an evaluation of the specific materials under fire. Search for the objectionable materials alleged to have been present has been made in the spirit of free inquiry and investigation.

International news is being stressed by student teachers in the upper elementary grades. They have reported their techniques of handling current events. Critical analyses of the relative value of current events items was instigated by one student teacher in the sixth grade, in which a series of cards was devised, with a check list for evaluating three current events in terms of world importance. As a result of this research students soon improved the selections which they shared with the class. Another student teacher who asked his pupils to give current events in their own words noted a marked increase in attention from the class.

In the placement of student teachers in public elementary classrooms, the university has had excellent success in sending members of racial minorities to schools where no students of these groups were in attendance. When two Negro women student teachers worked in such schools, the principals reported no adverse comments from teachers, students, or parents. Other students of differing national backgrounds complete their work without discrimination of any kind. In recent years student teachers of Chinese, Japanese, Korean, and Mexican descent have thus been placed in public school teaching situations. Supervising and demonstration teachers are chosen by the university in terms of competence and often represent, in consequence, minority groups.

Each summer a workshop in international relations is held at the university. Here many teachers inservice as well as student teachers and pre-student teachers work together, often with authorities in the field.

Community service is encouraged as a pre-student teaching activity, especially in such situations as the House of Neighborly Service in Redlands, which is an activities center for Mexican-American townspeople. One university student accepted the responsibility for leading a group of teen-age boys who chose to study etiquette during their weekly evening meetings. He reported great benefit in understanding and appreciation from the experience. Such community activities are included in the extracurricular program of the secondary teachers. Many school activities, including the sponsorship of clubs and the preparation of assembly programs, often of an intercultural nature, are included as well.

Basic to the education of student teachers at the University of Redlands is the belief that America should be considered realistically in both its historic and present world settings. The nature of American world leadership must be examined freely and issues must be clarified, even where controversial aspects are apparent. We assume that it is not enough to believe in democracy. We must also know how the principles of democracy work, both in and outside of the classroom. Through this interaction, we believe we will learn better to know how other people think and feel. Thus, it is hoped a sound basis for the development of both good human relations and international understanding will be laid.

Foreign Languages as Bridges to Other Cultures

Many linguistic approaches to foreign cultures are possible. In a secondary school or college there is no need to postpone these until the third year, when a comparatively small number of students are ready to read an advanced cultural reader. Several practical approaches are used in the first year of French, German, and Spanish at the State University Teachers College at Oneonta, New York.

At Oneonta the language teacher believes in intensive pronunciation practice from the first day, connecting the words with tangible objects. Before they attempt to write students must achieve coordination of the eye, ear, and vocal organs to utter the strange sounds with ease. They must realize from the beginning that they are dealing with a living language, spoken by real people. After a few weeks of fundamentals they listen to and imitate recorded voices of cultured natives discussing a variety of practical situations which an American would encounter abroad. Just as different people speak English correctly but with a variety of intonations and speech habits, the students rapidly discover that this is likewise true for other languages. The records are graduated in difficulty and the students use printed texts with them.

Students at the State University Teachers College also use a basic text which combines graded conversations and readings, set in the appropriate foreign locale, with the necessary minimum of grammatical principles. Some of the written exercises are assigned, but the primary emphasis remains on the oral-aural skills. After a few months the students are ready for carefully selected foreign language films. These can greatly broaden student understanding of other cultures, even though some parts of the sound track may not be clear.

The *Encyclopedia Britannica* has issued two very effective short films for first-year use: *Une Famille Bretonne* in French and *La Familia Sánchez* in Spanish. Both are simple but authentic. The first depicts the daily activities of an average family in Britanny. The second does the same for a rural family in southern Spain. The sound tracks, each prepared by a native professor with long American experience, encourage the students because they are deliberate and clear. Although limited to the 1000 most frequently used words, they successfully present foreign family life in adult conversation. The viewer begins to realize that one need not acquire a 10,000-word vocabulary before attempting conversation.

The University of Wisconsin has recently produced five German teaching films of graduated difficulty. They have proved helpful even in the first year at Oneonta. Each presents a normal situation in Germany, showing a man and a woman conversing at average speed. The speakers then utter each sentence slowly in a closeup, with the German text flashed the second time. An English translation accompanies the spoken German the third time.

After the basic classroom vocabulary is mastered, travel posters and particularly large, detailed maps printed in the foreign language under study are valuable conversational props. Geography takes on new meaning as the teacher discusses cities and rivers in simple French or German, asking the students to repeat the names and some of the basic facts, and encouraging questions.

A popular conversational device for the second semester of first-year Spanish is "La Carretera Panamericana"—the Pan American Highway—a discussion which gives unity to the very diverse Latin-American republics. The complete projected highway route is traced in red on a large map, with discussion in simple Spanish of the scenery, peoples, products, and cities along the route. The fact that members of the student body have actually toured parts of the highway enlivens the discussion.

Oneonta students are surprised to learn that there are over 20,000,-000 loyal Americans whose mother tongue is other than English.

Maintaining their cultural ties, these people create a demand for foreign language newspapers of high quality, such as *France-Amérique, La Prensa,* and the *Staats-Zeitung und Herold,* all published in New York City. Enough copies of a single issue can be purchased to supply a class. Even a first-year group enjoys guessing the meanings of headlines and advertisements because of their timeliness and their resemblance to those in English-language newspapers. Again the class is dealing with living people and events, not dead disciplines.

Foreign nationals who visit Oneonta also motivate undergraduates to meet the French or the Spanish mind on a common ground. Ten young French people who spent two weeks here, under the Experiment in International Living, aroused more interest than a whole library of books. Oneontans were impressed with their maturity and at the same time were agreeably surprised to discover that French boys and girls enjoy tennis, swimming, bridge, and dancing just as much as young Americans do.

Almost every sizeable college has a few students who speak European languages. Their possible contributions are often neglected. Such students have successfully taught full semester units in both French and Spanish in the fourth and fifth grades in the Bugbee School of Practice at Oneonta. A native of Dijon in the Oneonta student body gave a talk about his lovely province which kept students on the edge of their seats. On another occasion a second-year Spanish class had difficulty understanding some rapid-fire musical records imported from Seville. A student of Spanish parentage listened with the class and carefully explained the emotional and social background of each song. Some had been brought to Spain in remote times by the gypsies. Others, with complex Oriental rhythm, dated back to the Moors and still others, called *romances,* were derived from Spanish folklore of the fifteenth century. Thus, the students caught a glimpse of the history of Spain through the panorama of its music and gained a new appreciation of a colorful culture.

To teach effectively, language specialists should make a serious study of the history, folklore, arts and crafts, proverbs, and particularly, the anthropology of the areas where their languages are spoken. Possibilities for experimentation in the language classroom are limited only by time. Suggestions from students can be very helpful. The alert language teacher should always be on the lookout for new laboratory devices to broaden students' understanding of foreign peoples.

Comparative Education in New Perspective

Anyone familiar with the field of Comparative Education knows of the fruitlessness and futility of the task of studying each of the national systems of education as if it were an isolated entity. The foundations of the course, if they are to be fruitful, must be laid in the broader areas of cultural development and the economic, social, and political trends of the past century.

Since the close of World War II the course in Comparative Education at the University of Missouri has been under constant revision with the following objectives in mind:

1. To orient and more completely sensitize the student to our present international situation, especially with reference to educational conditions and needs

2. To study organized efforts in the field of international education, with special emphasis on the work of UNESCO and its program of Fundamental Education

3. To make a comparative analysis of various national systems of education representative of varying broad cultural areas throughout the world

In achieving our first objective pointed reference is made to the following:

1. Recent industrial and technological developments and their educational and social effect on world cultures

2. The movement toward nationalism and the rise of national systems of education (The Nazi-Fascist and Communist movements are compared with the liberal and democratic traditions in France, England and the United States.)

3. Twentieth-century intellectual developments in the fields of the physical, biological, and social sciences, as well as in philosophy and the arts

Materials for a study of each of these areas are plentiful, but the amount of time devoted to their use must be limited by the nature of the course. As basic material for this area, I. L. Kandel, *Comparative Education,* chapters I, II, and III, has been used, along with James Mulhern, *History of Education,* chapters 13, 14, and 15.

To supplement the numerous materials available for a discussion of organized efforts in the field of international education, the Eleventh Yearbook of the John Dewey Society, *Education for a World Society,* and the UNESCO publication, *Fundamental Education, Common Grounds for All People,* were found to be most useful. Here fundamental education for all peoples is considered as the core of our international needs. The John Dewey Society study has been found to be particularly valuable for an analysis of the varied nature of our present international education efforts. Major consideration has been given to such areas as human rights, the creating of attitudes conducive to international understanding, world trade, world religions, mass communication media, political activities, the scientific movement, the educational efforts, and the relation of all these areas to the problem of world peace.

In making a comparative analysis of the various national systems of education, the world is treated in terms of seven basic culture areas: (1) Anglo-Saxon, including the United States and Canada; (2) Northern countries of Europe, including Germany; (3) Area of the Romance languages, including countries of South America; (4) Union of Soviet Socialist Republics; (5) The Orient, especially Japan, China, and India; (6) Countries of the Mohammedan world; and (7) African colonial cultures.

To implement our study in this area each student carries on individual research and investigation in one of the countries in these areas. In addition, class reports are given, at which time students or individuals from representative foreign countries are invited to attend and participate in the class discussions. To obtain maximum group responsibility and initiative in these studies Arthur H. Moehlman's and Joseph S. Roucek's, *Comparative Education,* is used as a basic outline.

In studying a national system of education primary emphasis is placed upon present educational conditions, especially as they have been determined by the religious, political, social, and economic conditions of the country. Every effort is made to understand the people in terms of their needs, interests, and cultural origin.

An Experiment in International Understanding

On August 1, 1953, a group of eighteen students and two instructors boarded the Missouri Pacific Texas Eagle out of St. Louis bound for San Miguel de Allende, a town of 10,000 people located in central Mexico, to begin a four-week study of Mexican life under the direction of a Mexican anthropologist. The group lived and studied together at the Instituto Allende, a school of fine arts which is affiliated with the University of Guanajuato. All were housed and had their meals in a modern hotel on the grounds of the Instituto, which overlooked the town of San Miguel.

The Seminar was organized as a course for four units of credit in the Summer School at Washington University in St. Louis and was open to both upper classmen and graduate students, at a cost of $275.00 for each student. This included tuition, transportation, room and board. It had been estimated correctly that another $50.00 would be needed for incidental expenses, including meals on the train and transportation charges on field trips while in Mexico.

In planning and organizing the Seminar the primary objective was to contribute to international understanding. This was to be done by providing students with an opportunity of studying at first hand a culture quite different from their own. The plan was to have the students spend this month in Mexico studying the country, the people and their institutions, under the direction of a competent scholar.

The reason for selecting Mexico as the foreign culture was its proximity. The reason for selecting San Miguel de Allende was, first of all, its size and location. The idea was to get a community small enough so that students could get acquainted, but large enough so that 25 Americans would not be conspicuous. The town had also been highly recommended on the basis of a personal experience.

The idea of having the students spend the month touring Mexico had been considered but rejected. It was decided that the objectives of the Seminar could be more fully achieved by having the group live and study in one community.

The Seminar was planned largely for teachers or prospective teachers. If it is important for the average citizen to have a better understanding of the world in which he lives, it is even more important for teachers to have this understanding. This was a basic belief underlying the whole program. There are many ways of building understanding and of contributing to world peace, and certainly any and all efforts are desperately needed. But no area of endeavor would appear to offer greater potential for developing understanding than working through teachers. Each has some influence over a generation of children.

The academic program of the Seminar centered around four major areas: A broad survey of Mexico, the land, its people and their institutions from an historical standpoint; a concentrated study of the language, with the accent on speaking and understanding and, hence, a de-emphasis on grammar; a study of San Miguel as a Mexican community; and a series of field trips designed to relate what was being learned in the classroom to the actual conditions of Mexican life. In addition, the students were encouraged to participate in the Instituto's full program. This included classes in painting, sculpture, weaving, silverwork, ceramics, and photography.

In the third major phase of the academic program, the Community Study of San Miguel, the idea was to have students make a relatively intensive analysis of the community in which they were living. One side of the educational logic was that they could thus probably understand more of what they had actually seen and experienced. They were urged, therefore, to use their spare time in the first two weeks to get acquainted with the town. In the third week, guided visits were made to schools, churches, factories, and homes. A series of lectures also began at this time in which an instructor analyzed San Miguel as a community.

The other side of the educational logic was that a general survey of Mexico would become more meaningful if it could be focused on specific experiences of the students. For example, the breakdown of the haciendas, which occurred on a national level, also occurred in San Miguel. The group saw the old haciendas around San Miguel and the instructor discussed the effect of the change on the individuals concerned. In short, it was hoped that students would learn a great deal about Mexico as a nation. It was felt that focusing attention upon the community with which they were familiar might avoid the pitfall of superficiality and facilitate the development of a maximum of understanding.

During the first week the students became acquainted with the town and most of the shops. The evening after arrival a reception was arranged by the wife of the owner of the Instituto. In attendance were the staff, the students, and many of the prominent figures in the community, including the mayor. As a result of this evening, some of the students received and accepted invitations to visit homes in

San Miguel. From that time on all were free to attend concerts, dances, fiestas, and had an opportunity to see Mexicans in action and to meet them personally.

On Sunday most of the group attended church, although only a few were members of the Catholic faith. After the service on Sunday many went to the market place. In San Miguel, as in many other towns visited, including Mexico City, Sunday was the big market day, being the day when all the farmers from the surrounding countryside came to town. Going through the market and bargaining with merchants in poor Spanish proved to be an education in itself.

On Sunday afternoon the feature attraction was a band concert in the Plaza. Most of the inhabitants of San Miguel seemed to be out in their Sunday finest. The American visitors sat in the sun and watched. On Sunday evening the promenading began around the square, the girls going one way and the boys the other—a rather different approach to courtship than in Missouri. In the old days the best families promenaded in the inner circles with the poorer Mexicans on the outside. Since the revolution this is no longer compulsory, yet the custom is still observed.

It is impossible to measure the value of these experiences. An intelligent, alert, and friendly individual who works at his Spanish can learn a great deal about Mexico through such first-hand contacts. Most of the visiting students came to like the Mexicans. They were so friendly and cheerful, despite their poverty, it was hard not to like them.

As a result of this entire experience, the visiting instructors became convinced that such a program is of great value in the education of teachers and that every effort should be expended to make it available to as many teachers as possible. It is certain that the students learned a great deal about Mexico and that many of them developed a positive, human interest in the Mexican people. All gained some insight into the nature and complexity of the race problem inherent in the situation, especially as five of the student group were Negroes. Most students improved their attitudes in this respect. Moreover, a new interest in international affairs became apparent. Many realized their inadequacies in terms of knowledge and have been stimulated to begin studying in these areas. There seems no doubt that these students will be better teachers because of this Mexican study experience.

The organization of the Seminar seemed to be sound. The basic elements in the pattern were:

1. That the group be limited to twenty-five students
2. That most of the instruction be given by a scholar who is an English-speaking native of the country being visited
3. That the group be based in one place and live and study there as opposed to a travel tour
4. That the academic program be directed toward an understanding of the way of life of a people as a whole and therefore that such areas as art, religion, philosophy, and education be included

At least three changes might be made, however. The first is that the time of the Seminar be extended from four to five weeks. The credit should remain at four hours. The second recommendation is that a more extensive preparatory program be undertaken. If students could enroll in language or area study classes and begin studying months in advance, this would be excellent. Third, textbooks, maps, and other materials of instruction should be purchased in advance and taken along. A good text, especially, could serve as a source book. Such materials are not available in Mexico.

There should be no illusions concerning the results to be expected from taking twenty-five teachers to Mexico for one month. But it is one way of giving substance to the task of training teachers who can help build a world community based upon mutual respect and understanding. If enough American teachers could have such an experience, the next generation of Americans might have a better chance of creating the conditions necessary for men of all nations to live together in peace.

Forums on World Affairs

The forum program is the answer of Long Beach City College to the growing desire of the many families of World War II servicemen and defense workers to learn more about world affairs. At first, qualified full-time teachers were sent out to the different branches of the public library to lecture and to lead discussion groups on world affairs. In 1954 this forum program filled two entire pages of the school's catalog and public response called for further expansion.

Under the jurisdiction of the School for Adults three kinds of forum are offered: Forum Discussions, Forum Celebrity Series, and

Forum Film Lectures. All classes are held in accordance with the rules of the California State Department of Education to "provide free discussions of public affairs under qualified leadership." The discussions are weekly three-hour sessions, which take place in the best located school and library buildings throughout the city during morning, afternoon, and evening hours. Two courses, World in the News and Cultural Backgrounds of Current Events, are offered. Any citizen may take one or both classes for credit toward graduation from Long Beach City College but these credits are not transferable.

The lecture and discussion methods are supplemented by audio-visual material, such as films, slides, and news pictures. Copies of the monthly bulletin, *Foreign Affairs,* are provided for additional reading. Forum leaders are fully qualified and under full-time contract. In selecting instructors the school not only considers training in international relations but recent travel experiences.

The Forum Celebrity Series, is a community-wide undertaking. Long Beach City College attempts to bring personalities prominent in the news to the city for lecture engagements. Thus, in the fall of 1954, direct information on world affairs came from such speakers as Drew Pearson, Eleanor Roosevelt, and Douglas R. Stringfellow. These lectures have become so much of a public institution that available accommodations are usually exhausted long before the semester opens.

The Forum Film Lectures, during the fall of 1954, were concerned with countries currently in the news. For each country that appeared prominently in the news the best available all-color film was selected. The author of the book upon which the selected film was based was invited to Long Beach for a series of lectures. In this manner, as many as seven countries were presented during one semester. Each film was shown on successive evenings in an uptown, downtown, and suburban location. The school's catalog for 1954 listed among other films: *Southeast Asia,* with Joe Fisher; *Hongkong,* with Phil Walker; *Pakistan,* with Hal Linker; and *Austria,* with Robert Mallet.

The studious citizens attending these sessions total about 4000 per week. Again registration is of necessity closed weeks before the first lecture is offered. As stated previously, all forums are included in the college program. They are listed both in semester class schedules and college catalogs as available either for academic credit or for audit.

International Relations Education for New Citizens

The variety of nationalities, religions, colors, and creeds found in the New York City English and Citizenship Adult Elementary Classes establishes them as a fundamental place for instruction in international relations. The writer is a teacher in this program.

The goal of the classes extends beyond the mere preparation for naturalization. Effort is made to augment the basic skills and attitudes needed for living in present-day America. Attempts are made to help the individual adjust to changing national and international conditions. The role of international relations education in the present curriculum, then, becomes very significant. The curriculum includes the study of such aspects of living as: the home, the occupation, health, safety, intergroup relations, international relations, recreation, and leisure-time activities.

The students are classified as Beginners, Intermediates, and Advanced. These classifications are based on levels of literacy. Units utilized are:

1. The United Nations: charter, structure, affiliated agencies, accomplishments

2. Brotherhood: neighborliness, permanent international friendship, ties that bind humanity, living in a diversified community, people of different nations work together for peace and security and international peace

3. America and Europe: social, economic, and cultural ties, common struggle for nationalism and democracy

4. Current Affairs: news items, American military and financial aid, famine, earthquake, storm, flood, volcanic eruption, revolution, persecution

5. The United States and the Immigrant: past and present policy, when and why they came en masse, where many nationalities concentrated, occupations, the culture, science, and knowledge they brought

6. International Relations in New York City: Melting Pot theory, native neighborhoods, China Town, Lower East Side, Little Italy, Harlem, Puerto Rican problem, art and cultural center of the world

Methods of teaching depend largely upon the membership of the class and the level of students' literacy. Teachers prefer to teach non-English-speaking students through a direct method of conversation and dramatization. They use the theme approach when all class members do not understand the same language. Some examples of themes used are: "I buy a United Nations stamp," "I go on the subway to China Town," "I greet a German friend," "I buy an imported pair of shoes," or "I go to church." Each theme easily lends itself to dramatization.

Teachers are not bound by ironclad rules in reference to either subject matter or method. They frequently must disregard literacy levels in the process of meeting the learner's personal and social needs and in guiding them into an understanding of the American way of life. Wherever possible learning experiences are provided in the area of international relations, for it is thought that if the emerging citizen is to be brought to some understanding of the United States today that understanding must include the larger world of which our country is but an important part.

A World Affairs Class for the Community

Junior colleges are community colleges. An excellent way of attaining a portion of this aim is to provide a weekly series of evening discussions on world affairs for the community. For the last four years, Orange Coast College in California has operated such a program with increasing success. When the project was first planned, only a handful of people enrolled and the initial meetings were almost tutorial sessions. Through trial and error there finally emerged a pattern which was successful in retaining old friends and reaching new ones. Average attendance rose from about 18 the first term to a current level of 45. As high as 68 people have attended in one night.

Yet more important than numbers is the type of personnel attracted. Doctors, military officers from nearby camps, elementary and secondary school teachers, Girl Scout officials, business men, and other professional people make up a substantial portion of the class. With the present boom in international travel, it is interesting to note that one member has been using the class to develop an appreciation of foreign cultures in her work as a tour leader for a local travel agency. Possibly one of the best ways to aid world understanding is to help the American tourist in the human relations of travel. Other members have used the class in preparation for their first trip abroad. The total number enrolled during the last four years has been over

650. Since some have re-enrolled, the number of different people reached is about 400.

The two-hour class period is divided into two parts. The first part is devoted to current trends. In reviewing the happenings of the week, informality is the keynote. Citizens of the community, attending such a class, are usually not concerned with grades or units of credit. Their interest must be aroused and kept by meaningful information. About twelve or fifteen items of significance are selected and discussed.

A PicQuiz has proved quite effective in learning to recognize the leaders of various countries. Large pictures such as those found on the colored covers of weekly news magazines have been mounted on cardboard and are held up or passed around for identification. Such leaders as Adenauer of West Germany, Malan of South Africa, and Nehru of India become real personalities when thus identified.

Filmstrips have been used with some success. The most effective have been certain strips in *The New York Times* and *Life* magazine series. Diplomatic offices of the various countries usually have films which are both attractive and informative. The one produced by the Turkish Information Center and a British film release on the locust problem are examples. Colored slides of travel done by class members and the instructor have proved stimulating. The use of films, however, can be overdone. In an age of television and third-dimension movies, it is difficult to hold a community group with mediocre material. The give and take of open discussion, which is neither feasible nor available in the realm of public entertainment, still remains one of the school's best assets.

By request, map work was introduced and was immediately successful. The identification of countries, rivers, and cities provided a challenge to the geographical knowledge, or lack thereof, of the members. Initially the instructor felt that this type of activity might be considered too elementary but fortunately the reverse was found to be true. Ditto-graphed maps, in several colors, which emphasize a particular trend, e.g., countries belonging to the Council of Europe, have become a regular feature of the class. Space for notes is provided. Some members have requested extra copies for their club or church groups. Once a ditto carbon is developed, it is easy and inexpensive to duplicate a hundred or more. Consequently, the college has usually granted such requests as a community service.

As a result of various trips by the instructor, letters from Europeans are received and have been read to the class. These letters represent an additional channel of information which supplements and enriches the material available through the usual diplomatic and journalistic avenues. The Europeans are requested to comment in their letters on certain world problems and answer questions raised by the class. In return, they have asked and received information from the American side. This activity could almost be termed a modern committee of correspondence. The members value highly the sharing of views with other people on the nongovernmental, noncommercial level.

Outside speakers have been used sparingly. As in the case of films, the problem seems to be that in the present sociological climate, most people have ample opportunity to hear outstanding speakers via television and radio. The technique of interviewing a guest speaker, rather than having him give a lecture, has been found fruitful. Leading questions are asked by the instructor and answers soon result in an open forum which is really open. Successful interviews of this sort have been held with such people as an exchange teacher from Holland, a Pakistani visiting the area, students from abroad attending the college, and servicemen who have returned from various parts of the world.

Based on the assumption that world understanding is something more than an attempt to keep abreast of changing trends, the second part of the evening class is devoted to background material covering some movement, tension point, or area. Through lectures, charts, filmstrips, maps, and blackboard demonstrations, the history and cultures of the countries of Southeast Asia are presented.

The theories or patterns of history have formed another series, e.g., the "Great Man Theory" of Thomas Carlyle, Toynbee's "Challenge and Response," the morphological thesis of Oswald Spengler, and the theory of progress. Tension points in the cold war were studied, including the future of Germany and Austria, European Defense Community, Formosa, the Saar, and the problem of world trade.

One evening was devoted to the study of price supports for wheat; another to the tariff on tuna, which is a local industry; and a third to the Bricker amendment. These topics may seem national in nature, yet each has ramifications in international affairs. How America solves her farm surplus problems, and, in particular, whether the world price structure is affected by that solution, is vital. The tariff and its by-products are full of opportunities and pitfalls for our country, her friends and the world. And the famous "which" clause of the Bricker amendment has profound implications in the realm of diplomacy.

Reaction of class members has been encouraging. Some have attended for years. Others attend for a time. A good deal of esprit de corps has developed. New friendships are made as Americans in all walks of life sit, listen, and talk together about their country and its world. A recent survey showed that 58 per cent of the class had first learned about it through a friend. At the close of each term the members usually arrange an informal social of coffee, cake, and cookies. A final examination is given and, although the number of auditors compared to credit-earners is about ten to one, all are urged to attempt the test and most do so.

Several suggestions arise from this experience. In starting such a group, leaders should not be too easily discouraged if the initial response is small. Unlike many night classes, attendance at the world affairs course start low and grow slowly. Classes in cake decorating, lampshade making, or ceramics have effective pulling power so that groups are large and demands seems high. But the turnover is great. Once the lampshade is made, the cake decorated, or the dish glazed, the student may want to turn to something else. World affairs can and should be a continuous hobby which grows with age. A small beginning can pay large dividends eventually.

The teacher selected for the course should not only have an adequate academic background but should, if at all possible, have done some foreign travel. Foundations which administer hundreds of thousands of dollars each year to improve instruction might well investigate the need and opportunity for establishing some sort of a program which would enable alert social science teachers to experience other cultures rather than merely read about them. Travel provides insights which are obtained in no other way. In addition, the community will react more favorably to a class which is led by a person who speaks from the experience of having trod upon the streets of a few world capitals.

It is difficult to measure growth of international understanding. No claim is made that world conflicts are nearer solution merely because knowledge of the field has been imparted. But student interest is high. It is refreshing to find a class that does not want to take a holiday. Twice the weekly class session has been moved to another night in order that a national holiday would not interefere with the program. Such action was entirely student-inspired. As can be imagined, the teacher could have had mixed emotions. Yet why should learning take a holiday, particularly in the field of world affairs where no holidays occur?

CHAPTER 10

Out-of-Class Activities

THERE are many ways by which colleges, teacher education institutions, and adult education agencies can further an understanding of world affairs through out-of-class activities. Student organizations of various kinds, such as international relations clubs, come to mind, as do debating societies, conferences, forums, and assemblies which deal with world affairs. Such other approaches as the following appear promising: assistance to foreign students, the sending of student and teacher representatives abroad, active participation in international organizations, the use of community resources, and cooperative programs with community groups. Only a small number of such possibilities are here presented.

The reader will note, as elsewhere in this study, that various devices have been worked out by which people are enabled to learn by direct experience. Students from abroad are brought into American homes, Mexican teachers visit the United States, and American teachers go to Mexico.

Exchanges developed through community-wide participation and assistance have obvious advantages over those which are carried out as between educational institutions. At all events, it appears desirable that bi-national visitation should enable participants to see and learn to know people who are engaged in occupations similar to their own. Identification is thereby facilitated. It should be added, however, that visitation should include people from other walks of life as well.

It appears appropriate, finally, to observe that these descriptions center directly upon the large job of building the peace. They serve as evidence of the fact that there are in American colleges today people who stand ready to utilize research and local mass media to resolve the greatest task of our age, namely, finding ways of learning how to live peacefully together.

A Collection for Peace

The Swarthmore College Peace Collection was founded in 1935 in memory of Jane Addams, the famous social worker of Hull House and 1930 winner of the Nobel Peace Award. Her papers, which form the nucleus of the Collection, begin with a letter written in her tenth year from her home in Cedarville, Illinois. They cover her long life and are filled with records of her work for the betterment of humanity.

The Women's International League for Peace and Freedom, of which Miss Addams was the founder and president from 1915 until her death in 1935, has designated the Peace Collection as the depository for all its papers. Five other leading peace organizations likewise send their papers to Swarthmore for permanent safekeeping. Holdings relating to many important peace leaders at home and abroad add to the value of the Collection. Records of William Ladd, the Maine sea captain, founder of the American Peace Society; Elihu Burritt, the learned blacksmith; and many other significant American figures are represented.

A book and pamphlet collection on subjects such as disarmament, nonresistance, conscientious objection, conscription, and peace education forms an important part of the Collection. Some of the titles date back several hundred years and many carry inscriptions of important peace workers at home and abroad.

The periodical section of the Peace Collection is rich in its variety of languages represented. Some of its titles date as far back as the first half of the last century when the American and British peace movements first flourished.

A useful tool for students of peace is the subject file at Swarthmore. In it are folders containing printed and processed material on over 100 subjects relating to the peace movement, civil liberties, interracial questions, and education for peace. Here are to be found programs and bibliographies on peace, adult study outlines, material for discussion groups, Sunday School programs, and suggestions for celebrations of national holidays along peaceful lines.

Unusual features are a large set of posters of about 2000 items, which include special collections, as well as boxes of peace plays, both adult and juvenile. Among the greatest treasures are 25 manuscript letters by Gandhi and the Nobel Peace Prize gold medal awarded to Jane Addams in 1930.

Cataloged books and pamphlets in the Peace Collection may be borrowed through interlibrary loan. Other material is available for use only at the Collection. Reference questions by mail are given prompt attention.

A Social Science Foundation

Just over thirty years ago, James H. Causey established the Social Science Foundation at the University of Denver. Its purpose was, and continues to be, to bring capital and labor into closer relationships through a better understanding of international relations problems. Its program is both community and college oriented.

The community program strives to alert adult citizens of Denver to their responsibilities in the world beyond America's borders. Through the years, the Foundation has brought to the Rocky Mountain area more than 800 visiting experts in the field of international affairs. They have spoken at public meetings and served as a resource for discussion groups, institutes, and conferences attended by Denverites. These experts have included ministers of foreign affairs, newspaper reporters and publishers, educators representing all academic disciplines, radio commentators, religious leaders, and social workers.

Usually the focus of meetings is on the background of a currently important issue in world politics. For example, in 1932–33 all of the Foundation's lectures and conferences dealt with the problems of Japan and Manchuria. In 1937–38 the emphasis was on Latin America. The international political implications of the development of atomic energy held the spotlight in 1945–46. The foreign policy of the Union of Soviet Socialist Republics was the theme of the community program in 1949–50.

America's mid-century year, 1951, was devoted to a year-long inquiry into "The Prospect for Freedom in the Last Half of the Twentieth Century." Citizens' committees representing every phase of the Rocky Mountain region's life participated in the study which culminated in a ten-weeks summer institute on this problem. Statesmen, educators, and industrial, labor, and cultural leaders, drawn from here and abroad, took part and more than 40,000 people participated in the program.

By means of radio and television, the Foundation attempts to bring an understanding of world affairs to that portion of the public which does not participate in its conferences and lecture-discussion series. Each week for sixteen years it has presented a fifteen-minute analysis of world problems under the title *Journeys Behind the News*. This program is broadcast by two stations in Denver and by recordings on numerous other stations throughout the United States. In addition, approximately 17,000 mimeographed copies of the radio scripts are distributed to libraries, schools, and individuals throughout the United States.

With the introduction of television into Denver in 1951 the Foundation began to make use of this new medium for adult education. The first fifteen minutes of the telecast is an analysis of a single international problem, utilizing films, charts, maps, and dramatic sketches. The final fifteen minutes is a discussion by guest experts of the current issues involved in the problem. Regularly conducted scientific polls indicate that each telecast commands an audience of 10,000 viewers. Approximately 6 per cent of the residents of Denver listen to *Journeys Behind the News* on the radio.

In its community program the Foundation also works closely with educators and students in Colorado public schools in a joint exploration of America's responsibility in international affairs. In cooperation with the World Understanding Committee of the Colorado Education Association, the Foundation prepares study outlines, bibliographies, and teaching materials for high school social studies teachers and sponsors of International Relations Clubs. Annually since 1933 the Foundation has convened a High School International Relations Conference which brings approximately four hundred teachers and students from high schools throughout the state to the University campus for discussion of major issues of international interest, and consultation on teaching projects and activities.

Within the University of Denver itself the Foundation is designated as the Department of International Relations. It maintains a separate library of materials on world affairs and six members of its staff offer a wide variety of courses in International Relations.

In the undergraduate area, the primary objective has been to give a maximum number of students in the University an adequate understanding of international relations for effective citizenship in the modern world. On the graduate level, the objective is to prepare students for careers in international service, in diplomacy, politics, and public administration, in commerce, education, cultural relations, journalism, and radio, as well as other areas of endeavor which transcend national boundaries. The Foundation, in cooperation with the University, offers unusual training possibilities in the combined fields of adult education and international relations.

Another unique possibility is combined training in radio-television and international relations. Here leaders can be trained in the content of world politics, and at the same time acquire some of the skills needed to make that content palatable to nonspecialists and adult education groups. Experimentation is also under way in the application of the behavioral sciences to the study of world affairs. This is an attempt to discover what insights psychology, sociology, and anthropology may provide for the understanding of international relations.

Research Exchange on the Prevention of War

The Research Exchange on the Prevention of War with head-quarters at the University of Illinois, has been in existence since September, 1952. It was organized by a group of social scientists who have been concerned with the problem of war prevention and whose members believe that social science research can contribute to the elimination of war. It is felt that the complexities in the study of the causes of war and their implications require the joint efforts of people from all social science disciplines.

The primary purpose of the Research Exchange is to provide a means of communication among individuals interested in research relevant to war prevention. During the past two years one of the major activities has been the publication of a bulletin. Ten issues have been published. They contain research ideas, articles suggesting directions which research should take, reviews of past works, and announcements of on-going projects.

Another function of the organization is to arrange meetings at professional conventions. A symposium was sponsored at the Eastern Psychological Association meetings in April, 1953. Another was sponsored at the joint meetings of the Society for the Study of Social Problems and the Society for the Psychological Study of Social Issues in February, 1954. Other informal meetings and discussion sessions have been held in various parts of the country. The first year was brought to a close with a workshop in which the emphasis was on building a specific framework for research. The workshop is planned as an annual event.

The members of the Research Exchange hope that these efforts at communication will encourage and improve individual research projects. They should also foster collaborative research studies, joint editing of publications, and coordinated projects for the application of social science knowledge. The eventual goal of such intercommunication and collaboration is the development of an integrated and usable body of knowledge about the elimination of war.

The organization invites all social scientists to join. At the present time about 200 social scientists from different disciplines are associated with the Research Exchange. Not nearly all of these people are active participants in the work of the Exchange. As the work progresses, however, it is believed that there will be many more active members. The active contributors make up the administrative and decision making body of the organization which is called the Working Committee. The Working Committee is open to any one who expresses an active interest in the organization. Anyone who is associated is invited to make suggestions about policy or functions of the organization.

Students from Abroad Teach Us

To promote a better understanding of international affairs in the local community, the International Center of the University of Louisville works with many and varied groups in terms of age, education, beliefs, and social standing. In this description attention is especially drawn to ways by which university students from abroad become the teachers of the many adult groups of the community.

Experience has shown that not talk in itself, but the person who does the talking, is of greatest importance to an audience. Consequently, a meeting was held with all foreign students to discuss the value of mutual understanding among the countries of the world. It was pointed out that in spite of superficial differences, all human beings seek the same essential things, such as: security, shelter, food, freedom, justice, and recreation. Regardless of color, or appearance, all people basically are the same. If, therefore, students from abroad would agree to speak about their native countries, basic similarities rather than differences should be stressed. Through this emphasis the students would be enabled to create many personal contacts with different groups in the community. The response was very good.

A booklet was prepared which listed all students from abroad who volunteered to become community speakers. It included also photographs, educational backgrounds, countries, and the subjects on which each would be willing to speak.

In Louisville, there are about 300 civic clubs and women's organizations. The booklet was sent to each program chairman with the offer of free speakers on international subjects. The response was most gratifying. There is not a week when university students from abroad do not speak to two or three groups. Many students have become quite popular in the community and invitations to private parties and homes are many.

Louisville is decidedly an inland city. Only four to five years ago, it was very difficult to find rooms for Indian students because of the color problem. They have meantime become so popular that there is little trouble in arranging social contacts for them.

In the promotional work in the community, there is no ulterior motive. University authorities want merely to have facts presented to local citizens who cannot themselves go abroad. They consider it desirable that citizens learn from visitors who are temporarily residents in our country. Many patriotic organizations appreciate this nonpartisan stand and cooperate fully.

Into American Homes

Students from abroad attending the University of California in Berkeley desired to become acquainted with Americans who live in nonurban communities. They wished to learn of their home life. The Redding Rotary International Service Committee learned of this interest and established a project that was built around a group of hosts who opened their home to lodge and feed the students. In February, 1952, 22 students made the visit which lasted from Monday afternoon until Thursday afternoon. The following year 25 students came to Redding on a Sunday evening and stayed until Thursday. In February, 1954, 26 students came and stayed four full days and nights with a total of 24 hosts. While the majority of these hosts each year were

Rotarians, some non-Rotarians from the community joined in opening their homes to the visitors from abroad.

The public schools have had an active part in the program. During 1954, for example, a program was produced at the local high school by a local radio announcer in which the high school students gave a typical high school program to inform the visitors. Then the International House guests were interviewed and they told things about their lands or gave impressions of America. A similar program was produced at Shasta College in Redding. One of the college organizations, the Campus YMCA, sponsored a reception on Sunday afternoon when the visitors arrived. Several of its members also accompanied the visitors on a number of trips and attended a folk dancing event with them.

The foreign students ate breakfasts and dinners with their hosts, reserving Sunday evening and most of Monday to visit. Most of the hosts went with the students when they were guests of a local folk and square dancing group on one of the evenings. Many of the visitors from abroad proved quite adept in the dance routines and these occasions have been most successful each year.

Over the three-year period 41 countries have been represented by the 73 foreign guests. During the 1954 trip a group visited classes at the Redding Elementary School. One student went with the daughter of her host to her eighth-grade class. Two girls visited and talked with a Girl Scout group.

Each year the students have taken trips to Shasta Dam and Powerhouse. They also have visited Lassen Volcanic Park and were shown through two large lumber and plywood mills. On these trips a group of local junior college students assisted in explaining American life and activities.

Understanding American life by seeing Americans informally in the home atmosphere has certainly been significant. Seeing the dishwasher and the clothes dryer in many homes was one of the material wonders, but after the first thrill these were not the chief interest. The guests were impressed by American hospitality. On the other hand, the Americans were impressed by the high calibre of intelligence, personal charm, and character represented by the visitors. Many a midnight hour was passed before guests and hosts retired.

These visits became well known in the community. The city newspaper entertained the visitors at press time and showed them the operation of a newspaper. Each year the editor has written about these "Ambassadors of Good Will." Students have been interviewed on the radio station, while many have spoken before clubs, both in Redding and neighboring communities.

The climax to the visit each year has been the production of the weekly Rotary program by foreign guests. This program generally includes an invocation in a foreign language by a student, some musical novelty or variety number, and several talks by representative students.

As the University of California bus leaves Redding each year, on a certain Thursday afternoon, there are always many sad adieus from both hosts and from the new college friends. Generally a few tears rush to the cheeks as partings are made. In the hearts of all there is a solid feeling that we have come to know well those who were, but days before, complete strangers—that friendship knows no limitation of border or breed or birth.

A College-Community Program of Tutoring and Guidance

Pasadena, California, a residential and small-industry community of 115,000 residents, each year has thirty to forty persons apply to the city schools for help in learning English. Approximately two-thirds are citizens or citizens-to-be. The others, international students, are guests or relatives of Pasadenans and have come to this country for an education. Their abilities in English range from those who have not yet learned our alphabet to those almost able to carry regular class work. The placing of one or more students in each regular English class is not a satisfactory solution. There are, moreover, too few students to permit setting up classes at each level.

As a technique for obtaining individualized instruction, special classes were initiated in 1950 in which students from Pasadena City College and selected adults from the community provided private tutoring. After several semesters' careful observation, the College offered elective credit to student-tutors. Adult teachers from the community formed an organization to which they gave the name: Pasadena Intercultural Students' Auxiliary. During the past year PISA brought more than 200 tutors to work at the College.

Members of PISA include business men and women, doctors,

lawyers, club women, church and civic leaders, three retired college presidents, and more than sixty retired professors, counsellors, educational administrators, and teachers. Tutoring provides normative conditions for the learning of English. The best students advance from learning their first words in English to the ability to enter university classes in one semester.

Tutoring serves, also, as a method of integration into American community life. Students are assisted in obtaining homes and jobs, and in solving personal problems. Almost without exception, the tutors—some of whom hire baby sitters in order to have time to teach—have noticed changes in their own thinking on intercultural problems.

During the early part of the fourth year of the program, it was decided that, in view of the increasing numbers taking part in the program, and in view of the desirable results of adult participation, a community organization should be formed to assume responsibility for the nonacademic aspects of the program. It was believed that the provision of such services by the community would increase the effectiveness of the program as a two-way educational venture and that the pioneering of such an organization would facilitate the adoption of programs of tutoring and integration by other communities with similar problems.

It is the hope that the community group will acquire property immediately off-campus that will provide facilities in which volunteer workers can give students assistance in finding homes and jobs, as well as recreational facilities. Such a center would also serve as a meeting place for local citizens and persons from other cultures.

Community participation during Thanksgiving and Easter vacations, includes group excursions to points of interest in California and neighboring states. A private bus is chartered by a local service club. Other activities include the adoption of one international student each month by a second service club; the giving of membership in the local YMCA to more than 100 students from other countries; the arranging for the full facilities of the "Y" to be available only to international students and their guests each Sunday afternoon, culminating in a social hour with a different community group each week; and the providing of opportunity for individual and small-group social activities, many of which result in lasting personal friendships and valuable interchange of personal ideas and international cultural concepts.

One of the main objectives of the community group will be to study each incoming student, to consider the facets of American life of which each should be made aware, to offer to each a variety of experiences which will enable him better to understand this country and to decide what of our culture can be of value to him as an individual, as a citizen of his country, and as a member of his profession. It is believed that group-based activities alone are not sufficient for giving intercultural students the many potential benefits of their presence in America.

Bi-National Teacher Exchange

In the spring of 1952 a representative of Pasadena City College formed a committee which included sixteen service clubs, a number of churches, and interested individuals. The purpose was that of carrying out a project in improving understanding between the people of California and the Republic of Mexico. Believing that teachers are a key group, the committee invited the teachers of English of the State of Jalisco to be the guests of the City of Pasadena for four weeks during the summer.

Since the average Mexican teacher receives between forty and sixty dollars monthly and usually holds additional positions to supplement his income, the committee hoped to secure transportation for the guest teachers from the Mexican government. It was not possible, however, to achieve this aim.

Selection of participants was arranged through the American Consul in Guadalajara. Preference was expressed for younger teachers of English at the secondary, college, and adult educational levels. With the assistance of the Cultural Attaché, folios of biographical data were sent to Pasadena in advance for publicity.

The program was divided into three parts: Participation in Home Life, Study of Community Life, and Academic Instruction. Home hospitality was arranged through local churches. In order to gain insight into American home life, each guest was to remain two weeks with each of two families. The second part of the program was the responsibility of the service clubs. It was planned to show the organized facets of American life in the areas of government, business, industry, service and social groups, as well as places and events of cultural, historical, and sociological interest. The third part was arranged by the College, which provided facilities for academic instruction. Funds for the payment of teachers were acquired by private donation in order that the guests should realize the personal factor in everything arranged for them.

The teachers from Guadalajara, who had obtained special rates from Pan American Airways, were met at the border and brought to Pasadena by bus. A brief meeting was held at the College in which guests were introduced to their host families.

To realize maximum educational results, the program had been planned to involve the largest possible number of organizations and individuals in Pasadena. From 9 to 12 o'clock daily, classes were held at the College. The first hour was devoted to study intended to deepen the guest teacher's interest in an understanding of American literature and culture. Discussion of the preceding day's experiences was included. From 10 to 11 o'clock teachers were provided individual tutoring in pronunciation, grammar, or whatever study of English they desired. Tutors were drawn from the membership of PISA, Pasadena Inter-Cultural Students Auxiliary, an organization of local citizens who provide volunteer tutoring to international students. They were augmented by professors and teachers from the Greater Los Angeles area. Although many tutors spoke fluent Spanish, instruction was in English. Tutors often accompanied the guests on excursions and took part in social meetings. From 11 o'clock until 12 o'clock guest lecturers drawn from universities, government, and industry addressed the group on subjects of professional and cultural interest.

Meetings were always informal, with opportunity for questions and discussion. Films were shown and audio-visual materials demonstrated. An authority on the teaching of English as a foreign language demonstrated techniques, utilizing materials which would be available in Jalisco.

During the morning hours, educators were available for conferences and for the giving of individual attention to the needs of the guests. A library of professional and technical books, a collection of folk songs, tape recorders, and other equipment were available for use before and after class periods.

The afternoon program began with luncheon at a service club. The speaker and other parts of the program were usually selected for their value to the guests. The Mexican group often contributed songs, dances, and addresses. Such contacts led to home entertainment. After lunch excursions were in order. The club provided transportation in a chartered bus, in cars driven by members, or in station wagons supplied by the American Red Cross. These trips provided a detailed background in nearly all facets of organized community life. Minority group areas, as well as more highly developed residential sections, were visited.

Home hospitality included not only participation as a member of several Pasadena families, but also visits to many homes for swimming parties, the showing of private films, and seminar-type discussions. Evening meetings were rarely purely social. They often centered around a learning situation and they proved to be extremely popular both with guests and with members of the community.

It was hoped that the sum of these three experiences—formal study, observing the organized phases of American society, and the sharing of home life—would result in the removal of type concepts. It can be anticipated that these experiences will be reflected in the visitor's teaching. As the study of English in Mexico begins in the earlier grades and is continued by a number of students throughout secondary school and college, the total effect on guest teachers should, over a period of several decades, be considerable.

The effect on Pasadena was observable. Not only did the group receive favorable publicity in newspapers, over the radio, and on television, but the teachers became known as individuals through extensive personal contact. The head of one institution stated that this group had made the best impression of any ever to visit his establishment. He added that his understanding of Mexico was changed by this experience.

In the spring of 1953 letters were received from the group indicating they had formed an organization in Guadalajara. An invitation to visit Guadalajara was received by teachers of Spanish and Latin-American studies in Pasadena schools, and in early August the Pasadena teachers met in Guadalajara. The program there provided for many classes in Spanish at the University. Mexican folk songs and dances, together with outstanding lectures on the history and culture of Mexico, were also arranged. Service clubs were visited and trips made to see industry, government, and tourist attractions in the state of Jalisco. The American group agreed that the hospitality of the people of Guadalajara could hardly be equalled.

As a result of the contacts made during the summer of 1952, an international service club arranged for the exchange of students of Spanish in Pasadena's schools with families in Guadalajara. The student in the host family returned for a comparable visit in Pasadena. An organized program was presented by the service club in each community.

Individual exchanges also resulted. Three students from Guadalajara studied in Pasadena during the school year 1952–53 and an increased number during the following academic year. One American student first went to Guadalajara but several others followed. The number of individual visits exchanged by persons of the two communities has increased considerably.

During the Christmas vacation of 1953–54 an exchange was begun between students of the University of Mexico and Pasadena City College. With the assistance of Professor Gabino A. de Palma, representing the Intercambio Estudiantil de las Americas, a student from the University of Mexico, whose vacation is during the spring, joined an American family for a period of two and a half months. The following summer the student from Pasadena lived with the family in Mexico City and attended the University of Mexico.

After the visit of the Pasadena teachers to Guadalajara an attempt was made to assess to what extent the exchange had benefited, not only those who took part, but also those who cooperated. It was decided that the total experience in the two communities had furthered understanding and friendship among all concerned and it is expected that intercity exchange will continue. There is general agreement that serving as hosts was a most rewarding adventure in international friendship and that other communities would similarly profit from such a proect.

A Student Club Implements International Understanding

A student organization known as the Cosmopolitan Club at Sacramento State College, California, has as a primary purpose the implementation of international understanding.

It has become traditional that this group sponsor the College Assembly program on United Nations Day. A typical program, that of

1952, included a guest speaker from the United States Office of Immigration with students or residents of the community native to Japan, China, Pakistan, the Republic of Philippines, Greece and India participating. These students represented their countries through songs, dances, and other typical presentations of their cultures.

Members of the Club also take an active interest in the Model United Nations, and largely at their instigation this is now a campuswide activity sponsored by the Student Council. Currently, attention is being directed to the promotion of other activities like the World Affairs Council of Northern California.

The Club brings to the College, once or twice a semester, distinguished foreign speakers. The most recent address was given by a professor from the University of London, who discussed the crisis in the Near East.

Local talent is utilized for informal talks and discussions. Returning veterans have spoken of the problems of Korea. A German student told of her impressions as an observer at the Nürnberg trials and a Nigerian student discussed the problems of Colonial Africa. This utilization of community resources is not confined to the student body, as is exemplified by the Air Force instructor, a native of Central Europe, who spoke on his education under four flags.

Under the auspices of the Clubs, groups of foreign-born students present panel discussions for the Parent Teacher Association and church group audiences averaging three hundred persons. Sponsors of the Club receive more requests for this kind of community service than can be granted.

The Club membership includes students interested in foreign languages for whom special tables have been set aside in the College cafeteria where different languages are spoken at lunch time. Social activities are planned which will bring different races and nationalities together at parties and dinners. Efforts are being made to establish the tradition of an International Ball which will have a different country as its theme each year. It is planned to have interested members study the culture of a country throughout the year. The details of the decoration and program at the Ball will be an outgrowth of such study.

Part V

EVALUATION AND A LOOK AHEAD

A NUMBER of clear impressions emerge from a close analysis of the descriptions of practice in this book. First, it is apparent that a considerable number of teachers in American schools are dedicated to the education of children, youth, and adults for world affairs. In a period of uncertainty, of rumors and threats of war, and of faltering faith in organized world cooperation, these teachers remain convinced that democratic ends can, and must, prevail. They believe that educators have a vital part to play in achieving the desired ends. The emergence of these programs demonstrates both faith and courage.

A second major impression is the encouraging degree to which schools and communities are cooperating in international educational programs. In the early stages of the study it was believed that examples of such mutual effort could be reasonably well presented in one section of the study. But as more descriptions of practice were received it became clear that this could not be done. Classroom work, student activities, and school administration were frequently enriched by the efforts of parents and citizens. Indeed, many programs were planned and carried on cooperatively, with schools and community groups vying with one another in initiating cooperative relationships, both human and institutional.

An analysis of the examples also shows that conceptions of education for world affairs are becoming more realistic. When the United

States had relatively few responsibilities and commitments abroad, the emphasis seemed largely confined to conceptions of "human brotherhood." Enlightened self-interest and survival values are now coming to be powerful motivating forces. Self-interest, as well as democratic ideals, are beginning to lead teachers, as well as other citizens, to reappraise the world and its peoples. A study of the illustrations reveals that the content and method employed rests upon a recognition by teachers and pupils that they must think in world terms.

Readers may also be impressed by the numerous examples which reveal the effect upon practice of travel and foreign service. Many school people who return from abroad find that their old responsibilities must be seen, and executed, from the point of view of a broader world experience. First-hand experiences in foreign countries seem to be most effective in inducing changes in educational practice at home.

The extensive degree to which attitudes are felt to be important in education for world affairs in both school and community is clearly apparent in this study. Again and again writers state that they have found that knowledge is not enough in effecting behavior. Widespread child study programs, as well as increasing awareness of the importance of basic attitudes in practical foreign relations, are apparently helping to change practice. Many teachers are developing appropriate techniques for the development of desirable attitudes.

Some school systems are in the process of developing system-wide teacher education programs for promoting education for world affairs. They are also utilizing established community organizations and services more effectively. Such conscious efforts seem for the most part to be in the early stages of development nationally. Doubt might well be expressed about the widespread effectiveness of the type of education sought, unless and until inservice programs are increased in number and efficiency.

Many examples cited, splendid as they are, seem too often to lack depth of research and understanding of many basic issues. In many senior high schools, for example, more extensive research should be possible. Reliance is still placed too largely on good will alone. The hard realities of national self-interest, the clash of vested economic forces in the Western world, the dangers inherent in holding intransigent nationalistic positions, the threat to guaranteed freedoms in the United States, the appeal of Communism to the hungry millions of Asia, the revolutionary surge of colonial peoples, and the ever-threatening expansion of Communistic power—these are seldom sensed in their stark reality. Major weaknesses of this kind in educational programs, wherever they exist, will need to be remedied if American schools are realistically to introduce children and youth to the actual world.

Limitations which have been pointed out, or those which may be sensed by readers of *Teaching World Affairs in American Schools,* may undoubtedly be traced to inexperience in educating for world affairs. We ar eat the beginning of living in what one of our authors calls a "36-hour world." Teachers, as well as national leaders, are in the same situation. They find themselves ill prepared to understand and to deal effectively with new situations and new ideas. Necessary knowledge, insight, and skill develop slowly, at best, in both schools and society at large. Yet the need to hasten our gains is great.

Great faith will be needed in the years ahead. We shall need to deepen our faith in the efficacy of the principles which undergird the democratic way of life, if the challenge of an emerging world society is to be met successfully. Coupled with this strong faith in the soundness of democratic principles, must be an awareness and functional knowledge of the basic problems of our world, a world undergoing major, and as yet unpredictable, changes. At stake are the institutions which have been built at great sacrifice through centuries and millenia of history. The challenge of Communism must be faced, not by driving it underground, but by meeting it openly in the market places of the world with better ideas, better because they are ever addressed to man himself, to shaping his physical, moral, and spiritual growth toward a full humanity.

We look forward, then, to achieving everywhere in the world those democratic values which have meant so much to participants in this study. We can reasonably expect that major efforts will be made in individual schools, and in American school systems generally, to incorporate into their entire programs some of the knowledge, insights, and skills which these pioneers have achieved in the examples cited. Like all true pioneers these individuals have ventured forth with vision and courage into a new and different world. Their efforts are a challenge to the rest of us to swell this caravan and work diligently, in concert with all men everywhere, to achieve for all peoples those qualities of life that result when free men freely share the common concerns from which humanity emerges.

LIST OF AUTHORS

CHAPTER 1

"The Heart Can Push the Sea and Land"
Ruth McDonald, DuPont Primary School, Old Hickory, Tennessee
Beginning American Life in an American School: The Story of Tikva
Estelle R. Roddy, Oak Lane Country Day School of Temple University,
Philadelphia, Pennsylvania
Developing a Democratic Climate
Eleanor Mackinnon, Robert J. Vance School, Hartford, Connecticut
Spot the News
Pauline Hood, William Randolph School, Asheville, North Carolina
Teaching World Affairs in a University Elementary School
Corinne A. Seeds, University Elementary School, University of California, Los Angeles, California
Pacific Peoples Made Meaningful
Robert E. Greene, Ynez School, Alhambra, California
How Japanese and Americans Depend upon Each Other
Charles H. Friedman, McCall School, Philadelphia, Pennsylvania
Note: Donald Cain, Curriculum Office, Board of Education, assisted
in the preparation of materials submitted from the Philadelphia Public Schools.
Chinese Are People
Hazel Carey, Forbes School, Pittsburgh, Pennsylvania
A Study of Today's India
A. Edith Kelley, George Gray School, Wilmington, Delaware
How Young Americans Attempted to Solve the Trieste Problem
Rose DeMarco, F. Read School, Philadelphia, Pennsylvania
Hi Neighbor
Delwyn Lindholm, Platt Elementary School, Grand Island, Nebraska
Sixth-Graders Study Foreign Lands
Maurice A. Lucas, Belvoir School, Topeka, Kansas
How Air Transportation Affects Social Living
Herbert Cullen, Clara Barton Elementary School, and Loyd M. Landes,

253

Riley Elementary School, Long Beach, California

SIXTH-GRADE CHILDREN STUDY EUROPE

Mrs. H. W. Haden, William Randolph School, Asheville, North Carolina

CHAPTER 2

ATTITUDES BASED ON VALUES HELD IN COMMON

Charles J. Brauner, Tappan Junior High School, Ann Arbor, Michigan

IT IS INTERESTING TO BE DIFFERENT

Marie Murray, Cecil Avenue School, Delano, California

FIRST STEPS IN WORLD UNDERSTANDING

Robert C. Kelly, Lake Arrowhead School, Cedar Glen, California

COMMON ENDS ARE SOUGHT IN DIFFERENT WAYS

Doris Nash, Tappan Junior High School, Ann Arbor, Michigan

MEXICAN PUPPET SHOW

Mavis Bridgewater, Langley High School, Pittsburgh, Pennsylvania

"LIGHTS! CAMERA! ACTION!"

Charles M. Shapp, Junior High School 52, Bronx, New York City

FROM THE UNITED NATIONS TO THE UNITED STATES

Isobel S. Friedman, Bartlett Junior High School, Philadelphia, Pennsylvania

A UNITED NATIONS BUILDING PROJECT

Russell C. Gates, Arroyo Grande Union Elementary School, Arroyo Grande, California

A NINTH-GRADE CLASS STUDIES THE UNITED NATIONS

Helen M. Stelzriede, Lincoln Junior High School, Santa Monica, California

WHY WE BELIEVE AS WE DO

Isobel S. Friedman, Bartlett Junior High School, Philadelphia Pennsylvania

THE WORLD'S LIVING RELIGIONS

Sadie B. Udstuen, Metcalf Laboratory School, Illinois State Normal University, Normal, Illinois

A NINTH-GRADE UNIT ON THE U.S.S.R.

Agnes C. Armstrong, Johns Hill Junior High School, Decatur, Illinois

INTERNATIONAL TRADE CAN LEAD TO WORLD UNDERSTANDING

Edna Martin, Cavert Junior High School, Nashville, Tennessee

WORLD TRADE: ONE APPROACH TO INTERNATIONAL UNDERSTANDING

Edythe J. Gaines, Junior High School Division, New York City

CHAPTER 3

Helen G. Matthew and Barbara Keyser, Hunter College High School, New York City

CHAPTER 4

A JUNIOR UNESCO CLUB'S FIRST YEAR
Edwin Feldman, City Elementary Schools, San Mateo, California
A WORLD FRIENDSHIP CLUB PROMOTES INTERNATIONAL UNDERSTANDING
Esther A. Hunt, Chaffey Union High School, Ontario, California
AN INTERNATIONAL RELATIONS CLUB ACCOMPLISHES MANY PURPOSES
Ruth R. Crockett, Bristol High School, Bristol, Connecticut
STAMPS TELL THE STORY OF CULTURES
Icyl M. Kramer, Marshall High School, Chicago, Illinois
THE EAGLE ROCK HIGH SCHOOL HELPS EDUCATION IN KOREA
Vida N. Shields, Eagle Rock High School, Los Angeles, California
STUDENTS HOLD A YEARLY CONFERENCE ON INTERNATIONAL AFFAIRS
Morris R. Buske, Oak Park and River Forest High School, Oak Park, Illinois
THE HIGH SCHOOL UNESCO COUNCIL IN THE CITY OF NEW YORK
Alfred H. Wheeler, Forest Hills High School, New York City
DEMOCRACY IS LEARNED THROUGH MEMBERSHIP IN JUNIOR STATESMEN OF AMERICA
Alan Aldwell, Carmel High School, Carmel, California
JUNIOR COUNCILS OF THE CLEVELAND COUNCIL ON WORLD AFFAIRS
Bette Daneman, Council on World Affairs, Cleveland, Ohio
HIGH SCHOOLS IN OHIO HOLD CONFERENCES ON PUBLIC AFFAIRS
Margaret Willis, The University School of The Ohio State University, Columbus, Ohio
TWENTY YEARS OF INTERNATIONAL RELATIONS CONFERENCES IN COLORADO
Lulu M. King, West High School, Denver, Colorado

CHAPTER 5

STUDENT ORGANIZATIONS ARE UTILIZED TO WELCOME PUPILS WITH FOREIGN BACKGROUNDS
Raymond J. Milton, Lowell High School, San Francisco, California
SEEING IS BELIEVING
Anna E. Cebrat, Oak Ridge High School, Oak Ridge, Tennessee
A SCHOOL-COMMUNITY PROJECT ON AFRICA
James H. Young, Vaux Junior High School, Philadelphia, Pennsylvania
INTERNATIONAL DAY IN A SENIOR HIGH SCHOOL
Ben Lundquist, Edina-Morningside High School, Minneapolis, Minnesota

CHAPTER 8

INTERNATIONAL RELATIONS EDUCATION FOR NEW CITIZENS
  Joseph Brain, New York City Schools, New York, New York
A WORLD AFFAIRS CLASS FOR THE COMMUNITY
  Giles Brown, Orange Coast College, Costa Mesa, California

CHAPTER 10

A COLLECTION FOR PEACE
  Mary Cary, Swarthmore College Peace Collection, Swarthmore, Pennsylvania
A SOCIAL SCIENCE FOUNDATION
  Dale Fuller, Social Science Foundation, Denver, Colorado
RESEARCH EXCHANGE ON THE PREVENTION OF WAR
  James Carper, University of Illinois, Urbana, Illinois
STUDENTS FROM ABROAD TEACH US
  George Brodschi, University of Louisville, Louisville, Kentucky
INTO AMERICAN HOMES
  G. Collyer, Shasta College, Redding, California
A COLLEGE-COMMUNITY PROGRAM OF TUTORING AND GUIDANCE
  Robert Yeaton, Pasadena City College, Pasadena, California
BI-NATIONAL TEACHER EXCHANGE
  Robert Yeaton, Pasadena City College, Pasadena, California
A STUDENT CLUB IMPLEMENTS INTERNATIONAL UNDERSTANDING
  Dwight Baker, Lyman Glenny, Joe McCullough, Willard Smith, Sacramento State College, Sacramento, California

APPENDIX

The following material was compiled in an analysis of the John Dewey Society 1951 Yearbook, *Education for a World Society*. It was done with the hope that it might be helpful in suggesting individual items (with reference to purposes, content, and activities) that would be appropriate for inclusion in the new *Case Book*.

QUESTIONS WHICH SUGGEST PURPOSES THAT MIGHT BE STRESSED IN THE CASE BOOK

1. Does the conception of the self which the learner develops involve faith in other people, a sense of security within himself, a questioning attitude of wanting to explore many questions and many ideas?

2. Does the learner develop a sense of social responsibility for the welfare of others—mother, father, brothers and sisters, classmates, teachers, his neighborhood?

3. Does he realize his dependence upon the achievements of other nations past and present?

4. Is he led to wonder at the vastness of the world, its myriads of peoples, their ways and customs?

5. Does he begin to sense that his interests are at one with mankind, caught up as we all are in a world of human beings trying to work out a happier destiny?

6. Does the learner begin to develop the social and intellectual skills necessary to living, playing, working with other people?

7. Does he develop the knowledge necessary to growth as a person and as a member of a world community?

8. Is the concept of enlightened self-interest used in evaluating national policy?

9. Is freedom of inquiry stimulated?

10. Is there tolerance in the face of abuse?

11. Is the value of cooperative solution to world problems stressed?

12. Are local community, economic and social problems analyzed in relation to foreign policy?

13. Are local people and appropriate organizations sufficiently utilized in the study of international problems?

14. Is the idealism of all people who search for "the good life" sufficiently recognized?

15. Does the school seek to cooperate with community groups in adult education on international problems?

16. Are careful methods of research utilized?

17. Are the emotions of learners as well as their intelligence involved in questions relating to human values?

18. Are the horrors of modern war realized?

19. Is the question of whether war is ever justified raised and explored?

20. Are the achievements, as well as the limitations, of international organizations known?

CHECK LIST OF IMPORTANT CONTENT FOR STUDY AND DESCRIPTION

1. Foreign national and cultural groups of importance in the world today.

2. Underdeveloped countries in relation to national and international policy.

3. Fundamental Education as carried on by UNESCO.

4. Propaganda and scapegoating in relation to international questions.

5. Totalitarian states ancient and modern.

6. The struggle for freedom in the many countries of the world.

7. The development of democratic institutions in the United States.

8. Attempts throughout history to solve cooperatively international problems.

9. The history of Russia.

10. The story of colonial peoples seeking independence down to the present day.

11. The Universal Declaration of Human Rights.

12. The contributions of the countries of the world to world culture.

13. Totalitarian threats to freedom, ancient and modern.

14. The concepts of "the melting pot" and "cultural pluralism" in the development of the United States.

15. Ways in which basic attitudes involving international questions are formed.

16. Current prejudices of groups and nations.

17. Changes in warfare to the present, when no one is safe.

18. The impact of science on peoples' conception of freedom.

19. The place of trade in relation to imperialism, the spread of ideas and the search for peace.

20. The contribution of religion to peace.

21. In literature the struggle to achieve self-realization and freedom.

22. Worldmindedness through the study of foreign languages.

23. Worldmindedness and art.

24. The results throughout history of countries seeking to dominate the world.

25. The study of modern regional groups such as the Norden Association, the Arab League, the Pan American Union.

26. Analysis and evaluation of the current news.

27. Study of the hot spots of the world, i.e., Germany, Indo-China, the Middle East.

28. The United Nations.

29. The specialized agencies of the United Nations.

30. Changing patterns of power in the world.

31. The tenets of communism compared to those of democracy.

32. Folk tales, music and games of many lands.

33. Map study.

34. Economic geography.

35. Atomic fission and its uses in peace and war.

36. History of transportation to the present day.

37. The study of stamps.

38. Analysis of cultural backgrounds of a school class, a school, or a community.

CHECK LIST OF POSSIBLE ACTIVITIES TO BE REPORTED

1. School and community forums.

2. Discussion groups and panels on international topics.

3. Use of people with foreign culture backgrounds.

4. Correspondence with people of other lands.

5. Interchange of school art with schools abroad.

6. Schools promote adult education programs on international problems.

7. Dramatizations which promote international understanding.

8. Playing of games and singing of songs from many lands.

9. Student and teacher exchange between countries.

10. International seminars and work camps for students.

11. Pupils work out codes of behavior.

12. Films on foreign countries and United Nations activities.

13. Use of radio and TV internation news.

14. Newspaper analysis of foreign news.

15. Murals on the theme of freedom and other democratic values.

16. International school clubs.

17. Community visits to ethnic groups and historical points of interest.

18. Preparation of foreign dishes.

19. School bazaars featuring the products of foreign countries.

20. Visits to the United Nations.

21. International travel.

22. Utilization of foreign teachers and students.

23. Cooperation with community and national agencies to further international understanding.

INDEX

Germany
contact with, 140–41, 143–45
exchange students, 145–48
games of, 34
Graduate curriculum, in social and
technical assistance, 209–10

Haverford College (Haverford, Pa.),
209 f.
Hawaii, teaching brotherhood in high
schools, 71–73
Hawaii Calls, 18
Hersey, J., 85
Hogan, Inez, 5
Holland, 32
games of, 34
Human Rights Day, 115
Humor, in teaching acceptance of
peoples, 132
Hunter College High School (New
York City), 97 f.
Huntingdon, Harriet, 5

India, 27
college study of, 211
correspondence with, 140
unit on, 22–24
Indo-China, 79–80
International Art Exchange, 193–94
International Day, in high school, 126–
28
International Friendship League, 41
International peace, unit on, 174–75
International politics, 204–5
International Red Cross, 184–86
International Relations Club, in high
school, 105
International trade, units on, 60–63,
63–69
student reaction to unit, 68–69
Iron County School District (Utah),
156 ff.
Israel, 29
Ithaca Schools (N.Y.), 160 ff.

James Fenimore Cooper Junior High
School (New York City), 134 ff.

Japan
correspondence with, 140
exchange of teen-age art, 150–52
interdependence with United States,
19–20
John Marshall High School (Chicago,
Ill.), 107 f.
Johns Hill Junior High School (De-
catur, Ill.), 57 ff.
Johnson, Crockett, 6
Joint Distribution Committee, 66
Junior Council on World Affairs, 114–
16
Junior High School 52 (New York
City), 48
Junior high schools, teaching world
affairs in, 36–69
Junior Red Cross, 184–86
Junior Statesmen of America, high
school activity, 112–14
Junior UNESCO Club
in elementary school, 101–4
in high schools, 101–12

Kandel, I. L., 218
Kansas, 29, 31
Kindergarten-primary grades
developing respect for religious
backgrounds, 176
developing world understanding,
167–71
Kipling, R., 88
Koestler, A., 85
Korea
helping children of, 108–10
project for, 138
Korean Club, 108–10
Korean Relief, 115
Korean War, 19, 50, 51, 166
Krauss, Ruth, 4, 5, 6

Lakewood Junior High School (Long
Beach, Cal.), 129 ff.
Languages, approach to foreign cul-
tures, 215–18
Lapplanders, 44